BOOKS AGAINST TYRANNY

Books against Tyranny
Catalan Publishers under Franco

LAURA VILARDELL

VANDERBILT UNIVERSITY PRESS
Nashville, Tennessee

Copyright 2022 Vanderbilt University Press
All rights reserved
First printing 2022

Library of Congress Cataloging-in-Publication Data

Names: Vilardell, Laura, 1986– author.
Title: Books against tyranny : Catalan publishers under Franco / Laura Vilardell.
Description: Nashville : Vanderbilt University Press, [2022] | Includes bibliographical references.
Identifiers: LCCN 2021055326 (print) | LCCN 2021055327 (ebook) | ISBN 9780826504401 (paperback) | ISBN 9780826504418 (hardcover) | ISBN 9780826504425 (epub) | ISBN 9780826504432 (pdf)
Subjects: LCSH: Censorship—Spain—Catalonia—History—20th century. | Publishers and publishing—Spain—Catalonia—History—20th century. | Catalonia (Spain)—Intellectual life—20th century.
Classification: LCC Z658.S7 V55 2022 (print) | LCC Z658.S7 (ebook) | DDC 070.509467/0904—dc23/eng/20220224
LC record available at https://lccn.loc.gov/2021055326
LC ebook record available at https://lccn.loc.gov/2021055327

To Efren Domènech (1918–1993),
who experienced oppression firsthand

CONTENTS

Illustrations ix
Acknowledgments xi

INTRODUCTION. THE DISGUISES OF CENSORSHIP   1

1. "If You Are Spanish, Speak Spanish": The Evolution of Ideology in the Francoist Censorship Apparatus   10
2. Publishing Illicit Books during the Onset of the Dictatorship (1939–1959)   24
3. Publishers' Willingness to Publish Books in an Oppressed Language (1960–1975)   61
4. Writers Speak Up about Censorship   110

Notes   135
Bibliography   161
Index   185

ILLUSTRATIONS

FIGURES

2.1.	Evolution of books authorized and published in Catalan, 1946–1959	52
3.1.	Comparison between the number of Catalan books produced and the number of translations into Catalan, 1962–1977	68
3.2.	Translations into Catalan in 1962 and 1963, organized by categories	73
3.3.	Time delay between the completion of a work in Catalan and its publication, 1950–1970	80
3.4.	Number of books published in the Isard series, by year	90
3.5.	Comparison between the number of new releases and total availability of books in Catalan, 1967–1970	97
3.6.	Books in Catalan; percentage of new releases compared to the total books available, 1967–1970	98
3.7.	Number of publishers issuing books in Catalan, 1967–1970	99
3.8.	Number of publishers of Catalan books distributed geographically, 1967–1970	99

TABLES

2.1.	Control mechanisms and response strategies for issuing books in Catalan, 1939–1945	35
2.2.	Control mechanisms and response strategies for issuing books in Catalan, 1946–1951	54
2.3.	Control mechanisms and response strategies for issuing books in Catalan, 1951–1959	58
3.1.	Incidence of book censorship in Spain as a whole	79
3.2.	Availability of books in Catalan according to the geographic location of their publishers	100

3.3.	List of publishers and their companies' liabilities	101
4.1.	Documentation of the censorship process of *Incerta glòria*	127
4.2.	Contrasting publishers' and authors' strategies to overcome censorship	133

ACKNOWLEDGMENTS

Writing a book about this topic and in the midst of a global pandemic, with libraries closed and difficulty obtaining bibliographical resources, can only be possible thanks to colleagues and friends across the world who helped me selflessly. The first acknowledgment goes to my mentor, professor, and advisor Manuel Llanas. Without him, this book would not exist.

I appreciate the generosity of Elisenda Boix, Maria Boix, Pere Julià, and Zum Boix. All of them opened the doors of their houses and took the time to speak to me about Josep M. Boix i Selva.

Many thanks also to my institution, Northern Illinois University, to support my research. Thanks also to Stephen Vilaseca, Rosa Flotats, Montserrat Bacardí, Pilar Godayol, Ramon Pinyol i Torrents, Josep Mengual, Adelina Plana, Emili Boix, and Jeremy Rehwaldt.

I extend special thanks to Vishal Kamte, who helped me tirelessly in every step of this process.

And finally, my gratitude goes to my parents, Joan Vilardell and Antònia Domènech, for their unconditional support.

INTRODUCTION

The Disguises of Censorship

In April 2018, I organized a talk for my class at Georgetown University on Catalan culture with the famous Catalan journalist Miquel Calçada i Olivella. The title of his presentation was "Solidarity, Information, and Independence: Catalan Television and Its Impact on Its Society." I was aware that it touched on a complex subject—the controversy after the self-determination referendum of Catalonia held on October 1, 2017.[1] However, my students had asked me specifically to speak about this topic, and the guest agreed.

At six o'clock in the morning on the day of the talk, I received a call from the sponsor located in Barcelona asking me to remove the word "independence" from the title in order to "avoid being offensive." Calçada's reaction was that we were being censored, and he declared he was not willing to go through censorship *again*—obviously referring to Franco's earlier censorship. However, for the sake of the class, he gave the talk, finally retitled "Information and Social Justice: Catalan Television and Its Impact on Society."

This was the first moment in my professional career that I had dealt with censorship firsthand, and the oddity was that the directive did not come from the university where I worked, but from Barcelona. Why? It is no secret that today in Spain some subjects remain sensitive, such as political events related to the unity of the country—as in the case of the example mentioned above—or any reference to the dictator Francisco Franco, whose thirty-six-year regime ended in 1975. This is proved by the article "No Laughing Matter: Making Jokes about Franco and ETA Is Off the Table in Spain if You Want to Avoid Trouble with the Law," published in *Index on Censorship* (Nortes 2017, 85). One of the cases the author mentions is from 2017, when the journalist and comedian Dani Mateo, on the late show *El Intermedio* shown on the Spanish private television station La Sexta, opened a section called "5 Things Never Explained about Valle de los Caídos (Valley of the Fallen)."[2] One thing was that "Franco wanted that cross to be seen from afar." Mateo commented, "Normal because . . . who's going to want to see that shit up close?" (LaSexta.com 2017). He was denounced by the Association for the Defense of the Valley of the Fallen and brought before a judge. The director of the show, El Gran Wyoming, referred to William Wallace: "Before they can silence our mouths, we will shout freedom!" (LaSexta.com 2017). The case was eventually shelved.

In 2019, as a result of the already mentioned self-determination referendum in Catalonia, the Provincial Electoral Board of Barcelona prohibited the public media from mentioning "expressions such as *exile*, *political prisoners* or *the repression trial* [because] they violate 'information neutrality'" (Redacción 2019).[3] The director of the public Catalan radio station Catalunya Ràdio denounced the prohibition: "This has only one definition: censorship. It is a direct attack on freedom of expression and freedom of the press. The magistrates have exceeded their powers and have become a figure that we thought was forgotten" (Redacción and Agencias 2019). He was obviously referring to the repression in Franco's times, but without mentioning it explicitly. Why has the word "Francoism" created such a huge trauma in Catalan society? What is the evolution of censorship in Spain? What was the repression against written material like? Why were there still books written in Catalan if the language was forbidden in public areas? What is the role of publications and translations in the cultural recovery of Catalonia? Did Catalan society overcome all the obstacles of censorship and repression from the Franco era? Since the start of the twenty-first century, more and more monographs related to Francoism have been published, many focusing on memory, identity, and repressed authors. Journalists have also been keen to discuss more modern concepts, such as digital censorship (Carrasco 2020), self-censorship (Nortes 2020), and freedom of the press in Spain (Schweid 2011). Surprisingly, though, some of the previously mentioned questions remain understudied. In order to answer them, this book engages in historical and social analysis of three basic concepts: dissemination, censorship, and resistance.

To tackle dissemination I focus on literature, using the struggle of publishers of Catalan books and translations in the context of the dictatorship of Francisco Franco (1939–1975) as the main topic, as they were doubly oppressed—both the Catalan language and the introduction of foreign ideas were banned by the regime, which was preoccupied with creating a "one, great and free Spain." The publishers' actions are true acts of resistance that some paid with severe economic penalties and book sequestrations. This study aims to examine the behavior of Catalan-language publishers and to compare it to the experience of writers by using first-person accounts by those who spoke up about that period.

By censorship I mean the suppression or modification of a message to make it align with the guidelines of the government—or in this case, the regime. I examine censorship laws and censors' accounts by means of firsthand sources from both sides, aiming to shed light on the evolution of Francoism's ideological and political thought. My motivation is to provide and analyze a unique list of strategies used to overcome censorship in Spain during that era.

Resistance in this case refers to the reaction of those who are oppressed. This book shows that resistance against cultural and linguistic oppression is a universal topic. Both the censoring apparatus and those who suffer from it have similar patterns of action, no matter where, when, or under what pretext it was produced. For example, Burma's censorship is based on a completely different ideology from Franco's, yet the guidelines for publishing are extremely similar (Allott 1994, 6, see also 1–20). Repression from censorship is becoming an interesting topic everywhere and for everyone. For example, the movie *Manto* (2018), directed by Nandita Das, tells the true story of the Indo-Pakistani writer Saadat Hasan Manto in 1940s India; today the film is available on Netflix in the United States. Thanks to globalization, local issues become concerns of a broader audience.

In 2007–2008, the last year of my undergraduate studies in translation and interpreting at the University of Vic (Barcelona), I received a grant, awarded by the Agency for Management of University and Research Grants (AGAUR), to assist in the research group "Editorials, Traduccions i Traductors a la Catalunya Contemporània" (Publishers, Translations, and Translators in Contemporary Catalonia). One of the main jobs of this scholarship was to index a documentary collection of one of the most relevant Catalan publishing houses during the years of the Franco dictatorship (Edicions Proa Collection); the collection included letters, censorship files, original works, authors royalties' agreements, and translation manuscripts. I was fortunate enough to have as a mentor for this project Dr. Manuel Llanas, a key scholar in the study of the publishing history of Catalonia,[4] who taught me the value of the archive and the love for research. At that moment, I realized the vicissitudes and the pressure under which publishers during the dictatorship lived; they had to make a living while trying to keep alive a forbidden language. Back then, I put the idea in a drawer, and I initiated my graduate studies. In July 2010, after I had already started my doctoral thesis focused on a completely different topic, Pompeu Fabra University held a session on translation and postwar Catalonia. My thesis supervisor, Dr. Ramon Pinyol i Torrents, together with Dr. Llanas, thought it would be a good idea for me to participate, and they mentioned a series, Isard (1962–1971), that remained understudied. I was lucky enough to be able to contact three of the children of the literary director of the collection, Josep M. Boix i Selva (1914–1996), and they showed me their father's personal archive, which included letters, censorship files, documents, translations, and copyright contracts (Josep M. Boix i Selva Collection). Being in contact with those two archives throughout my early academic life made me realize that publishers had well-thought-out strategies aimed at overcoming the obstacles of censorship, and they were aware of their role as cultural preservers. This finding, along with the lack of studies in this field, led me to write this book, where I share their strategies publicly as a historical document, contributing to studies on memory and cultural heritage.

Once my thesis was finished, I dedicated myself fully to my great passion—discovering the concerns of the Catalan publishing sector and its problems with censorship. Therefore, in July and August 2014 I took a research stay at Archivo General de la Administración in Alcalá de Henares, near Madrid, where all the censorship files are kept. I consulted around one hundred files, all either translations or original works in Catalan that had problems with censorship, such as those written by authors the regime deemed controversial, as in the case of Manuel de Pedrolo. While reading the files, I confirmed that any book needed to be evaluated by *at least* two or three censors before final approval. The "readers," who were the lowest category of censors (above them there were directors and ministers), could belong to three different groups: civil, military, and ecclesiastical.

Guided by the judgment of those readers, one can reach two conclusions: First, some of the readers were intellectuals, but others were definitely not. Second, the censors who read what they called regional languages or foreign languages, mostly at the beginning, were "from the right-wing ideological branch, old monarchic lords, Catholics. They applied much more censorship to sexual and religious matters, etc. than in Spanish, where they were also there, but there were many more people" (Porcel, interviewed in Beneyto 1975, 102). When it came to books written in Catalan, it was even more suppressive: "Here there has been normal censorship and censorship for being Catalan" because "being Catalan has meant being a citizen, in principle, suspicious" (101). Publishers, aware of this fact, began to use strategies to survive and see their books published.

Spain had two book censorship regulations for nonperiodical publications, one an order passed during the Spanish Civil War, on April 29, 1938, and the other the Press and Printing Law, approved on March 18, 1966. Gabriel Arias-Salgado, vice secretary of Popular Education (1941–1945) and head of the Ministry of Information and Tourism (1951–1962), was the main architect of the first regulation. Publishers were required to submit two copies of the book—or the original, in the case of translations—before publishing. In 1962, Minister Manuel Fraga Iribarne came to power, and he promoted the Press and Printing Law, approved in March 1966. Although it was intended to show a kinder face of the regime, it was a Machiavellian apparatus that punished even more harshly: having a book published did not exempt it from denunciation, and its author could end up in front of a judge in handcuffs. This is close to what happened to Manuel de Pedrolo once his book *Un amor fora ciutat*, a novel about homosexuality, was published and distributed in 1970. The writer exposed himself to "six months of major arrest, a fine of 25,000 pesetas, special disqualification for nine years, legal bonds and additional costs and the confiscation of the copies of the book" (Oliver, interviewed in Beneyto 1975, 211).[5] However, what happened to Pedrolo did not happen out of the blue—such repression was common.

While I was clear about the ideological distinction of the laws, what perplexed me was that in 1965 more than half of the books produced in Catalan were translations but later, in 1973, only 8 percent were (Bacardí 2012, 50). While some scholars spoke of a boom in translations (Bacardí 2012, Cornellà-Detrell 2013, Vallverdú 2013), others spoke of an increase of books in Catalan (Llanas 2006; Serra d'Or 1966, 19), and this apparent disagreement left me to navigate a sea of uncertainty. However, two different concepts were blending: on the one hand, there was a boom in translations beginning in 1960 and ending in 1969; and on the other hand, more and more books authored by writers of the new generation were being published in Catalan, starting in the last years of Franco's regime. The boom in translations was the seed that created the ideal climate that gave way to a new generation of Catalan-language authors.

I still had to determine to what extent publishers were a key part of cultural promotion in the Catalan language. In July 2019, I was accepted to participate in the International Research School for Media Translation and Digital Culture at the Baker Center for Translation and Intercultural Studies, Jiao Tong University, Shanghai. During one of the sessions, I revisited the theory of attention economy and ecology of attention (Citton 2017) from the point of view of the humanities. I also investigated eco-translation (Cronin 2017), and, looking for common ground between these concepts, I realized that Catalan publishers actually used the theory of the attention economy, which focuses on the target audience and using marketing strategies to increase sales, without naming it as such. After 1963, they began to believe more and more in advertising campaigns to catch the readership's attention, and they also based their catalogs on the preferences of their readers, rather than having an internal plan guiding their publication strategies. Therefore, there was a real boom in translations that could be explained through the same theory that describes the behavior of multinationals and the race for attention today. A boom that ended up with a supply bubble and a subsequent crisis was necessary to guarantee the future of the Catalan language.

This book has three main goals: (a) to give voice to the censors and the censored, to editors and writers, in order to analyze and explain their experiences during that period; (b) to study the strategies used to circumvent censorship—such as gifts to the censors, creating titles that could be read in both Spanish and Catalan, or having a translator pass as the author of a work; and (c) to rely, as much as I could, on primary sources in order to convey to the reader the effect of lived experiences.

The book is a chronologically organized trip with the historical setting as the common thread. It begins before the end of the Spanish Civil War (1938), when the first censorship law was approved, and ends with the death of the dictator and its consequences (1975). Due to the diversity of sources analyzed, my approach is multidisciplinary, based on historical, sociological, and cultural studies. My goal is to provide a rigorous, empirical, and critical analysis of both primary and secondary sources to arrive at insightful conclusions. In addition to published material, I use accounts from firsthand witnesses, correspondence, memoirs, censorship files, newspapers, my personal interviews, and unpublished material from several Spanish archives.

In the first chapter, I invite the reader to take the red pen and dive deeper into a censor's mind to better understand the historical context. By means of a historical and social approach, this section analyzes the censor's profile, sensitive topics, and the evolution of Francoist ideology throughout the years of the regime.

The second chapter focuses on the period from 1939 to 1959. This was the most traumatic phase because the Catalan intelligentsia was fragmented; many went into exile, lived an internal exile, or simply changed their ideology as a means of survival. Some writers and artists risked their physical integrity to hold secret meetings and even publish books and magazines clandestinely, sometimes using four or five different printers for one single publication. In addition, because the mail could be intercepted, they had to go house to house to invite attendees. There is no doubt that the poet Carles Riba, after returning from exile in 1943, played an important role unifying the Catalan intelligentsia in Barcelona until 1959, the year of his death.

According to Griffin (1993), Spain was a para-fascist country because its main objective was to stay in power indefinitely, even abandoning its ideological principles to do so. This is exactly what happened in 1945, with the defeat of the Axis troops in World War II. This conflict brought much hope to the Catalan publishers, who were optimistic that international organizations would be able to remove the dictator from power. However, the opposite happened—Spain used its visceral anticommunism to ally itself with the United States and to be recognized by the Holy See. There is no doubt that 1945 brought a bit of openness, albeit within the confines of the country's economic, social, and cultural self-sufficiency. Around this year, Catalan publishers experienced the "privilege" of seeing their books crossed out, instead of being directly nonauthorized for the sole reason of having been written in Catalan. One of the first historical milestones of Catalan publications was the authorization in 1943 of the complete works of Jacint Verdaguer, considered the Catalan national poet, though the edition used a shameful nonstandardized spelling. Its editor, Josep M. Cruzet, of Editorial Selecta, metaphorically removed the first of many stones from the wall. By the end of the 1940s, some publishers tried to publish in Spanish and also a little bit in Catalan, although in 1954, "the mechanical composition of texts in Catalan was 10 percent more expensive than those written in Spanish" (Albertí 1994, 225).

Chapter 3 talks about the *apertura* (openness) years of the 1960s. Spanish society's exposure to American culture and a generation of young adults who had not lived through the war led to a "soft dictatorship," with protests led by young people, some influenced by the hippie movement. The tourist boom broke the Spanish autarky, and publishers began to see the real possibility of issuing books in Catalan. However, the situation was not ideal: Catalan was not a language for public use, nor was it for school use (apart from clandestine classes). The already mentioned boom in translations happened at this time, bringing about an increase in the number of books written in Catalan. For the first time, this volume uses historical documentation to analyze the boom and its sociological effect through the theory of attention economy. In the 1960s, more than ever before, attention was paramount to selling foreign books written in a language that was not officially recognized. Based on the principles of Yves Citton (2017) and of Tim Wu (2017), I establish the different phases that align with the behavior of editors, both those who published exclusively in Catalan and those who published in Spanish and jumped on the bandwagon of translations into Catalan once the boom had already started. For the latter, my hypothesis about that decision is double-sided: the reading public was growing, and the editors channeled more of the economic benefits granted by the government when they exported their books abroad. Using as a case study the evolution of one of the most important publishing houses in Barcelona, I establish the decline of the translation boom, its causes, and its consequences. In the final years of the dictatorship, censorship continued to be fierce, and many publishing houses went out of business.

The last chapter is intended to give writers a voice. At the end of Francoism (1975), all parties agreed on a "Pact of Forgetting" (1977) to look aside instead of facing the truth. After more than forty years of democracy, it is time to reveal to the world the struggle of writers in Catalan and their survival strategies. Why did Catalans keep writing in a language condemned to die? What was their motivation? What was the price they paid? Are their strategies the same as those of the publishers? The usual procedure for collecting fees for a work was conditional on passing through censorship. However, some publishers, even before knowing the censorship verdict, paid their fees to support the authors' contribution to the language and culture.

The efforts that the sector had to make to break even were titanic. While the role of publishers remains in the historical shadows, they were essential in facing the Ministry of Information and Tourism to justify the existence of a work. Using unpublished documentation, this book sheds light on the real struggle of publishers.

Now more than ever we need to speak out about censorship to let citizens know its different forms and dangers. I hope that readers around the world can extrapolate from the Catalan context to connect the events to their own struggles. What matters is who holds the power, not the power itself. People in countries in Asia, Africa, and the Americas can also understand the repression of their authors and their thoughts. This book aims to open up the field, using theories, such as that of the attention economy, that go beyond those usually employed in the humanities. Thus, I aim to engage other scholars' investigations in cross-border, colonialist, memory, cultural heritage, or war studies.

CHAPTER 1

"If You Are Spanish, Speak Spanish"

The Evolution of Ideology in the Francoist Censorship Apparatus

Ideological Censorship: Political and Religious

In February 1936, Spain celebrated the third general elections of the Second Republic (1931–1936), which was won by the Frente Popular (Popular Front), the left-wing party coalition. Given this result, General Emilio Mola and "a significant portion of the Spanish army" (Alonso 2020, 75), who called themselves "the only true Spaniards" or *Nacionales* (Preston 2006, ch. 4), organized a military uprising (*alzamiento*) in Melilla (Africa) on July 17, 1936.[1] In order to organize it successfully, they relied on social and financial support from political parties, centers of economic power, social welfare sectors, the hierarchy of the Catholic Church, and external allies, as well as "mass violence against any civilians or combatants who interfered with the progress of the columns" (Alonso 2020, 75).

The plan had been to rapidly conquer Spain, as Preston explains: "Their plans had been for a rapid *alzamiento*, or uprising, to be followed by a military directorate like the one established in 1923 [Primo de Rivera's dictatorship], but they had accounted for the strength of the 'working-class resistance' that 'would turn into a long civil war'" (2006, ch. 4). After the coup, a state of emergency was established, and a number of generals committed to sacrificing their lives for the victory of the Bando Nacional (*Nacionales* Front) against "a broad socio-political collective identified as the 'other,' in this case the 'reds'" (Alonso 2020, 75), or defenders of the Second Republic.

General Francisco Franco laid out two main reasons for the uprising: *regionalisms* and *the exploiters of politics*. By *regionalisms*, the rebels referred to those who defended the three historical communities within the Spanish territory: Catalonia, the Basque Country, and Galicia, each one with an autochthonous language, culture, and tradition. During the Second Republic, these territories were ruled by their own regional law, along with the Spanish Constitution. In the case of Catalonia, Estatut de Núria was approved in 1932; in the Basque Country and Galicia, the regional law was approved in October 1936, after Franco's coup d'état.[2] The second aim was to attack the *exploiters of politics*—that is, those who belonged to the Second Republic or any other left-wing party or ideology.[3]

THE NEW STATE'S IDEOLOGY

The rebels faction was very heterogeneous.[4] Though they shared common ideas, the means by which they sought to achieve their targets were varied and sometimes discordant. In order to channel their efforts, Franco unified them on April 19, 1937, into the only legal political party, FET y de las JONS (Falange Española Tradicionalista y de las Juntas de Ofensiva Nacional Sindicalista). That gave Franco unprecedented power to control all sectors of society. He called its duty "Movimiento" (Movement) and established unity and repression as its main goals.[5]

According to Cisquella, Erviti, and Sorolla, once the war ended, the "two key ideas—the only truth of the established regime—were: inner order and survival at any price" (2002, 21). The following quotation spoken on October 12, 1936, by Fascist general José Millán Astray, confirms the statement, "Catalonia and the Basque country—the Basque country and Catalonia—are two cancers in the body of the nation. Fascism, which is Spain's health-bringer, will know how to exterminate them both, cutting into the live, healthy flesh like a cold scalpel." (Millán Astray in Portillo 1941, 396).

The Spanish state under Franco was a totalitarian state that controlled all institutions, giving no room for any opposition. It controlled a parliament that was a façade, manipulated trade unions, suppressed free elections, persecuted dissidents, and severely restricted freedom of expression. Unlike Mussolini or Hitler who justified their ideologies in manifestos, though, Franco never thought that a doctrinal justification was necessary, and according to Serrano Suñer, the regime "never missed it" (1978, 145). The new state failed to create a political ideology (425), "so it had to fight against everyone" (Cisquella, Erviti, and Sorolla 2002, 21). Indeed, Francoism was initially a counterreaction that sought to destroy everything its leaders considered to be Republican values: secularism, parliament, free elections, left-wing parties, concessions to the autonomous regions, and so forth. The fastest and most evident consequence was, according to Prof. Juan Beneyto, director general of the press (1957–1961), a "cultural vacuum" (1987, 11) especially during the first phase of Francoism. Later, more or less fortunately, it copied some of the regulations of Italian fascism. German fascism remained in the background because it was anti-Catholic.

To differentiate the Francoist regime from Italian and German fascism, I base my argument on the concept of the para-fascist state described by Roger Griffin in *The Nature of Fascism* (1993, 124) and used by other scholars, such as Rundle (2018, 31). According to Griffin, Franco's regime in Spain had to be considered para-fascist because, unlike fascists, who come to power through elections, have an explicit ideology, and are populists, para-fascists take over in a coup d'état to establish a regime based on the mythification of a glorious past and, most importantly, they aim to stay in power by all means (1993, 124). Paul Preston argues similarly: even though those who opposed Franco "reasonably described themselves as anti-fascist" (Preston and Attar 2020, 24:19), Franco cannot be "technically considered as a fascist" (2020, 24:03); rather it was the aim of Mussolini to define the Francoist regime as fascist, "to put pressure on France" (Preston 1994, "VIII Franco and the siege of Madrid").

LLEIDA, MARCH 27, 1938. THE MILITARY REBELS ABOLISH THE AUTONOMY OF CATALONIA

The military occupation of Catalonia began in 1938, specifically in the region's west, and the idea was to reach the sea by all means necessary (Solé i Sabaté 1985, 31). As soon as the Francoist troops bombed Lleida, in the western part of Catalonia, on March 27, 1938 (34), they immediately abolished the autonomous law, Estatut de Núria (*Official Bulletin of the State* [*BOE*], April 8, 1938, no. 534, 6674), and restricted the use of the Catalan language in public (Massot i Muntaner 1978, 80–81).[6]

BARCELONA, JANUARY 28, 1939. MILITARY OCCUPATION

The arrival of Franco's troops in Barcelona meant the end of Republican rule and the defeat of Catalonia, as reported by Gaziel (the pseudonym of Agustí Calvet) in the Jocs Florals contest in Exile in Havana, 1944: "Nothing was left standing of what was ours: neither the government, nor the institutions, nor the culture, nor the language, not even the *senyera* [Catalan flag]. All that remains is our defeated Catalan land, like a body cut up and without a soul." (Sayrach and Sayrach 2007, 28). A fierce repression began against the fields of culture, communication, and education, in which the Catalan language had played a key role.[7] On January 28, 1939, the Barcelonan newspaper *La Vanguardia Española* published a disposal signed the day before by Eliseo Álvarez Arenas, brigadier-general of the Spanish Army and assistant secretary of public order, which stated, "All vehicles and media of any nature, radiophonic stations, showrooms with their facilities, printers and engraving workshops and all kinds of paper stocks are declared confiscated at my disposal."[8] Article 18 stated "two copies of all printed materials or documents intended for advertising will be submitted to the previous censorship" (Álvarez Arenas 1939).

Álvarez Arenas also added, "Catalans, the use of your language in private and familiar environments will not be persecuted" (1939), clearly implying that it was better not to speak Catalan in public circles. Indeed, in Catalonia, repression focused on two areas: ideology and language, with the consequent annihilation of Catalan publishing and the purging of bookstores. Wenceslao González Oliveros, the civil governor of Barcelona in 1939 and 1940, ordered that officials who spoke a language other than Spanish in their job "shall be ipso facto terminated" (Martín de Pozuelo and Ellakuría 2008, 79).[9] They even changed the names of places and people and reduced the language to a mere "dialect."[10] Despite this, intellectuals used a number of strategies to keep the culture alive, sometimes even risking their lives, as described in the next chapters of this book.

The Need for the Dictatorship to Fit into the International Reality after 1945

The tides turned when first Italy and then Germany surrendered in May 1945 to the Allies. After the suicide of the Führer on April 28, 1945, and the execution of Mussolini two days later, Franco had to react. In order to keep the "Movimiento" alive, he decided to show the entire world that the country had changed its restrictive model, removing Falangist groups from public power and also from the Tribunal de Responsabilidades Políticas (Tribunal of Political Responsibilities), which, applying the eponymous law, was charged with punishing those who "had not actively supported the 'National Movement' from October 1934, the date of revolutionary insurrection" (Ruiz 2005, 132).[11] On July 18, 1945, through the Fuero de los Españoles

Law (*BOE*, July 18, 1945, no. 199, 358–360) he determined the proper behavior of citizens and officially adopted a transition to National Catholicism.[12] As a consequence, "the majority of key positions [were granted] to Catholic politicians" (Ruiz 2005, 100). This new model also brought social and economic changes based on national pride and self-sufficiency (autarky), which is characterized by not allowing any trade beyond a nation's borders (Evans 2018, 604–6). As a result, citizens struggled to get food, which led the country to an emergency situation (López Burniol 2010). At the international level, institutions rejected this system, and their unanimous response was to isolate the country. On December 12, 1946, the General Assembly of the United Nations, in Resolution 39(I), "condemned Franco's dictatorship and recommended withdrawal of all embassies in Spain" (Carrasco-Gallego 2012, 94). Spain was also excluded from the European Recovery Plan (ERP), which provided for free trade between the countries aided by the Marshall Plan. According to Carrasco-Gallego, the main reason for this response was not Spain's current situation, but "the origin of Franco's dictatorship" (94).

1953. SPAIN'S INTERNATIONAL PARTICIPATION: THE AGREEMENTS WITH THE UNITED STATES AND THE HOLY SEE

Franco was aware of the alarming situation in the country, but the response of international organizations urged him to react quickly. His successful strategy was to show the regime's visceral anticommunism to international institutions. As a result, 1953 brought two crucial international pacts: the first was the Concordat signed with the Vatican by which Spain empowered the church to establish Catholicism as the unique religion of the state (in line with the principle of National Catholicism found in Fuero de los Españoles Law, 1945) and gave it the right to intervene directly in all parts of society (Franco's Concordat 1953). The second one was the Madrid Treaty with the United States, signed on September 26, that injected $465 million into the Spanish economy.[13] In exchange, the United States established four airbases in Spain in its effort to beat the USSR during the Cold War.[14] That "openness" would also bring the United Nations to accept Spain as a member on December 14, 1955. In 1958, Spain joined the International Monetary Fund (IMF), the World Bank (Carrasco-Gallego 2012, 100), and the Organization for European Economic Co-operation (later OECD), becoming a full member of the last of these in 1959 (Luelmo 2010, 2).

SPAIN, FEBRUARY 25, 1957. OPUS DEI VERSUS FALANGE

A group of technocrats belonging to Opus Dei formed the eighth government of the Francoist dictatorship with who else but Franco as president.[15] With the Catalan economist Joan Sardà i Dexeus as a leader, this group drew up a Stabilization Plan to regenerate the Spanish economy, as per the requirements of the IMF and OECD (Riquer 2019), while "removing the shadow of the Falange" (Hilari Raguer, in Bru de Sala and Dropez 2003, 61). Mariano Navarro Rubio, minister of finance from 1957 to 1965, found it difficult to convince Franco and the Falangists of the viability of the project, as they argued that the "economy is subordinated to politics" and that "there is no development without inflation." They expressed pride in "the work done by INI" (Spanish National Institute of Industry) and "a distrust, almost allergic, towards any relationship with international organisms." These arguments were fed by their autarkic mentality, their nationalist pride, and "the political doctrine of Falange" (Navarro Rubio 1989). Finally, the Stabilization Plan was approved in 1959, bringing international confidence in the Spanish market (Serra Ramoneda 2001, 9) and economic growth within a dictatorial political structure.

1960S. THE RISE AND FALL

In 1964 the Development Plans, inspired by a French model, were approved.[16] They had three phases: (1) Primer Plan de Desarrollo (1964–1967/9) (*BOE*, December 30, 1963, no. 312, 18190–18198), which focused on budgetary stabilization;[17] (2) Segundo Plan de Desarrollo (February 1969–1971) (*BOE*, February 12, 1969, no. 37, 2137–2142), which sought financial stabilization; and (3) the unconcluded Tercer Plan de Desarrollo (May 1972–1975) (*BOE*, May 11, 1972, no. 113, 2137–2141), aiming at economic stabilization, "which would have to be carried out in agreement with international bodies" (Navarro Rubio 1989). The Development Plans also brought what was called "Polos de Desarrollo" (Development Poles), to stimulate industrialization in the less-industrialized cities of Spain.

The 1960s, considered the years of *apertura*, brought a social and artistic turn. The influence of rock and folk music, in particular that of Bob Dylan and Pete Seeger, along with exposure to tourism, Hollywood movies, and the struggle for equality (especially that of Martin Luther King Jr.), made Spain's citizens dream of a free country. One of the most acclaimed examples was the protest song movement, Nova Cançó (New Song). Born in 1959, it gained momentum from the first concerts of the group Setze Jutges (Sixteen Judges) in 1961.[18] The key factor in its success was self-censorship, along with the complicity of the audience, who understood perfectly what the group was trying to say and sometimes even finished the songs during concerts so as not to put the musicians in the spotlight. The social movements made the regime react, as they recognized that the dictatorship would end unless it had a planned response.

In 1973, the Third Development Plan had to stop because of the great world energy crisis. Thus, Franco gathered a new cabinet, with Luis Carrero Blanco, who exercised great repression, as head of the Spanish government. However, the dictator's plans were shattered when on December 20 of the same year the terrorist group ETA attacked the leader's successor and killed him.

In 1974, the execution by *garrote vil* (strangulation) of the Catalan anarchist Salvador Puig Antich is especially relevant because "Franco refused to commute the death sentences" (Preston 1994, "XXVIII The Long Goodbye"). On November 20, 1975, Franco died and his regime was agonizing. The response of the leaders across the political spectrum was to sign the "Pact of Forgetting" in 1977, an agreement to hide and forget what happened. However, it is hard to ignore deaths, shootings, and cultural repression in the blink of an eye. This book's purpose is to open up the discussion about Francoist censorship to a wider audience, allowing the reader to relate it to other realities in the world today.

Book Censorship in Spain: Laws, Censors, Criteria, and Consequences

Franco approved a "provisional measure" on book censorship as early as April 1938, when the Spanish Civil War was still ongoing. While Italy and Germany showed at the beginning of their regimes "a less systematic censorship of books" (Rundle 2018, 38), Spain found it crucial to establish control as soon as possible. Proof of this rush is the fact that it had to be approved in Burgos, in National territory, since Madrid was still under Republican rule. Once Franco's allies conquered Madrid in July 1939, they relocated the censorship office to the capital of Spain.

The Law and the Order of 1938, inspired by Mussolini's censorship apparatus, established prior-to-publication censorship for printed material to be published, as well as a system of control to prevent citizens from acquiring prohibited books, using the excuse of paper scarcity.[19] This "provisional measure" lasted twenty-eight years. The next—and last—censorship law was called the Press and Printing Law and was passed by Minister Manuel Fraga in March 1966. It fostered freedom of speech and also switched prior censorship to *voluntary consultation*, but with countless restrictions, as will be discussed in Chapter 3 of this volume. It survived until 1977, two years after Franco's death.

CENSORS' PROFILE

According to Abellán, there were three levels of censors. "At the first level are the simple 'readers,' who clear the bulk of the works. These are generally civil servants with very poor cultural backgrounds, with the exception of the 'glorious' early post-war period" (1980a, 115). In the files we can find the annotation "pase al lector no. [X]" (pass to reader number [X]). This number, randomly assigned to each new book, determined who would assess it. "At the second level are the people who issue the dictamens, with whom the writer or editor usually discusses or negotiates as much as possible. This interlocutor is, in Madrid, the head of the Editorial Ordinance and, in the provinces, is the provincial delegate" (115–16). And, finally, "at the third level are those who are effectively responsible for censorship policy, who pull and slacken at the mercy of changes or internal conflicts in the regime, even using their position to influence them" (116).

Especially in the first years, with the Falange at the head of propaganda, the public image of an author was decisive for the verdict of that author's book. Thus, if the publication was written by someone in exile, this was definitely more than enough evidence to avoid having to read it. There were also books that could not be prohibited because they were written by authors who were closely linked to the regime. In such cases, censors were bound hand and foot, as one censor explained: "I think that by covering one's ears, I would authorize it. In the end, it is not the ears that define good and evil" (Larraz 2014, 83).[20] Readers were divided into three groups—civil, military, and ecclesiastical. While the former two saw works as ideological discourse, the last evaluated material as moral discourse.

The body of religious censors was made up of deacons, priests, and friars (Larraz 2014, 89) with substantial academic skills; some, such as Saturnino Álvarez Turienzo, even had a doctoral degree. Contrarywise, military censors were "poorly educated and given to outbursts" (91). The verdict of General Luis Martos, commenting on *Leña verde*, a work by Luis Berenguer, illustrates this point. He wrote that the book "reflects the mentally handicapped nature of the author when he wants to be funny" (96).

In an effort to determine the character of the civil censor, I follow Larraz's judgment. He stated that half were teachers, literary critics, or frustrated writers who were jealous of those who knew how to write (2014, 87). There was also room for a few intellectuals. The other half were simple public employees or lawyers who read books as a mechanical exercise. Censors scanned the book, looking only for words or expressions to cross out, without considering the content of the work or the spiritual or intellectual message it conveyed (101). For this reason, the censor has been characterized as having no intellectual zeal. However, though they enjoyed little prestige, they had "more power than the minister or the general director" (86) because they were responsible for permitting or banning most nonperiodical publications in Spain. If the first reader was not sure about the verdict, the publication went to the table of another censor, with the goal of reaching an agreement. However, when readers came into conflict, there were two possibilities, either to trust the one that had the most prestige (85) or to call the head of the section (and in rare occasions even the minister). There are cases where the same book had up to four different reports if the initial reader did not clearly determine the verdict.[21]

Readers were paid per file (Arroyo-Stephens 2015; Abellán 1980a, 93; Martínez Rus 2012), and sometimes, due to time constraints, they based their judgments on previous verdicts or on the author's ideology more than on the content of the book itself. The censors had a heavy workload, as Larraz explains, referring to a letter from a reader asking for a salary increase in 1956: "There was talk of a burden on the censor of no fewer than 500 books a month" (2014, 101). This explains the poor use of the censorship criteria by the readers, who prioritized quantity over quality.

In 1951, Franco created the Ministry of Information and Tourism, and one year later the body suffered a reorganization, splitting the readers' group into two subgroups, fixed and specialists. The hiring criteria were the same for both groups (the minister himself appointed the candidates directly), but the contractual status was different. Fixed readers enjoyed a contract with the ministry, while specialists did not have any legal relation with it. Instead, specialists were paid for work done. According to the Order of March 7, 1952, specialists were paid 100 pesetas ($0.68) per reading unit, about two hundred pages: "Works in regional languages, French and Italian will be counted as 150%; in English, or presenting extraordinary difficulties due to the subject or theme, as 200%; and works in German and Slavic or Oriental languages, as 300%" (*BOE*, March 21, 1952, no. 81, 1282).

To illustrate the profile of the censor, Mireia Sopena describes the experience of Saturnino Álvarez Turienzo, one of the religious censors during Franco's reign, in these terms: "As a specialist reader, he could never choose the titles to read. . . . He came to receive eight works in a week and, at the end of the month, he could earn around one thousand pesetas, according to the length and languages of the book (he read in Greek, Latin, German, English, Italian, Portuguese and Catalan)" (2013, 149–50). It should not be forgotten that they were still enforcing the Order of April 29, 1938.

CENSORSHIP CRITERIA

According to Abellán, there were fixed and variable criteria for censorship. The fixed criteria included the *protection of institutions*, *laws*, and *ideology*; these remained in force until 1977. Among the variable criteria were *morality* and the *use of proper language* (banning references to sex, abortion, divorce, and homosexuality), *political opinions* that differ from those of the "Movimiento," and the protection of *religion* above all (1980a, 88–89).[22] Even though these were the main concepts, the criteria, as Beneyto stated, were volatile: "The well-known volubility of certain forms of censorship—normally attributed to the whim of the censor on duty—is much more indicative of a discontinuity between cause and effect than a plausible justification. . . . The text is grafted onto the continuous flow of other texts and the censorship phenomenon into the broad framework of social phenomena" (Abellán 1987, 10). Larraz also hints in this same direction: "Even at the same time, phrases, scenes and themes allowed in one novel could very well be censored in another without obeying the concretion of these more or less predictable variables" (2014, 79). Ángel Crespo, poet and translator, referred to the reasoning behind this volatility: "Since the current Spanish regime lacks ideology and its only aspiration is the indefinite and permanent holding of power, its criteria have never been fixed or based on permanent ideological assumptions or logically evolutionary ones. This makes Spanish censorship opportunistic, and it lacks any intellectual nuance" (qtd. in Abellán 1980a, 91).

In order to make the censorship process less chaotic, the Francoist regime relied on an index of banned books (Beneyto 1987, 27–40) that prevented citizens from reading the works of *disaffected* authors, some of whom were in exile (Larraz 2014, 63). According to Abellán, in "any legislative text a black list of authors is mentioned" (1980a, 139). Another mechanism for censorship was the *Index Librorum Prohibitorum* (Index of forbidden books) issued by the Roman Catholic Church.

In an effort to standardize the censorship guidelines, on March 15, 1940, Juan Beneyto, at that time president of the National Press Council, a post he had held since 1939, summarized the censorship criteria in nineteen points (Beneyto 1987, 33). It is worth mentioning the summary's second point, about surveillance, which "should also be carried out on anything that might be disturbing to military, civil, ecclesiastical or political institutions" (38). The image of Spain and the *caudillo* (leader) abroad was also controlled and protected.

In 1940, Beneyto also crafted a questionnaire to be included in all censorship files (1987, 33): "Literary or artistic value / documentary value / political nuance / deletion (with references to the pages) / other observations" (Lázaro 2004, 25). Taking the same information as a base, it changed a little bit in 1946: "Does it attack dogma or morals? / To Regime's institutions? / Does it have literary or documentary value? / Circumstantial reasons supporting the resolution / Observations" (26). In the 1950s it was even more detailed: "To the regime and its institutions? / To the people who collaborate or have collaborated with the regime? / Do the reprehensible passages qualify the total content of the work? / Report and other observations" (27). However, the questions do not seem to have been of any use, as the majority of censors left the form blank, only writing their own judgments under the title "observations."[23]

CENSORSHIP PROCEDURE

The 1938 Order was based on the concept of "prior censorship," in which the publisher had to submit two copies of the text to the corresponding body before publishing it (Santos Recuenco 2016, 44), either in galley proofs or in the original version, if it was a translation. Once this was done, each new book was assigned a number whose last two digits corresponded to the year of submission. A form was completed with the following information:

> Name and address of the publisher
> Author
> Title
> Name and address of the publishing company
> Number of pages
> Formatting
> Print run
> Price
> Series (if applicable)

The print run was especially important, as it sometimes determined the fate of the book. If the publisher forecast a long print run, it was very likely that the book would be censored or even banned because the goal was to keep citizens' minds as "safe" as possible. While information about the target language of translations was required, there was no specific spot to write this information on the petition. The form did include a section dedicated to "background," where censors mentioned the previous times the book had been submitted to censorship and the verdicts it received.[24]

Nonreligious books were generally censored by civil censors, but the censors would commonly ask for a "religious assessor" when unsure about a decision. Dionisio Ridruejo, director general of propaganda (1938–1941),[25] described the ecclesiastical power in censorship decisions: "A more or less secret Board of Governors, with abundant ecclesiastical participation, established rules and drew up lists of exclusions. These were decisions that could not be discussed. I fought once for the publication of certain works by Goethe, Kant, Stendhal, etc. And I was almost always defeated. Even my minister was defeated. A little later—already without the pretext of war—the betrayal increased. Relaxation did not begin to be felt until 1963" (Ridruejo 2007, 435). After consulting the Archivo General de la Administración in Alcalá de Henares, beginning in 1937 and continuing in the years that followed, Abellán stated, "We believe that Dionisio Ridruejo was wrong. What he wanted to indicate, without a doubt, was the degree of identification of the criteria between the state censorship . . . and the criteria of the Church" (1980a, 112n77). Religious books received an exception to this procedure since they were reviewed by ecclesiastical censors in order to receive the *nihil obstat* ("nothing hinders" it from being printed).[26] After April 1944, liturgical publications or church texts, Spanish literature from before 1800, and technoscientific and musical texts were not required to pass through prior censorship (Lima Grecco 2014, 368; *BOE*, April 7, 1944, no. 98, 2786). Other books were classified in the following categories: "Politics, history of Spain and political pedagogy; Religion and Catholic pedagogy; Scientific and textbooks; Military history and technique, and Entertainment and recreational reading" (Lima Grecco 2014, 368).

BOOK CENSORSHIP STAGES EXPLAINED: CONCLUSIONS

The book scene in Spain throughout the dictatorship was different for books written in Spanish and those written in Catalan. While the persecution of books written in Spanish was partial, since "only a part of the books or authors are prohibited," in the case of Catalan books "all . . . are at first prosecutable, because the underlying purpose is to destroy the Catalan reading public" (Vallverdú 2013, 10). Equipo Reseña and Alcover's reasoning was that "the Catalan language was left on the losing side" (1977, 84, qtd. in Bacardí 2012, 13) because "they were building the ideological pillars of the regime" (12). Bacardí also identified two types of censorship: *ideological*, for both Catalan and Spanish books, and *linguistic*, only for books in the regional languages (12). As the censorship criteria were different, the timelines do not coincide. While Abellán establishes only two stages of censorship for books written in Spanish, 1931 to 1966 and 1966 to 1976 (1980a), Vallverdú establishes five in Catalonia: 1939 to 1945, 1946 to 1951, 1952 to 1962, 1962 to 1966, and 1966 to 1976 (2013, 9–16). My proposal, as I will argue throughout the book, is to divide the censorship into four fundamental periods: 1939 to 1945, 1946 to 1959, 1960 to 1966, and 1966 to 1975.

1939–1945. During the first phase, the Falangist leader Millán Astray created the motto "Una patria, un estado, un caudillo" (a fatherland, a state, and a head of state), with which the regime tried to eliminate all regionalisms, and it punished them following the same scheme as the Inquisition. Thus, they fought to deconstruct the ideals of the regime's enemies through violence, betrayals, and revenge. Juan Beneyto confirmed this hypothesis: "The censorial mechanisms were not so much intended to remodel or create a new culture as to retaliate against undesirable outbursts and to prevent, as a precautionary measure, the dissemination of literary products whose ambiguity was excessive" (Abellán 1987, 11). The regime controlled the population in "two directions": Falangist and religious. The first guaranteed the defense of the army, the government, and the nation (Larraz 2014, 47); the second maintained the "moral puritanism" that, according to the regime, the "Reds" had lost.[27] In these first years, the aim of building an empire was still alive, and members of the Falange chaired the most important government offices. This stage, called "the desert,"[28] was the most devastating one for books issued in Catalan: such books were almost nonexistent, and translations remained a dream. By 1946 the regime was a little bit more flexible regarding regional languages.

1946–1959. The fate of World War II was crucial for establishing the new regime and rethinking the founding ideals of the "Movimiento." The government was restructured, and Falange members were removed from some key government positions. The National Tribunal of Political Responsibilities was also eliminated. Franco relied on the Holy See to disseminate

National Catholicism. Through the Concordat signed in 1953, religion was protected in Spain and made mandatory in schools (Franco's Concordat 1953). It became a very powerful monopoly in all aspects of the society. Gabriel Arias-Salgado, minister of information and tourism starting in 1951, tried to establish the "information theology" to justify the arbitrary censorship, basing the ruling system on Catholicism and more specifically in the precept of Saint Thomas. Certain publications in Catalan were permitted, provided they were literary works—in other words, "everything that is not linked or linked only a little to the realities and daily needs of the general buyer" (Gallofré 1991, 20–21).

The arrival of Opus Dei technocrats in the government in 1957 brought a drastic change to the country, as they opened it to tourism and to European and international organisms. Even though at first glance it looked more liberal, the censorship was still harsh, though it was more tolerant regarding regional languages and manifestations of culture. National Catholicism was the main doctrine.

1960–1966. In the 1960s, with the Stabilization Plan in force, many publishers wanted to issue books in Catalan, bypassing censorship and fostering "foreign" thoughts. Given the social context of Catalonia at that time, publishers had varying missions. Even though books had been issued in Catalan, it was not considered an academic language (Fuster interviewed in Beneyto 1975, 225) and was not taken seriously. As a result, publishers sought to regain the prestige that the language had lost during the dictatorship, as well as to find a standard linguistic register to which people could attach their identities (Coromina and Vilardell 2019, 146–47).

1966–1975. During this fourth phase, censorship was even more controlling as the government recognized its weakening position. The "Movimiento" died with the dictator in 1975 along with his wish to "leave the country tied up." The Press and Printing Law of 1966 encouraged freedom of expression, but, in reality, repression against publishers and Catalan translations was brutal. A "Pact of Forgetting" was signed in 1977 by all the political groups as a way to turn their heads away from the past and toward the future. One year later the constitution was signed, and democracy was established.

CHAPTER 2

Publishing Illicit Books during the Onset of the Dictatorship (1939–1959)

1939–1945: In a Hostile State—The Most Restrictive Phase

The social, economic, and cultural scene right after the end of the Spanish Civil War was devastating. In order to monitor publications, the regime used three weapons: repression, censorship, and propaganda. *Repression* can be driven by ideological, social, cultural, ethnic, or racial reasons and is defined as the restriction of the citizenry's freedom, with consequences ranging from bullying to murder, imprisonment, or torture.[1] *Censorship* is the suppression, modification, or distortion of ideas, thoughts, writings, or messages that may be found to be improper, offensive, or harmful by the power structures within a society. Lastly, *propaganda* is a tool of power with a directed intention to create in the citizens a new or modified thought, whether conscious or unconscious, according to the dominant doctrine. It can occur in a repressive context of dictatorship, but also in advertising, when the information breaks the layer of consciousness and makes us fall into unwanted behaviors (Manent 1984, 10).

The outcome of these strategies was clear: in the particular case of Catalan books, from 1939 to 1943 only ninety-nine were published, most of them clandestinely, and only four prewar collections in Catalan survived.

PROTECTING READERS

Both repressors and the repressed argued they *protected* readers against the threats posed by their enemies, whether those threats were foreign thoughts or the fascist doctrine. Thus, in order to better understand the consequences of the first censorship law, I find it essential to identify the four groups of readers.

Censor as a reader. Abellán quoted a pamphlet for the internal use of censors, that says, "Our work must be directed to destroy everything that could be harmful and prejudicial to our morals and to all the concepts mentioned above" (1980a, 108n73). According to Portolés, the censor "identifies himself . . . with the recipient of the message. He tries to protect him with his prohibitions on speeches that he sees as a threat to him" (2016, 119). For me, the only censors were the ones that worked at censorship services, who by means of a red pen decided what should be authorized.

Writer as a reader. It is the decision of the writer to adopt, consciously or unconsciously, the imposed guidelines, to practice self-censorship, or to publish abroad.[2] Spanish-language writers could easily resort to publishing their works in Latin America. In contrast, for those who wrote in Catalan, the possibilities of publishing abroad were few, as exiles were the only target market overseas.

Publisher as a reader. While Abellán (1980a, 97), Estanislau Torres (1995, 55), and Francesc Vallverdú (2004, 181) consider publishers to be censors, I disagree, since the actions of publishers should be considered as a means of self-censorship. To me, both writer and publisher have the same aim—to see the book published. Indeed, maintaining "an editorial line by a private company is a legitimate option and can never be considered properly censorship" (Vallverdú 2013, 10). It is undeniable that publishing houses are guided by economic reasons, and sometimes they had no choice but to "conveniently prune the text," even though unfortunately this sometimes still resulted in its nonauthorization (Arbonès 1995, 91).[3]

General Audience. This was the part of the Catalan society—shrinking as the days went by, given the fact that Catalan was not taught at school and was forbidden in public spheres—that expected the publication of books in Catalan and that hoped to encounter literary "new trends" in Catalan (Vallverdú 2013, 10). However, given the repression, many writers decided, some against their will, to switch to Spanish and wait for better times to come.

THE "PROVISIONAL" LAW OF APRIL 22, 1938, AND ORDER OF APRIL 29, 1938

The Law of April 22, 1938, on Press and Printing, was complemented by the Order of April 29, 1938, which addressed the sale and distribution of nonperiodical publications with a special emphasis on foreign book translations and imports.[4] This is the order that I will refer to from here onward.

The Order of April 29, 1938, popularly known among the writers who suffered under it as the Arias-Salgado Law, was named after the secretary, vice secretary, and minister who created it and enforced it for the longest time (from 1941 to 1962). It came into force during the Spanish Civil War and was signed by Ramon Serrano Suñer, minister of the interior at that time. The law was inspired by its antecedent, the Order of December 23, 1936, about pornographic and "unsettling literature" (Morcillo 2010, 226). The 1938 Order's main aim was to control publications, establishing prior censorship and regulating nonperiodic publications issued after July 17, 1936. The rules, "subject to the requirement of authorization by the Ministry in charge of Propaganda Services," can be divided into two scopes:

> **Commercial production and its circulation.** This area governs both publications from the national territory and those produced abroad.[5] Thus, in order to be approved, a printing or reprinting authorization form was required.[6] This had to include the number of sheets of paper that would be required for each book, the number of copies that would be printed, and the type of paper.[7] Once the first step was completed, the applicant needed to fill out a petition to obtain the authorization to print the book. This form was very detailed, including the addresses of both the publishing office and the publisher's home, in addition to the price, the series, and the print run, the last of these being decisive for approval. Prior censorship required that two copies of the work be submitted before publication.
>
> **The sale and circulation of foreign works on national territory** was totally prohibited, unless authorization had been obtained from the ministry. To this end, two copies and the petition had to be submitted before circulation, including the number of sheets, print run, and type of paper.

To avoid the legal loopholes that the administration encountered with the Customs and Border Services for book imports, the Order of June 24, 1938 (again approved during the Civil War; *BOE*, June 24, 1938, no. 610, 8002), had different criteria, depending on whether the request was made by importers or individuals and on the type of book:

Importers. For technical or liturgical publications it was sufficient to send, in duplicate, the catalogs or lists for approval, while for novels and historical or doctrinal publications the importing authorizations needed to be included as well.[8]

Private individuals or travelers.[9] Private individuals who were travelling with books were stopped at the border, and the Section of Censorship of the National Service of Propaganda was consulted about whether the publications were allowed on national territory. Books, pamphlets, and doctrinal periodicals in "German, Italian or Portuguese," from 1923, 1926, and 1932 would be authorized if they were published in the countries where those languages were spoken, since these countries were ideologically close to Franco's regime. For Spanish, "works written in Spanish and published outside Spain were suspicious." If it was a matter of "technical, liturgical or professional works," no prior consultation was required, and authorization could be obtained from the service in charge.

THE REASONING BEHIND NONAUTHORIZATIONS

According to the Order of April 29, 1938, nonauthorizations were caused mainly by the scarcity of paper stock (Manent 1984, 215–38; Baró Llambias 2005, 53) and improper doctrine:

> The body responsible for censorship may refuse to authorize printed matter, not only for reasons of doctrinal nature, but also in the case of works which, without being considered necessary or irreplaceable, may contribute to the present circumstances of the paper industry to hindering the publication of other printed matter which meets with preferential treatment. (*BOE*, April 30, 1938, no. 556, 7035–36)

According to Gallofré, *doctrinal nature* could refer not only to political concerns but also to the "use of non-Spanish languages in the state" (1991, 14). Once the Law of Political Responsibilities was passed in January 1939, the regime felt powerful enough to do and undo as it pleased. As Solé i Sabaté recalls, "Anyone can be accused of being *red-separatist*. . . . People everywhere are controlled. Everyone is analyzed by their past and their ideas. The authorities in each locality pass on reports" (1985, 53–54).[10] Authorities of the new state rushed to make a list of disaffected publishers, authors, and translators (Gallofré 1991, 21).[11]

Laws left ample room for censors to act based on the "criteria" I mentioned in Chapter 1. The application of the rule posed great difficulties for publishers, who, on top of having to overcome censorship and the export of foreign currency to pay foreign royalties, "went through an excessively complicated application procedure [that] forced publishers to indicate the number of copies sold in order to fulfil the payment of the corresponding royalties" (Baró Llambias 2005, 53). The surveillance "of the availability of paper" was another tactic of control, which led to "the proliferation of the black market" (53) since "the distribution . . . was rigorously assigned by portions" (Mengual Català 2013, "La industria editorial barcelonesa") and became much more expensive.[12] The only thing that remained, according to Ainaud, were the films that "came from Italy and Germany" (interviewed in Gabancho 2005, 26). However, even there, the regime's strategy was to dub movies, a compulsory practice from 1941 until 1967, in order to modify music, dialogue, sounds, and so on.[13] According to Joric, it "became the most powerful weapon of the censorship" (2015, 62–70).

BARCELONA, 1939: THE BOOK PURGE IN CATALONIA

Barcelona was in the spotlight because the regime knew that "the meridian of literary publishing activity was located in Barcelona, against the most political and official profile of the capital" (Gracia and Ródenas de Moya 2011, 45). During the Spanish Civil War, Barcelona had "supported . . . intense intellectual manifestations, the literature of classics and the usual rigor" (Santonja 2003, 132, 137). Thus, the city had "an infrastructure in terms of professionals, machinery and a network of bookstores that, even after the war, were very usable" (Mengual Català 2013, "La industria editorial barcelonesa retoma el hilo").

On March 5, 1939, *La Vanguardia Española* published a "book censorship note" (Servicio Nacional de Propaganda 1939) indicating, per the National Service of Propaganda, that all publishers must submit a list of the works published since July 1936 within forty-eight hours (Gallofré 1991, 19). Under the pretext of ridding the society of the "Marxist tendency," the ministerial body put an end to all the books *disaffected* with the regime, following the same strategy taken in 1936.[14] In order to eliminate "dangerous books," they established three categories. The first was *forbidden books*, which had to be handed over to the Departamento de Ediciones (Publishing Department) to become paper pulp.[15] The second category was *other books*, whose circulation was banned until further notice, and the third category was *allowed* (Gallofré 1991, 34). This is how Miquel Porter Moix, son of the antiquarian bookseller Josep Porter Rovira, remembers this episode of history:

Every day a couple of men came [to the bookstore], who looked around and said (in Spanish) "not this one, not this one either." They picked up the books from the bookshelves and carried them away. Without paying, of course. "It is seized," you know? This circumstance meant that the apartment where we lived suddenly became full of books because my father brought all those which were in danger of not being liked by those gentlemen. (interviewed in Gabancho 2005, 43)

However, as the process of "purification" was taking too long, the provincial head of censorship services of Barcelona informed its central office that the Barcelona Book Chamber had put itself forward as the controller of publishing activity in that area (Gallofré 1991, 34).[16]

On February 3, 1939, the official representatives of the Barcelona Book Chamber communicated to its members that from then on, the Chamber would belong to the provincial censorship services, and would thus be responsible for controlling which books were published and for monitoring the bookstores' editorial collections. Thus, "political power intervened in the Chamber, and it had no room to maneuver" (Llanas 2006, 33). Consequently, on March 6, 1939, Catalan publishers met again with the officials of the Barcelona Book Chamber to address their concerns (Baró Llambias 2005, 20). Josep Zendrera, from Juventud Publishing House, suggested exporting books to the Americas (Abellán 1980a, 18) as an alternative to destroying them.[17] With the majority agreeing, the president of the Chamber sent the official petition on April 11, 1939, to the National Service of Propaganda. However, in the minutes of the Barcelona Book Chamber of June 22, 1939, the members were informed that the petition "to settle in America the forbidden works" was denied (Llanas 2006, 21).[18] Baró Llambias noted that by 1940 the export of books by members of the Barcelona Book Chamber was halved, and "they go in a decreasing progression" (2005, 54).[19]

Once they took full control of bookstores and publishing houses, the government still faced the problem of secondhand bookstores. In order to reduce their riskiness, authorities asked all merchants to submit the checkbook registers of bought and sold books. The problem was that the bookstores never kept any inventory. According to Gallofré, a bookseller, scared about the consequences, went to the authorities and told them that the lists did not exist. This small gesture became the spark that lit the great fire, since on June 27, 1939, *La Vanguardia Española* announced that the Book Chamber was "proceeding with the purification" of its funds. In other words, booksellers had to submit within seventy-two hours the list of books sold and proof the books had been "acquired during the red domain" (Gallofré 1991, 41 and *La Vanguardia Española* 1939), that is, during the Second Republic.[20]

By Order of July 15, 1939, the National Service of Propaganda was unified and moved from Burgos to Madrid, creating a censorship section with five subsections: "Periodic and non-periodic publications, dramatic texts, patriotic writings and lyrics of musical compositions" (Montejo 2013, "introducción"). In short, they established a "unique platform" (Gallofré 1991, 60) to control not only nonperiodic publications, but also cinematographic, theatrical, and musical scripts. Thus, with the order of July 15, the control of the "previous, centralized and unique censorship" (Gallofré 1991, 68) was tied up. On June 9, 1939, Juan Beneyto became the head of Spain's censorship services so the delegate for Catalonia, the poet Sebastià Sánchez-Juan, was informed that the services of the Barcelona Book Chamber were not needed anymore.[21] As a result, in the final months of 1939, "lists of authors and works explicitly forbidden will begin to be drawn up (lists of 7 September, 16 November and 6 December)" (Mengual Català 2013, "Janés y sus amigos").

INLE (NATIONAL BOOK INSTITUTE)

The regime wanted to disseminate its idea of protecting readers from the dangers of Republican-tendency books. Thus, as a part of the propaganda strategy, Franco created the National Book Institute (INLE) through the Order of May 23, 1939, signed by Minister Serrano Suñer. According to the second article, the most relevant duties of the body were as follows:

> To direct the domestic and foreign policy of the book; to intensify its propaganda through contests, festivals, fairs, exhibitions, and competitions; to take care of the representation of Spain in the International Book Assemblies and Congresses; to draw up rules to combat illicit competition; to publish periodically a Bibliographic Bulletin of the books that appeared in Spanish language; to continue the edition, interrupted during the war, of the General Catalogue of the Spanish and Hispanic-American Bookstore, and to contribute, in short, by whatever means are considered appropriate, to the best fulfilment of the National function of the Spanish book. (*BOE*, May 22, 1941, no. 142, 3836)

The implementation of INLE was not among the regime's priorities, and the decree regulating its functions was delayed until April 19, 1941.[22] Among its articles, I highlight two concepts directly related to the subject matter of this book: *funding* and *scope*. Article 10 stated that INLE was "made up of the assets resulting from the liquidation of the Official Book Chambers of Madrid and Barcelona."[23] Article 56 stated that the scope was "all natural and legal people involved in the production of books and their trade." Moreover, among the functions of the body was the organization of the National Book Fair, an annual gathering for publishers that began meeting in 1943.[24] Carlos Robles Piquer, director of the National Book Institute from 1962 to 1969, attributes to INLE the virtue of being governed by publishers, booksellers, and high-level administration officials—a feature, according to him, rarely seen in Europe or America at the time (Robles Piquer 2011, 206).[25] INLE met every week, alternating between Madrid and Barcelona (207).

Julián Pemartín, falangist and director of INLE, approved what became INLE's milestone achievement: the Spanish Book Protection Law in 1946, known as *ley giliana* (the Gilian Law; Llanas 2006, 51), as it was based on the guidelines written by the Barcelonan publisher Gustau Gili in his book *Bosquejo de una política del libro* (1944). The law was about "establishing an aid of two pesetas for each kilogram of paper they would need to purchase" (Arimany 1993, 250).[26] Herrero-Olaizola stated that the law established a "tax exemption given to publishing houses . . . and was later reaffirmed with tax refunds of about 5 percent to cover exportations tariffs on paper (Devolución del impuesto)"; however, "the refund policy did not take full effect until 1962" (2007, 179).[27]

After passing through different state agencies, in 1951 INLE ended up joining the recently created Ministry of Information and Tourism, which was large enough to embrace those organisms that didn't have much support.[28] Guillermo Díaz-Plaja became INLE's director from 1966 until 1970 (Fraga Iribarne and Díaz-Plaja 1966, 387–94). One of his first decisions was to publish a catalog of books available in Catalan, which he began in 1967 and continued until 1988.

Also noteworthy is the publication of INLE's monthly magazine, titled *El Libro Español* and issued from 1958 to 1986, the year INLE ceased to be an autonomous body (*El País*, 1984c).

REPRESSION TOWARD PUBLISHERS

In reference to repression toward publishers as citizens, Martínez Rus mentions the "letter from the Jefe del Departamento de Ediciones [Head of the Publishing Department] dated 14 July 1939" (2014, 113), in which he related the book purge to the Law of Political Responsibilities. Thus, the belongings of those publishers who had closed or who left the country for being "markedly reds" could be transferred to those who stayed and showed loyalty to the regime. In addition, the government "restrict[ed] their advertising," as Juan Beneyto stated about the Maucci and Bauzá publishing houses, as a consequence of the Law of Political Responsibilities (1987, 33). In one noteworthy example of the repression of publishers as individuals, one of the most outstanding Catalan publishers, Josep Janés, was condemned to death. However, he was saved by his colleagues who belonged to the rebel side. In another instance, Rafael Giménez Siles's house was searched, his furniture evaluated, and his publishing house's information seized. His whereabouts were unknown (Martínez Rus 2014, 113), and eventually a case was filed against him by the government.[29]

I have already mentioned the lack of definition in the criteria used for censorship. At that time, censorship verdicts were also delayed from one month to more than half a year (Gallofré 1991, 134). Besides this, in 1940, the legislation on publications changed and became even more repressive, since "the criteria that had been applied in the old editions were not considered valid for the new ones" (138). All those books reported in the inventory given to the authorities during the book purges of 1939 were governed by the old law. In contrast, all those books hidden by publishers for later publication were governed by the new, more repressive law. As a result, Josep Pla stated, "There was not a single book in Catalan on the market that had not been published at least ten years before" (Llanas 2006, 23).

In order to further control the work of editors, the Order of March 15, 1941, established that publishing houses and editors "are obliged to present their publishing plans every semester to the Dirección General de Propaganda [General Directorate of Propaganda]" (*BOE*, March 15, 1941, no. 74, 1818–19). In addition to this, the governing body switched the office in charge of censorship matters, which had been the vice secretary of popular education. The new regulation required that publishers "send to the Publishing Section . . . a copy of the work accompanied by an affidavit, expressing the day the work appeared in the bookstore" (1819). Reprisals included fines, publishing applications, and even "temporary suspension of publishing activities" (1819). The response from publishers, as explained in the next section, was to hold clandestine literary meetings and to publish books with a false imprint or no date of publication.

The First Book in Catalan

Mes de Maria Eucarístic, published in 1939 and written by Lluís G. Otzet, is considered the first book in Catalan to be issued legally after the Spanish Civil War. Given the fact that its author was a priest, the only censorship needed was the ecclesiastical one so that it could receive the *nihil obstat*. At that time, the ecclesiastical censorship of Barcelona could authorize publications of no longer than sixteen pages. Thus, the book's publisher, Jaume Aymà (Mengual Català 2013, "La industria editorial barcelonesa"), filled out the censorship petition stating that the book was a "commemorative card of first communion" (Galderich 2015). Because the censorship body assumed it was certainly shorter than sixteen pages, they didn't even bother to review it. As a result, according to Mengual Català, 125 copies of a 237-page volume in Catalan were printed (2017)!

After 1939, the first book "legally published in Catalan" was *Rosa Mística*, by Camil Geis, issued in 1942 (Civtat 2017).[30] Its title could be read in the same way in Catalan, Spanish, and even Latin (*Revista de Girona* 2000, 6), so "to know that it was in Catalan you had to buy it, which was a complicity" (Josep M. Ainaud, interviewed in Gabancho 2005, 26). The book went through religious censorship and received the *nihil obstat*, as its author was also a priest.[31] The genesis of the authorization, however, was not known until Geis explained it in his forgotten book *Pas i repàs* (1981). The priest explained that he sent three copies to Spain's censorship services in Madrid, and twenty days later received the authorization along with a warning: "It is forbidden to write: 'visado por la censura' [approved by the Censorship]" (*Revista de Girona* 2000, 6). However, Geis said that the provincial head of press and propaganda in Barcelona was surprised because "there was the tacit criterion of not letting anything be published in the Catalan dialect" (*Revista de Girona* 2000, 6).[32] Gallofré also ratifies this idea when she points out that for regional languages, "only editions of works of undoubted value and of a classical nature or of folkloric value and scientific merit will be authorized" (1991, 190). Thus, by the simple fact of a text being written in Catalan, censors were free to prohibit it or to require changes, as in the case of the collection of children's songs *Aplec de cançonetes de Nadal*. In order for the collection to be authorized, the censors forced the authors to translate its title and prologue into Spanish (Gallofré 1991, 195). It was clear that they sought to distort the edition (198). In 1943 the regime authorized the first nonreligious books, allowing Selecta Publishing House to issue the complete works of Jacint Verdaguer, but with nonstandardized spelling, arguing about "the philological value it can have, in addition to the poetic" (157). In reality, it was "a humiliating condition" (Llanas 2006, 22), as it was written in almost hieroglyphic language for an audience not used to reading in Catalan. "However, the book was soon sold out" (Bacardí 2012, 16). The series *Les illes d'or* was also authorized and issued by Moll Publishing House (from the Balearic Islands), and Cruzet (of Selecta Publishing House) "managed to publish ... *L'Atlàntida*, *Canigó* and *Montserrat*, by Verdaguer" (16).[33]

Translations and Strategies (1939-1945)

During this period, translations into Catalan were totally forbidden. On top of that, in 1942, the Cuerpo de Inspectores de Traducción (Translation Inspectorate) was created to "monitor the import of foreign books and was responsible for safeguarding the Catholic morality and orthodoxy imposed by Franco's policy" (Ruiz Soriano 1998, 28). As a strategy for resisting the regime, Catalan intellectuals tried to translate books with fresh ideologies from abroad, even if they were in Spanish, in order to expose readers to the social and cultural reality outside Spain's borders.

As an exception, I underline the authorization of Fundació Bernat Metge, a collection of translations into Catalan from Latin and Greek classics published by Alpha. As Serrano Suñer stated, "In 1940 we began to authorize the publication of books in Catalan. The 'Bernat Metge' collection ... reappeared with publications not only for its subscribers" (1978, 442). What the minister does not mention is the fact that the regime obligated the publisher to issue a parallel book translation in Spanish, since there was not such a collection in this language.

Based on my experience reviewing censorship files from that time, and using the studies of Abellán (1987, 1980a), Gallofré (1991), Bacardí (2012), and Llanas (2006), as well as the memoirs of publishers, in Table 2.1 I summarize the strategies used by the regime at that time to accept or deny a book written in Catalan, as well as the ingenious tactics used by the publishers to bypass the regime's repression. This list is based on general trends rather than on individual cases.

Strategies to Issue Books in the First Stage of Francoism

Publishers responded in several ways to the regime's control of Catalan publishing (see Table 2.1). Even though the shortage of paper was used as a justification for the strict surveillance of publishing in Spain, it was based in reality. According to a study made by Josep Zendrera in 1943, "the poor quality of paper was one of the causes of the loss of the American market; the other cause was the price which, according to the report, had increased from 3.5 to 5.8 pesetas." (qtd. in Baró Llambias 2005, 53).[34] However, even though there were some government financial incentives to support publishers, as in the previously mentioned Spanish Book Protection Law (or the Gilian Law, passed in 1946),[35] it was difficult to issue any publication

TABLE 2.1. Control mechanisms and response strategies for issuing books in Catalan, 1939–1945

Control mechanisms	Response strategies
Control paper distribution	Use the black market (*estraperlo*) for importing paper to be able to publish clandestine books
Nonauthorization of books written by "disaffected" authors	Use only the initial of the author's first name with the last name so the author's identity is masked
Require translation of the title, foreword, or footnotes into Spanish	Find a title that could be read in both Spanish and Catalan, as well as abbreviations that are the same in both languages (e.g., "col." to designate a collection)
Use spelling prior to Catalan linguistic normalization (as the case of Selecta, Verdaguer in 1943)	Switch to Spanish in order to make a living or accept the changes as a means of resistance
Require that a Spanish translation be published in parallel (Alpha)	Publish in a patois between Catalan and Spanish, what the poet Salvador Espriu called "estellà," which uses Spanish words and expressions in the text in Catalan
Increase the price of foreign currency and therefore the royalties to foreign authors	Use contacts with cultural centers or consulates to negotiate royalties
Control book imports	Use *estraperlo*, or illegal entry of goods, in this case, books
Allow only short print runs and subscriber-only editions	Publish clandestinely or without an imprint (Galderich 2009)
Delay censorship resolutions	State that the work had already been accepted before the war
Fail to define the regime's position on the publication of books in regional languages	Include a note praising the regime and blaming the Republicans for all the ills of Spain
Increase arbitrariness from 1940 to 1945	Disobey the regime and publish works until asked to explain
Veto all translations	Identify the translator as the author of the work

and to attract the attention of a sufficient audience, as they faced the analphabetism and low incomes of the proletariat. According to *Actividad y territorio: Un siglo de cambios*, "in 1950 just over a quarter of the population, 27.9%, could not read or write" (Azagra Ros and Chorén Rodríguez 2007, 33). On top of that, there was the cost: a book at that time cost between 25 and 40 pesetas (Arimany 1993, 173), while, according to González, "the average salary in the industry in 1945 was 12.27 pesetas a day" (2009). As a consequence, in order to afford a book, workers had to spend two or three days' salary. The regime, aware of this, only authorized books with short print runs, which were pricey and intended for scholars or subscribers (Gallofré 1991, 176). To make up for the economic problems of potential customers, some publishers, such as Josep Pedreira, who issued the poetry series titled Els Llibres de l'Óssa Menor (1949–1963), gave away a large part of the print run to students and friends, or through literary contests (Sopena 2011, 304). Thus, as the reader may infer, the business did not always generate a profit; Pedreira ended up selling only 204 copies out of four hundred.

Another constraint was the social prestige of the Catalan language, which was struggling to survive as the regime tried to discredit it. In the 1940s, as Ainaud pointed out, "there were families, groups, and people who spoke Spanish to make themselves look good to the ruling class" (interviewed in Gabancho 2005, 25), even though Catalan was spoken at home. But this was not only the case with Catalan: any language other than Spanish was persecuted in those times. Thus, the regime's aim was to corner books written by both suspicious authors and those whose names didn't sound Spanish, including foreign authors, a practice inherited from the Führer's repressive policy (Abellán 1987, 32).[36]

In order to publish translations, currency exchange was required, as was payment of royalties, a practice that was especially guarded in the 1940s, when autarky reigned. Thus, Miquel Arimany (1993, 204), for example, would go either to cultural institutions of the author's country or to the consulate of the author's country for particular cases to negotiate the royalties.[37] Once he got them, he followed the popular practice, started by Josep Janés, of publishing all the author's works—"the good ones, the medium-quality ones and, probably, some of the bad ones" (204).

THE POSSIBILITIES AFTER THE OUTCOME OF THE SPANISH CIVIL WAR

The historical context after the outcome of the Spanish Civil War is summarized by Manent in these terms:

> In Catalonia we suffered a double oppression, the general one of those who were Spanish subjects and the specific one that wanted the cultural and linguistic genocide of the conquered land of Catalonia. Clumsy, perhaps the Francoists; but above all the loyalty of the majority of the people to the language and to certain ways of thinking and living stopped for the moment and then diluted the attempt to Delenda est Catalonia. (1986, 10)

Following the theory of colonial studies and in particular that of Homi Bhabha, given the "contradictory and ambivalent space" (1994, 37) that occurred in 1939, Catalan intellectuals had two options for survival. The first one was collaborationism or, in Wilson Harris's terms, "assimilation of contraries" (Bhabha 1994, 38); the second one was exile, or creating a "third space" of encounter among those disconnected from Catalan culture. In this sense, whether they were physically abroad (external exile) or in the Spanish territory (internal exile), they tried to keep the spark of Catalan culture alive in different ways, either through illegal and clandestine activities or legal but uprooted means of surviving. As a result, the culture and literature in Catalan "produced throughout the 1940s and 1950s is the result of the interplay of relationships established between that produced in exile and that produced underground," along with "that one produced publicly by the country, promoted by the state, the municipality or private initiatives" (Molas 1991, viii).

Even though the meaning and symbols of a culture have no essential guidelines—since the same signs can be appropriated, translated, rehistoricized, and read anew (Bhabha 1994, 37)—people in exile tried to keep in mind the references learned in Catalonia to construct what Ferriz Roure calls "supra-text" (2001), based on the movements that took place before the Spanish Civil War.

Collaborationists

Collaborationists were people who, usually before or right after the war was over, decided to switch sides and started wearing the blue shirt (the emblem of the Spanish Falange). The reasons for this change of mentality are varied, although one reigned supreme: fear, whether for one's life, one's professional activity, or one's family. Indeed, repression in Catalonia was combined with terrible and Machiavellian emotional blackmail. Collaborationists can be divided into three groups: (a) the convinced ones, or those who really believed in the slogans of the movement and never wrote in Catalan again;[38] (b) the scared ones, or those who, fed by the fear of repression, wore the blue shirt and waited for better times to come;[39] and (c) those who sold themselves to the highest bidder.

For the first group, I quote José M. Gironella, who justified himself in these terms: "When I started to write (I applied for the Nadal Prize in 1945), Catalan was absolutely prohibited. *And I had the vocation of a writer, not of a hero.* The second reason is maybe a consequence of the above mentioned: I felt in love with the Spanish language" (interviewed in Beneyto 1975, 147). The italics are mine to emphasize that he opted for the easiest solution. Secondly, there were those who were scared for their own lives, as in the case of Jordi Solé-Tura:

> In the midst of that confusion of feelings, of normality re-discovered and normality violated, it was communicated to everyone that if they wanted to save their imprisoned relatives and they wanted to have more security in the face of the approaching massacre, it would be good for them to join the Falange. A lot of people did. They made me too. And with me many schoolmates who had parents, older brothers and sisters and relatives in prison. Then the sad years began. . . . People came out of the fear of the war and into the fear of a dark and threatening system that came with a thirst for revenge. (1999, 28–29)

Within this group there were countless people who suffered repression, death, and blackmail. Finally, there are those who, depending on the circumstances, changed their ideology. One of the best examples here is the painter Salvador Dalí. For example, in an interview for the French radio station France 1, he stated, "Franco is a wonderful being, I am against freedom and for the Holy Inquisition. Freedom is shit" (Arasa 2008, 358). After a while, he declared his apoliticism.

DESTINO

To show their "Spanishness," some of the collaborationist Catalans resident in Burgos—Ignasi Agustí, together with Joan Teixidor, Josep Vergés, and Juan Ramón Masoliver—founded in 1937 the weekly Falangist publication *Destino*, which fiercely defended rebels during the start of the Spanish Civil War and became the voice of Falangism.[40] In 1939, "those who would return in blue uniforms, and others who suddenly adapted, enjoyed the experience that the new official culture gave them" (Samsó 1994, 153). In order to fulfill the propaganda strategy of the regime, *Destino* was moved to Barcelona, beginning with issue 101 of June 24, 1939. It aimed to satisfy the Catalan bourgeoise's demands by creating a publication close to the prewar Catalan magazine *Mirador* (Samsó 1994, 136) and fostering a "nonpolitical Catalanness . . . although not a single article could be published in Catalan" (Manent 2010, "Polèmica a l'exili").[41] This new era was directed by Ignasi Agustí until 1958 (Corderot 2004, 209n12), when Néstor Luján took the lead.[42]

Franco's main objective was that Catalan speakers themselves would push their native language aside and switch to Spanish for any public or private event (Gallofré 1991, 213), even though there was an "explicit recognition of Catalan culture" (Samsó 1994, 84). Among the initiatives taken, we count not only this weekly magazine but also literary awards, such as the prestigious Nadal Prize for novels established in 1944 and still awarded today (Bru de Sala and Dropez 2003, 44). The regime thus tried to fight against the most powerful weapon of Catalans: their language.[43]

Exile in Europe and America

According to Larraz, between 1936 and 1950 "the Spanish publishing industry went through one of the most critical stages in its recent history" (2014, 62). In contrast, Argentina, Mexico, and Chile were living their "golden age" as they published a great number of the titles banned in Spain.

In the case of Catalan books, Manent and Crexell proved for the first time that the number of books in the Catalan language published in Catalan territory—mainly clandestinely or receiving the *nihil obstat* through ecclesiastical censorship—was always higher in comparison to the "six hundred books and booklets in Catalan" that were published in exile from 1939 to 1975 (Manent 2010 "Polèmica a l'exili").[44]

The general tendency among those who left the country leads me to divide the Republican exile into two stages: (a) from January or February 1939 until the end of World War II, and (b) from 1946 to 1975, with the most prolific period lasting until 1959.[45] This division has to do with psychological reasons: in the first stage, intellectuals were convinced that exile was temporary, and after the defeat of fascism in Europe, they hoped that European democracies would remove Franco from power.[46] The reality, though, was that they had to deal with an even stronger and endless regime. Their reaction was double-sided. According to Bacardí, some writers had the conviction that they would never use Catalan as a literary language again (2012, 14–15), but others found a way to create an element of struggle and resistance abroad. Besides this, Lluís Agustí explains, Catalan exiles had to assimilate to the target language and culture (2018, 20) (although not all of them did).[47] The writer Pere Calders, for example, left in 1939 with the aim of returning in three or four years (Coromines 2019, "pròleg"), yet ended up staying in Mexico City for twenty-three years (from 1939 to 1962):

> I was very homesick, I wanted to go back, so it was a kind of resistance that I don't find right, against a country that had generously welcomed me. I didn't want to stay there, I just thought about going back, this is not right but I did. So we made a kind of little glass-bell island, some groups of Catalans who lived in a great city in a great country, but made up of Catalan families, let's say. (Calders interviewed in TV3 1991, 1:10–1:31)

Catalan intellectuals saw their language as an element of resistance and an indisputable part of their identity. Their aim was to build a national political entity, gathering all Catalan-speaking territories, including the Balearic Islands and the Valencian Country. Apart from this, they did not want to renounce their ideology or the cultural references learned in Catalonia before the Civil War. The tendency in both groups of exiles was to keep their ideology while praising the past with a focus on Noucentisme, the movement that took place before the war and through which Pompeu Fabra standardized the Catalan language.[48]

WORLD WAR II

During the Spanish Civil War, many of the exiles crossed the Pyrenees and went to France. There is only a difference of five months between the end of the Spanish Civil War and the start of World War II, and thus those who sought refuge in France had to decide their fate. According to Ainaud, some of them left for America while others returned to Spain (interviewed in Gabancho 2005, 23). As an example, right after the end of the Spanish Civil War, Anna Murià, translator, writer, feminist, and poet, stayed at the Roissy-en-Brie castle with other great figures of Catalan and Spanish literature: "twenty Catalans and twenty Spanish, intellectuals. . . . We stayed very well there" (interviewed in Serra 1999, 15:50–16:00). However, after the start of World War II, she left for Latin America (Brenneis 2018, 120).

The epicenter of the European Republican exile was France and England, while the exiles in the American continent went to Mexico, Chile, Argentina, and, to a lesser extent, Uruguay.

JOCS FLORALS IN EXILE

One of the most important initiatives that lasted until the end of the dictatorship was the celebration in exile of the Jocs Florals, a Catalan poetry contest that finds its origins in the twelfth century (Boer 1952). Its celebration was not permitted in Barcelona or Catalan beginning in 1939.[49] Thanks to the entrepreneurship of Pere Mas i Perera and the approval of the Consell de la Comunitat Catalana a l'Argentina, the Jocs Florals was running from 1941 to 1977, each year in a different location of the world.⁵⁰ Both exiles and those who remained in the country participated, such as Albert Manent, who won the Natural Flower Prize at the Caracas Games in 1953 (Manent 2010, "Més notícies"). As Faulí stated, "no other activity in exile had such an impact" (CRAI 2009).

STARTING A NEW PUBLISHING HOUSE ABROAD
According to Mengual Català, there were three attitudes when it came to starting a new publishing house or magazine abroad: serve only the community in exile; start serving the community in exile, but afterward adapt to the target audience; and start a new project serving the target audience, but keeping one's own ideology (2019). Regarding the behavior of publishing houses, Mengual Català identified two trends: those who aimed to introduce, as much as they could, their books to Spain's book market, and those who published in other countries.⁵¹ Their main aim was to contribute to the enrichment of the Catalan literature, fostering translations and also originals in Catalan around the world. However, authors had to be aware that the publisher would not pay royalties for their work, given the current economic situation. In exchange, they got real freedom of speech (Ferriz Roure 2001). Publishers in exile became self-sufficient, acquiring the roles of publisher-editor-printer. For funding, they relied on their own finances, although associations that fostered Catalan language and culture could contribute by issuing some books and subscriptions by exiles.

MAGAZINES
Magazines were usually under the protection of some association or choral society, or sometimes they were initiatives that had been started at the beginning of the twentieth century and the publishers saw exile as an excellent way to sustain them. That was the case, for example, of *Ressorgiment*, from Argentina, started back in 1916, and *Germanor*, from Santiago de Chile, which started in 1912 and became "on a par with the best [magazines] of the emigration" (Manent 2010, "La represa"). The newly created ones were mainly started in Mexico in 1942 by great names of Catalan literature, such as Joan Sales or Agustí Bartra. These magazines included *Quaderns de l'Exili*, *Pont Blau*, *La Nostra Revista*, and *Lletres*. In 1944, in Perpignan, France, *Quaderns d'Estudis Econòmics, Polítics i Socials* was issued, and *Revista de Catalunya* was published in Paris. All this editorial production

arrived only very sporadically in Catalonia "because they did not pass the thick net of censorship." On very rare occasions, people had them secretly thanks to a traveler ("La represa").

DESTINATION: ENGLAND

Joan Gili i Serra (1907–1998), was a publisher who left Barcelona in 1934 to start a bookstore in London. His Dolphin Book Publishing House introduced some of the most celebrated Hispanic authors, such as Federico García Lorca and Salvador Espriu, to the English-speaking market beginning in 1935. He was also one of the founders of Anglo-Catalan Society. Between London and Oxford, he helped Republican exiles who were leaving Catalonia,[52] among whom were well-known writers such as Carles Riba and Marià Manent (Joan Gili / Dolphin Book Company collection, MS1197). "The Civil War . . . brings him closer to solidarity with the important exiles, Trueta, Pi i Sunyer, Batista i Roca" (Pol 1987). However, in 1938 the Spanish Embassy in London threatened him with consequences for his family in Barcelona if he did not stop these activities (Michael 1998, 18).

DESTINATION: FRANCE

In France, there were two different publishing houses that are worth mentioning for historical reasons and also for their influence on Catalonia.

Editorial Albor: Once Ferran Canyameres obtained the rights to publish the works of Georges Simenon in Catalan and Spanish, he founded the Albor publishing house in Paris in 1942, together with two other partners (Canyameres 1972, 182). The volumes were issued in a collector's edition, which bothered certain sectors of the Catalan exile community, who thought they were too expensive. In 1949, having just arrived in Barcelona, Canyameres "signed a contract with the publishing house Aymà to publish his translations of Georges Simenon" (Terrades and Erill i Pinyot 1999). Albor, however, closed its doors in 1958, after Canyameres had been imprisoned twice, in 1954 and 1957.

Editorial Proa: Josep Queralt i Clapés and Marcel·lí Antich founded Edicions Proa in Badalona in 1928. After passing through concentration camps, Queralt's aim was to move the publishing house to his new home, Perpignan (Camps i Arbós 2004, 45n1).[53] In 1949 Queralt received the letter that allowed him to start his publishing activities, and he chose Joan Puig i Ferrater, who lived in Paris, and Ramon Xuriguera, who lived in Mouleydier and

Bergerac (47), as his collaborators. Edicions Proa promoted their work by publishing translations by exiles, mainly from French into Catalan (with the permission of the mayor of Perpignan) and by offering prizes at public events. Indeed, despite the difficult economic situation the publishing house faced, in 1950 they offered a prize of one hundred thousand French francs in the Jocs Florals of Perpignan to the best novel; the award was won by Xavier Benguerel (61), at that time living in Santiago de Chile. From 1952 onward, the economic struggles became more serious (72).[54] In 1964 Editorial Aymà continued the series A tot Vent (Proa), and in 1965, the year of Queralt's death, Proa settled back in Catalonia under the label of Aymà, owned by Joan Baptista Cendrós and directed by Joan Oliver (74).

DESTINATION: AMERICA. CATALAN PUBLISHERS IN EXILE IN MEXICO

Those who decided to go to Mexico found a land of refuge, thanks to the Mexican president, Lázaro Cárdenas, who welcomed the exiles ("Conmemoración del 80 aniversario" 2019). After the country gave them the necessary tools so that they could work freely, the publishing, bookselling, and graphic design industries became, in part, controlled by committed Catalan refugees. Patricia Weiss Fagen (1973) saw it as a win-win: while the Mexicans "benefited from the experience and neatness of the foreign publishers, they in turn gave them a place to publish" (qtd. in Agustí 2018, 1144).

The final product was, according to Tísner (Avel·lí Artís-Gener), "well-made works" (Ferriz Roure 2001), written under normative grammar guidelines, that aimed to attain the attention of a broad audience by modifying, including, and excluding content; the publications were then advertised in national magazines and newspapers. The print runs of popular books, according to Ferriz Roure, were usually around five hundred copies, though they also issued some special collectors' editions with shorter print runs. Some authors, such as Josep Carner and Agustí Bartra, translated their own works, whereas the younger generation was able to publish in Catalan under a Mexican publishing label, as Ramon Xirau did. In the majority of cases, the readers were tied politically or culturally to Catalonia. The zenith of publications in Catalan in Mexico was in the mid-1940s.[55] Later the publications were a means of gathering the community, but they had a lesser impact overall.

In 1953, the origin "of the new editorial attempt in Mexico" was, according to Pere Calders in a letter to Joan Triadú, dated July 9 in Mexico City, as follows:

> The printer Guillem Gally, knowing that censorship had banned *Odisseu* by Bartra, a work of purely literary intention, had the idea of publishing it [in Mexico], annexing the censorship office, without any comment. Hence, by virtue of his progressive enthusiasm, the idea was born of publishing all those works that could not be published in Catalonia, but which were essentially forbidden without justification. (Calders and Triadú 2009, 39)

But there were limitations:

> But reality has shown us that there are multiple reasons that will limit the company. On the one hand, it seems that there are not as many works as we believed in the situation expressed, and on the other hand, the "censored" authors will decide not to authorize the publication of their works in Mexico. . . . All this made Gally a bit discouraged. (39)

The idea that the repression would not last forever was still very much in people's minds. Therefore, if the copyright was given to a Mexican publisher, it could "become an obstacle to the publication of my book in Barcelona—which is what fundamentally interests me" (Calders and Triadú 2009, 39). Publishers were looking forward to "a day in the future when they would be able to affirm their rigor, which always seemed closer than it [actually] was" (Arimany 1993, 238).

THE RESISTANT CORES: THE INNER EXILE

Given the virulent and oppressive context, the population of Catalonia was distributed in the following way: people in prison, dead people, collaborationists, those who informed on some acquaintance or relative to free themselves of charges, and those who were silenced forever by the repression. The expression "inner exile" refers to "those who, not having moved from Catalonia, tried to survive and rebuild the cultural fabric that Francoism had wanted to destroy" (Manent 2010, "Pròleg").

Immersed in autarky and struggling to make the paychecks last until the end of the month, many Catalan intellectuals used "literary bilingualism," or switched to Spanish for publication, as Ramon Folch i Camarasa did in more than two hundred translations, always signing under a pseudonym, because "I didn't want my name to be linked to the language that was picking on us at that time" (Lladó 2004, 217). The same was true for Carles Riba, who signed under the pseudonyms of Javier Barceló and Carlos Ibarra (Bacardí 2012, 20). According to Castellet, "to be Catalan, even if you live in Catalonia, is to be a translator" (1955, 30) because of the diglossia in which Catalan civil society was immersed—enhanced, of course, by the regime. Those intellectuals who remained loyal to Catalan language and culture often had another source of income (Flotats i Crispi and Boix i Selva 1994). Creating special collectors' editions was another means of intellectual resistance starting in 1946 (Manent 2010, "Més editorials en català"); this became a strategy for issuing books after World War II, as the censorship services seemed to be less strict in this area.

CLANDESTINE ACTIVITIES

In 1943, Carles Riba, recently returned from exile, became the leader of the reconnection movement (Molas interviewed in Gabancho 2005, 162). Clandestine meetings started, the first ones held in the home of professors J. V. Foix and Riba (Manent and Raguer interviewed in Gabancho 2005, 72).[56] They offered cultural groups and private "reading" sessions, particularly on Sunday afternoons, that "served to commemorate important events, pay homage to important people, listen to lectures or concerts, stage plays, and . . . to read recent works" (Bacardí 2013, 2).[57] Everyone was welcomed, and attendees included great figures of Catalan literature along with amateurs and young writers.[58]

The approval of the Fuero de los Españoles Law in 1945 along with social and political changes meant that after 1946 "it became 'fashionable' to hold 'semi-clandestine' sessions" (Samsó 1994, 176).[59] By 1948, some of them were held in public places, such as at Boliche Restaurant or on the ground floor of Llibreria Catalònia, renamed Casa del Libro by the regime (177). These meetings were part of a long process initiated by a group of people with a common goal: to keep the flame of Catalanism alive. The action to fulfill this objective was translated into the following areas:[60]

Writers' Gatherings. Once the Spanish Civil War was over, in the early 1940s, some writers' gatherings emerged, such as Amics de Rosselló-Pòrcel or Amics de la Poesia. Amics de la Poesia (1942–1945 and 1946–1953) was the first and most important one of them, because it became "one of the first instruments—more than clandestine, in the catacombs—to reunite people that meant something for Catalan culture during the Republic times" (Gabancho 2005, 258).[61] In March 1941, Josep Palau i Fabre, with Ramon Aramon, organized two poetic sessions that can be considered "the precursor sessions of Amics de la Poesia" (Samsó 194, 186). Palau decided to gather illegally in his father's house with about ten people.[62] The strategy of the

Catalan writer was to invite a former combatant of the Franco regime, Miquel Dolç, to the first meeting in case the police showed up (Palau i Fabre, interviewed in Gabancho 2005, 258). He had to personally invite the attendees, since "the mail could not be trusted, because the mail was censored. It was very serious, everything" (259). The second meeting of Amics de la Poesia had fifteen people (Samsó 1994, 181). "In the meetings, people entered one by one or in pairs and made sure that the meeting did not last more than two hours" (Samsó 1994, 188). They also issued clandestine booklets, called *Quaderns* (notebooks), that included the readings and normally were published with no imprint and sometimes with no date.[63] In March 1942, Amics de la Poesia started formally in the back room of the jewelry shop of Ramon Sunyer. This initiative resulted in about thirty readings (Samsó 1994, 190).

Taking advantage of the little allowances made by the regime, more than one hundred sessions were held between 1946 and 1953 (Arimany 1993, 250), still with the fear of having to disperse immediately if the police showed up.[64] According to Albert Manent, "they were very crowded meetings; there were sixty or seventy people" (interviewed in Gabancho 2005, 73). Miquel Gayà explained that after 1945, the members "paid a fee high enough to belong to the association" (1986, 262).

Magazines Written by Young People. Between 1939 and 1945, the Catalan intellectual scene was hitting rock bottom. There were fewer and fewer professors capable of teaching university classes, because the majority of intellectuals went into exile or were in hiding.[65] Instead, colleges were full of regime sympathizers with few pedagogical skills. However, a minority of these professors were true intellectuals who inspired and engaged students to create university magazines (Molas 1978).[66]

Following the victory of the Allies in World War II, Palau i Fabre saw that the Amics de la Poesia accepted everything that was written in Catalan, whether good or bad poetry, so he left the group to create the Amics de Rosselló-Pòrcel and the clandestine magazine *Poesia* (1944–1945). Due to the vigilance of the regime in monitoring the paper supply, though, he opted to use thread paper for his magazine. This is how he described the process: "I went from Can Guarro [where he got the paper] to the printer's. Nobody could think, if they saw me on La Rambla: this well-dressed guy is making a clandestine magazine. It was so obvious that no one thought about it" (Palau i Fabre, interviewed in Gabancho 2005, 261). The magazine, one of the first issued in Catalan, enjoyed an indisputable literary quality and about one hundred subscribers (Verrié, interviewed in Gabancho 2005, 131).[67] Palau i Fabre explained that he worked alone, as Miquel Arimany did in the early years of his publishing house, sometimes even working with more than one printing house (Arimany 1993, 178).[68] When Palau i Fabre left for Paris in 1945 thanks to a grant from the Institut Français, no one was in charge of the journal, as it was such a personal undertaking. For this reason, Joan Triadú, Miquel Tarradell, and Frederic-Pau Verrié founded the magazine *Ariel* (1946–1951) as a kind of continuation of *Poesia* that "represented the restart of the past from the dual perspective of classicism and the avant-garde" (Manent 2010, "La represa").[69] The big differences between the two magazines were the format and the fact that all contributions to *Ariel* were signed. According to Verrié, "it was a real provocation" (interviewed in Gabancho 2005, 133), although without an imprint.

As for personal initiatives, it is worth noting the crucial role played by ecclesiastics such as Mossèn Ramon Muntanyola, who created a clandestine magazine called *Ressò*. "He ended up with fines of 10,000 pesetas and two men in prison. As he was a priest, he did not go" (Manent, interviewed in Gabancho 2005, 73). Censorship services persecuted and eventually shut down two other journals: *Antologia* (1947–1948) and *Temps* (1948).

In 1949, Ramon Aramon started the journal *Estudis Romànics* from the "clandestine" Institut d'Estudis Catalans.[70] Those in charge of the publication emphasized that the magazine had a scientific scope, so it was able to avoid censorship: it "gave us international prestige" (Manent 2010, "L'escletxa"). The *Anuaris de l'Institut* also resumed, although issues were only published in 1952 and 1953 (Coll i Alentorn 1992, 505). The first authorized and legal journal aimed at a broad audience with a regular publication schedule was *Serra d'Or*,[71] published in 1959 and protected by the Monastery of Montserrat (Manent 2010, "La represa").[72]

Youth Debate Forums and Cultural Action. Grup Estudi was another outstanding cultural initiative from the early postwar years. Led by Maurici Serrahima, the group wanted to educate subsequent generations, putting senior writers in touch with younger ones. They met fifty-three times, from 1942 to 1955, and left behind a magazine, *Estimats Amics* (Dearest friends), signed with pseudonyms (Samsó 1994, 210), although in the last issues of the magazine, from 1944, some of the collaborators signed with initials or their whole names (211n27).

Another group, Miramar, was founded in 1945 by Maurici Serrahima, a "bridge man between the generations before and after the war" (Samsó

1994, 253), who encouraged harmony among the members. The aim of the initiative was to create a generation of young people from different sectors of society gathered by their opposition to the dictatorship and their love for Catalonia. The initiative was divided into different sections to offer plenty of short-termed courses (around thirty the first year) and conferences about diverse topics with the aim to "educate leaders" (Giró 2004, 102) and gather together different generations of intellectuals. Once the regime was recognized by UNESCO in 1952, the group no longer made sense, as it seemed the Franco regime would continue indefinitely, and it dissolved the same year.

Literary Prizes. Several literary prizes were begun during this period, among them Joanot Martorell (1947–), launched on the initiative of Aymà, and Nit de Santa Llúcia (1951–), initiated by Josep M. Cruzet, head of Selecta Publishing House (Sarsanedas, interviewed in Gabancho 2005, 118).[73] These prizes, together with gatherings and the help of editorial and personal initiatives, placed "Catalan culture on the surface of Barcelona's social and public life" (Samsó 1994, 176), although there were still some efforts that remained hidden, such as La Nit de Sant Jordi, held clandestinely "in the house of the architect Lluís Bonet Garí" (Arimany 1993, 251).

Organized Patronage to the Institutions. Ramon Aramon, disciple of the philologist Pompeu Fabra, became a key figure for the Catalan resistance: he reorganized the Institut d'Estudis Catalans (IEC; Institute of Catalan Studies) with new members, since the former ones were either hidden, dead, or in exile. The institution was *in public clandestinely*,[74] the expression used by Miquel Coll i Alentorn to refer to the fact that the authorities would not recognize it as an academic corporation, but "they did not deny its status" (Balcells 2012, 93) either.

Thus, according to Albert Manent and Coll i Alentorn, the plenary meetings and Sant Jordi celebrations were held in the dining room of the home of Josep Puig i Cadafalch, president of the institution.[75] In addition to this initiative, Aramon also relaunched the Estudis Universitaris Catalans, "an embryonic clandestine university" (Manent 2010, "L'escletxa"), at his house and that of Professor Jordi Rubió i Balaguer.[76] The Catalan bourgeoisie played an important role supporting clandestine cultural events. In 1943, Fèlix Millet set up an almost one-man company called Agrupació Benèfica Minerva (Coll i Alentorn 1992, 504).[77] Its aim was to ensure the publication of books in Catalan and also to support Catalan institutions financially.

Folkloric Associations. After 1945, folklore associations, mainly under the auspices of religious organizations, were authorized. This was the case for the artistic and cultural entity Esbart Verdaguer, founded in 1945, which intended to disseminate Catalan folk dances while defending the autochthonous culture and language.[78] According to Joaquim Carbó, the Esbart was the seed that brought together teachers, students, and organizers for Catalan classes, carried out "in secret [by] teachers Balot and Antoni Jaume" (2008, 64). But it wasn't easy to start a folklore group at that time. Miquel Arimany explained in his memoirs that when a group of people asked to create one, the governor advised them—secretly—to affiliate with an organization that already existed "in agreement with the board" (1993, 216), even though the main aim of the organization may have been completely unrelated. For example, some ended up being part of the Unió Excursionista de Catalunya (Catalan Hiking Union), "a group of people who mostly had nothing to do with hiking" (216).

Legal and Foreign Institutions. The meetings that found protection in foreign cultural centers, such as the London Club or the Institut Français, can be considered semi-clandestine meetings, since they "served as a refuge for Catalan cultural activities and groups" (Samsó 1994, 93). According to Jordi Sarsanedas, the Institut Français hosted talks on different subjects thanks to its director during the period from 1939 to 1962, Pierre Deffontaines, who also founded the Literary Circle, which ran from 1946-1947 until 1951-1952 within the same institution (Samsó 1994, 290). This initiative gathered Catalan intelligentsia in "a free entity ... promoted and welcomed by the Institute" (291n4). However, they didn't escape censorship, since Sebastià Sánchez-Juan was responsible for approving the sessions and sometimes also showed up at the meetings (Sarsanedas, interviewed in Gabancho 2005, 110).

Jordi Sarsanedas explained to Patrícia Gabancho that the Salvador printing house from Barcelona, which printed clandestine publications about UFOs, Protestant religious texts, and some issues of the Catalan magazine *Ariel*,[79] had a typesetter "who must have been clandestine. He was a policeman, one of the 'grays.' I mean that in that printing house working on unauthorized things, a man dressed in gray arrived and worked hourly as a cashier" (interviewed in Gabancho 2005, 115). Therefore, the regime not only was aware of what was happening but also allowed it. As long as they fulfilled their objective to eventually eliminate Catalan from the public scene, they did not care much about what was taking place privately.

However, that doesn't take away from the fact that clandestine actions were also sometimes forcefully punished (Gallofré 1991, 358).

The outcome of the Spanish Civil War implied that everything related to Catalonia fell on the side of the losers. As a result, the city of Barcelona, one of the most important epicenters of publishing before the war, suffered endless retaliation: book purges, government control over editorial plans, and the most restrictive laws on book publication. In this context, Catalan editors and writers had to decide their own fate, whether switching sides to defend the National cause (collaborationists; leaving in exile and publishing abroad, hoping for better times to come); or staying and resuming literary activities clandestinely, with countless secret activities, among them issuing magazines, gathering on Sundays, and publishing books without imprints. Given this scenario, it is not surprising that scholars such as Molas and Vallverdú named the period from 1939 to 1945 "the desert." However, the outcome of World War II produced a sense of hope the outcome of which will be seen in the next section.

The Rebirth of Catalan Letters: Publishing Books "of a Literary Nature" (1946–1959)

With the Allied victory in World War II, Franco decided to distance himself more and more from Falange, "because it was too closely linked to Italian fascism and German Nazism and therefore [became] a nuisance to the winners" (Vallverdú 2013, 10). Without the weight of this conservative sector, the dictator decided to show a "kinder" face, getting closer to "regional" cultures. Thus, in order to assess the current situation of the book market and to approach it without giving free rein, Franco sent the provincial delegate of popular education (at that time the body in charge of censorship) to Barcelona. The result was a "very complete" (Gallofré 1991, 234) report issued in May 1946. After the statement of facts, his verdict was as follows: "I consider advisable, as far as problems of book censorship are concerned, to ... a) Recognize and authorize the use of the Catalan language as a means of literary expression. Poetry and novels, as well as essays—typical forms of literary creation—should be included in this margin of authorization" (Gallofré 1991, 235). The concept of "literary creation" was another example of ambiguity and provided, as always, ample room for interpretation. As a result, Catalan publishers, in an effort to publish legal works in their own language, used this vague statement to their advantage by submitting historical essays or technical and scientific books with an introduction justifying their categorization as a literary creation.[80] One of the most curious cases was the publication of *La teca* by Ignasi Domènech, who tried to pass off a cookbook as a literary creation. When it was authorized in 1946, it set a precedent for technical publications in Catalan that was immediately resolved by banning them with rather colorful pretexts, such as "not in the language you want" (Bacardí 2012, 35). However, the guideline allowed publishers to issue books of poetry in regional languages, and the regime saw this as "suitable and desirable" (Gallofré 1991, 295) since poetry was not for everybody and could be considered part of the folklore.

The delegate's report mentioned earlier had a special warning for translations: "This is not the case of the translation of foreign works, except for those in which the translation has the value of literary creation—Carlos Riba's *La Odisea*, for example[81]—or when—as in the case of the Fundació Bernat Metge (Bernat Metge Foundation)—it is appropriate to save a considerable work, which has already been done and which has no equivalent in the Spanish language" (Gallofré 1991, 235). As a result, one of the strategies of publishers was to pass off the translator as the author and the content as literary creation (385). Another strategy was to visit the censorship services either in Barcelona or Madrid. Even though the delegate mentioned Carles Riba's *Odyssey* as an exception, Riba had to go personally to Madrid in 1948 to ask for authorization to publish three hundred copies of a special collectors' edition, with a price of 1,200 and 4,000 pesetas (Bacardí 2012, 36).[82] It was authorized because "in this case it was a work of literary creation" (Gallofré 1991, 383).

RESURRECTING FROM THE ASHES: THE ROLE OF PUBLISHERS

This new scenario of allowances and restrictions created a huge debate in Catalonia.[83] While some identified them as a betrayal ("we don't want crusts, we want the whole bread"[84]), others, such as the clandestine magazine *Redreçament* (May 1946), considered it to be the "First Catalanist victory."

However, compared to 1945, when the Catalan language was not an option for those who wanted to make a living out of publishing, 1946 "marks a point of inflection in the censorial attitude, which from then on was not that asphyxiating" (Llanas 2006, 24).[85]

In September 1946 Catalan publications for the first time had "the privilege of crossing out" (Gallofré 1991, 258) instead of being directly rejected.

FIGURE 2.1. Evolution of books authorized and published in Catalan in the period 1946–1959. Based on Hout-Huijben 2015, 69–70.

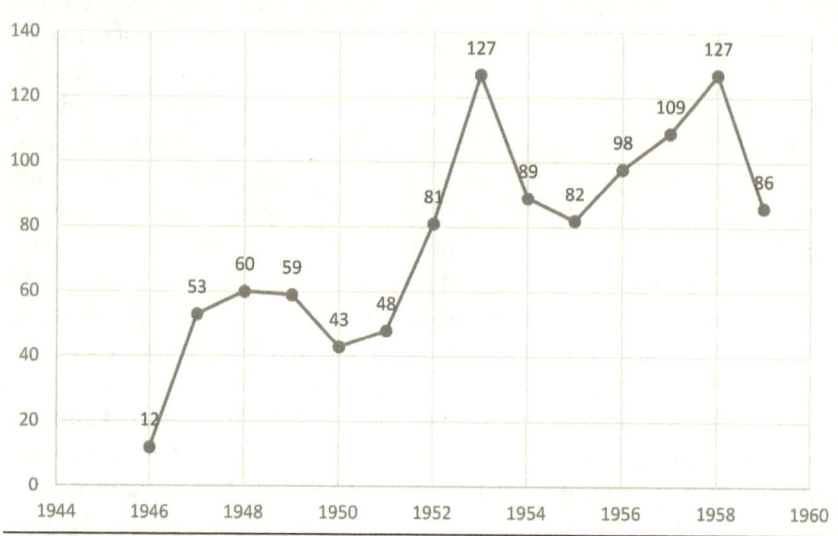

An element denounced by Spanish-language writers was seen as a small victory for Catalans.

Figure 2.1 shows the number of books "authorized" (Hout-Huijben 2015, 69) in Catalan and the corresponding years of publication. Despite this upbeat climate, only four series issued before the Spanish Civil War still survived in 1946: Fundació Bernat Metge, issued by Alpha Publishing and focused on translations of Greek and Latin classics into Catalan; Els Nostres Clàssics, published by Barcino Publishing and focused on Medieval Catalan texts; Col·lecció Popular Barcino, also published by Barcino, issuing general interest books in Catalan; and finally Catalunya Teatral, published by Millà, issuing plays by contemporary playwrights. In October 1945 the Orfeó Català was authorized to perform, and in 1946 some publishing houses and foundations started up again. Among those who published exclusively in Catalan were Selecta, which published Catalan literature of all time periods; Editorial Moll, located in Palma de Mallorca and focused on literature and history; and Fundació Bíblica Catalana, which published translations of the Bible.[86]

Among the newly created publishing houses was Rafael Dalmau focused on history and Catalan culture. In addition, a series of books, Col·lecció el Dofí, was published in Catalan by Edicions Destino.[87] In 1947, Aymà Editor began publishing novels in Catalan,[88] and in 1958 Miquel Arimany started issuing the first children's collection in Catalan: Col·lecció Juvenil Sant Jordi (Coromina and Vilardell 2019, 136).[89]

As publishers became "judge and jury at the same time" (Abellán 1980a, 97) in order to get their books authorized, they undertook a number of strategies to reach their goal (see Table 2.2). One of them was to send the books to the censorship services in Madrid, since the provincial censorship services of Barcelona were seen as stricter. The reasoning behind this attitude, according to Miquel Arimany and Josep M. Boix i Selva, is that those officers who sat in Barcelona were scared that the people sitting in Madrid would take their jobs if they granted too many permissions (Arimany 1993, 153). The downside to this strategy was that Catalan publishers could not stay in Madrid all the time. Thus, they had to hire a representative in the censorship services in Madrid to take care of the negotiations. In the case of Arimany, this person, Bernardo Crespo,[90] was "a former official of that ministry" who "represented several Catalan publishers" (Arimany 1993, 153).[91] As a result, a new occupation was created, as reported in *La Vanguardia Española*, in which a person advertised himself as a "solvent person who manages in Madrid the censorship of books, plays, etc." (*La Vanguardia Española* 1953).

Table 2.2 summarizes the strategies of publishers for the period 1946 to 1951. In it, I would like to highlight the addition of "deluxe, limited editions" (Godayol and Taronna 2018, 111). A great fortune of Catalan society is that its bourgeoisie always considered collector's edition books to be a socially respected element, a must for those entrepreneurs who wanted to be well-considered in upper-class circles (Manent 2010, "Més editorials").[92] That helped authors since many were also publishers: self-publishing was very common, as in the cases of Joan Amades, Carles Riba, and Maria Montserrat Borrat.[93] But it was not cheap. When Santiago Albertí acquired the "Nova Col·lecció Lletres" around 1954, he explained that "the mechanical composition of texts in Catalan was 10 percent more expensive than those written in Spanish" (1994, 225).

EVENTS AND RELAPSE

In order to foster the idea that the Catalan language was suitable only for folklore, Franco's government encouraged some regional festivities, such as the centenary of the birth of the Catalan poet Jacint Verdaguer (1845–1902) in 1945, who became "cantor of Hispanic letters." As part of the tribute celebrations, the regime authorized Selecta Publishing House to publish, in 1946,

TABLE 2.2. Control mechanisms and response strategies for issuing in Catalan, 1946–1951

Control mechanisms	Response strategies
Delay the verdicts, up to a year and a half (Bacardí 2012, 37)	Conduct negotiations in Barcelona and Madrid
	Use personal contacts (Gallofré 1991, 378)
	Directly address Franco (359) by letter
Veto all translations, "one of the basic underpinnings of *restrictive rules*" (Gallofré 1991, 380)	Pass off the translator as the author of the text: "It's a true poetic creation"
	Publish translations of works that carried an ideology into Spanish (Bacardí 2012, 40)
Institutionalize a diglossic situation. Implement suppression and nonauthorization	Refer to "literary creation," to folklore, and to studies without scientific basis.
	Argue that edits have already been made (Gallofré 1991, 359)
	Submit the work directly to the censorship services in Madrid by someone hired by the publisher to defend the submissions
Tolerate "literary creation"	Pass off other genres, such as cookbooks, as literary creations
	Literary contests
Do not authorize publications for general distribution	Produce special collectors' editions, expensive editions, and editions with short print runs
Veto foreign authors, "dangerous" authors, and those in exile (Gallofré 1991, 373)	Create and submit a list of Catalan authors without problems to be published in their language.
	Import books clandestinely, although only symbolic.
Tap the telephones of and monitor Catalan writers	Send messages in an eccentric way, like Miquel Arimany, who sent one through a private service crane, "of the kind used to remove cars" (Arimany 1993, 251)

his complete works in standardized spelling.[94] This gesture gave fresh air to Catalans, who saw books written in Catalan in bookstore windows (Gallofré 1991, 265). A key milestone was the Festivities of the Enthronement of the Virgin of Montserrat, that "served, with the help of the Comissió Abat Oliva, to resume, during 1946 and 1947, the public use of the Catalan language, in conferences and publications of all kinds" (Massot i Muntaner 2016, 12). The origin of the permission to hold the event was the request, from the Monastery of Montserrat to the civil governor of Barcelona, Bartolomé Barba, to print pamphlets in Catalan. Barba confessed that he could not deny an initiative coming from the Monastery of Montserrat, and he required only one condition: to print the pamphlets in Catalan along with the Spanish translation. By doing so, the monastery was able to circumvent the censorship that at that time prevented Catalan from being used in public spaces: it became not only the language of the leaflets, but also of conferences, presided over by a large Catalan flag (Aracil, Oliver i Puigdomènech, and Segura 1998, 288). As the reader may infer, this openness could not be tolerated by the regime. Once the celebration was over, Franco removed Governor Barba right away and replaced him with Eduardo Baeza Alegría. With this change, the regime fixed its objective again: leave Catalonia as a folkloric reality. Although the Catalan language was used in public for the first time since the end of the Spanish Civil War (Gallofré 1991, 300), the repression after the event was even more brutal.[95] Thus, "the prohibitions against books in Catalan during the final months of 1947 imply a spectacular backward step" (302). In light of the circumstances, at the end of 1947, Marià Manent decided to visit the head of the censorship services in Madrid, Juan Beneyto, offering a list of "harmless" authors to be authorized by the regime; the list had been created by the Aymà, Selecta, and Juventud publishing houses, as they had pending editorial projects (305). As a result, on December 6, a "list of Catalan authors sent by the Publishers" (303) was officially submitted.[96] However, Gallofré argued that even though the censorship services somehow accepted the list to avoid the noise of other interlocutors, it seems that it was only useful in "a few cases" and that it had "zero weight on most occasions" (306, 309).

The Consolidation of the Dictatorship and Publishers' Efforts to Reconnect with the Public: 1951–1959

After July 19, 1951, censorship was carried out by the newly created Ministry of Information and Tourism (MIT), headed by Gabriel Arias-Salgado, who was in charge of encouraging cultural policy. Thus, according to Moreno Cantano, the ministry passed new laws "of a more moderate nature" (2016; qtd. in Bacardí 2012, 38n95) about regional languages. The laws Arias-Salgado enforced became his "information theology," gathering together the censorship criteria to be less arbitrary. "They were the first steps in an attempt to ideologically bless the state of emergency" (Cisquella, Erviti, and Sorolla 2002, 23), since the 1938 Order was still in force. Creating an "information theology" through new laws was the perfect strategy for maintaining and promoting censorship without any qualms, thus fostering what was "normal, correct, convenient, right and opportune" (24). The 1950s "put an end to clandestine Catalan literature; it also reduced the literature of exile and, correspondingly, increased literature published in Spain with all the legal guarantees" (Molas 1978).

There were also associations of a particular and totally private nature, responding to a need for integration and democratization, such as Asociación de Cultura Occidental (Association of Western Culture), presided over by Agustín de Semir, professor at the University of Barcelona (Guzmán 1954, 42). This desire for dialogue was reflected in the movements of both Spanish and Catalan intellectuals in the period from 1951 to 1955, "led by Carles Riba and Dionisio Ridruejo" (Samsó 1994, 144). Together, they celebrated three poetry conferences, which "had constituted a para-official recognition of the Catalan situation," but at the same time it was a "period that consolidated the movements of Castilian expression" (Molas 1978) because, according to M. Aurèlia Capmany, "the Barcelona of 1952 is an absolutely Castilianized city" (Capmany 1971, 17).

TRANSLATIONS

History books, essays, and translations were part of the other side of the coin. In 1951, MIT gave "guarded permissiveness" (Bacardí 2012, 38) to translations into Catalan. However, after this initial openness, the status of translations didn't change until 1957, when contemporary works began to be translated (40n102); from the 1960s onward, translations "represented common currency" (Llanas 2006, 24).

In the case of theater, Jordi Coca explained some informal censorship rules of the provincial censorship services of Barcelona, from December 1957, which included the guideline that for every four original premiered works they could premiere a translation into Spanish. In the case of Catalan, no work could be premiered until two years after its premiere in the country of origin, although it seems that these rules were never applied (Coca 1978, 50–51). There were also sporadic initiatives, such as that of Bonaventura

Vallespinosa, who "organized performances at the Teatre Bartrina and Teatre Fortuny" (Bacardí 2012, 45) in order to import foreign plays into Catalan, and that of the Agrupació Dramàtica de Barcelona (1955–1963), which also published some "Quaderns de Teatre ADB" (1959–1963), more than half of which were translations (46). Thus, a "diglossic situation was being institutionalized" (43), which was affected by the difficulty of translating foreign works and by limits on the audience and on the number of premieres.[97]

In Table 2.3. the reader can find government control mechanisms on book publication in Catalan during the period 1951–1959 and the strategies publishers used in reaction.

The changes of this period culminated in the approval, on May, 17, 1958, of the Law on the Principles of the National Movement, where the fundamental rights of citizens, in terms of fatherland, family, and religion, were listed in twelve points (*BOE*, May 19, 1958, no. 119, 4511–12).[98]

Destino requires a special reference in this section because of the way its ideology evolved. It began by being the Falangists's voice in 1937. However, from 1939 and until 1950, it "balanced between serving the Franco regime and approaching the Catalan middle class, potential readers of the publication" (Ripoll Sintes 2015). From 1951 onward, the magazine had been increasingly converted into an "important support for public Catalan culture" in Spanish (Samsó 1994, 137).

In 1942 the editorial board of the magazine tried their luck in founding the eponymous publishing house Ediciones Destino. Even though at the beginning it only published in Spanish, from 1946 onward it also issued books in Catalan, with the series El Dofí, L'Àncora, El Trident, and Llibres a la mà.[99] Together with the magazine of the same name, it has been awarding the Nadal Prize since 1944 and the Josep Pla Prize for narrative since 1968. The two initiatives closely followed the trend of "de-Francoization" and "recatalanization" (Samsó 1994, 138), while at the same time seeking a "new model of reader" (Ripoll Sintes 2015). In 1989 Planeta acquired half of the publishing house (Tobarra 1989), and in 1996 the publisher became wholly owned by Planeta, but with "its full independence and identity as a company" (Piñol 1996).

Conclusion: The Difficulties of Regaining Contact with the Reading Public

The social changes after 1945 brought a little bit more openness, such as permitting books in Catalan to be issued under the label of "literary

TABLE 2.3. Control mechanisms and response strategies for issuing books in Catalan, 1951–1959

Control mechanisms	Response strategies
1951: Guarded permissibility "New Regional Language Guidelines"	Negotiations in Barcelona and Madrid, and friendships (Fundació Bernat Metge or Benèfica Minerva)
Civil versus religious censorship	Publishers such as Nova Terra and Estela (created in 1958) were subject to religious censorship, which was a little more permissive
Veto on magazines in Catalan	Arimany (*El Pont*): Present the content in the form of a booklet and at first do not make volumes of similar character and appearance (Arimany 1993, 263) Do not put the name of the magazine at the beginning, but in a small corner at the bottom, as if it were a collection (264)
Tolerance for literary creation	In 1956, Arimany (*El Pont*): In order to make the issues uniform, Arimany retyped the authors' speeches, to make it seem like a book (Arimany 1993, 263)
No authorization	Wait a few years (Arimany 1993, 265)
1957–1958: More permissiveness of translations	Increase of translations into Catalan, because Catalan literature was almost inexistent. Two first collections: "El Club dels Novel·listes" and "Nova Col·lecció Lletres"

creation," but in 1947 the regime became stricter after the celebration of the Festivities of the Enthronement of the Virgin of Montserrat. As the increased control and repression against books in Catalan became unsustainable for publishers, they started meeting with officials in Madrid in order to address the situation. Even though the aim of the regime was to corner the Catalan language by promoting literary contests in Spanish, there were also contests in Catalan, such as the Joanot Martorell Prize and Nit de Santa Llúcia. The fact that they could win a literary prize was the only incentive for Catalan writers to write in their language. However, it meant that for the first time since 1939, they could earn money writing in their native language. According to Molas (1978), that allowed different literary groups to emerge, such as those who wrote in Catalan after being inspired by a university professor, those whose language of expression was Spanish but took Barcelona as a main topic, or even those whose parents emigrated from other parts of Spain. Defenders and detractors of prewar trends reemerged, and new literary and artistic genres developed, as visible in the work of Antoni Tàpies and the group Dau al Set and in the creation in 1955 of El Club dels Novel·listes series. According to Pericay and Toutain (1986, 187) and Cornellà-Detrell (2011, 27), this started a new era that moved away from Noucentisme, which until then had been the reference point for the majority of both exiles and those who stayed.[100] Col·lecció Juvenil Sant Jordi, published by Arimany in 1958, is considered another milestone, as it is the first youth literature, whether original works or translations, published in Catalan after the war.

In the 1950s there were also some other changes for Spain on the international stage: an agreement with the Holy See, negotiations with the United States,[101] acceptance of Spain as a UN member, and membership in the International Monetary Fund (IMF). All these brought more openness to the country. However, even though the international image of the country was improving, the majority of translations speaking about current events (Bacardí 2012, 40) were banned until 1957–1958, which corresponds with the entrance of Opus Dei technocrats into the recently created government. Nevertheless, that did not mean the repression was over. On February 21, 1957, the visit of Torcuato Fernández Miranda, general director of university education, to the University of Barcelona was an ideal moment for students to raise their voice against the regime (Coll i Pigem 2017). Thus, "more than 600 University of Barcelona students gathered" in the assembly room of the university for hours "to celebrate the first Assemblea Lliure d'Estudiants [Free Student Assembly]" (Sàpiens 2017). The result was 22 detentions, 268 sanctions of missing an academic year, and files created by the authorities on 718 students.[102]

This chapter closes in 1959, considered by historians as the year that inaugurates Second Francoism.[103] The Opus Dei technocrats created the Stabilization Plan (1959), which brought progress and hope. The regime also embraced anticommunism as a way to get even closer to countries that shared that same idea and as a way to position itself in the Cold War (Estefanía 2014, ch. 1).

The announcement in 1959 and the subsequent convocation of Second Vatican Council (1962–1965) was a breath of fresh air for translations of religious texts, and it also motivated the creation of two publishing houses: Nova Terra (1958–1978) and Estela (1958–1971) (Bacardí 2012, 41). It was a golden opportunity to encourage the publication of translations, since religious books had to obtain the *nihil obstat* and pass through religious censorship, but often did not need to make it through civil censorship.[104] This greatly expedited the procedures and also made the *Nou testament de Montserrat* (1961) a bestseller, with more than one hundred thousand copies sold. And last but not least, 1959 marks the year of the death of Carles Riba, a key figure in maintaining the Catalan language during a period of internal exile.

CHAPTER 3

Publishers' Willingness to Publish Books in an Oppressed Language (1960-1975)

1960-1966, Transition to a New Press and Printing Law: An Opening Forced by the International Context

The Decree-Law of July 21, 1959, presented the National Stabilization Plan (*BOE*, July 22 8, 1959, no. 174, 10005–10007), which established unprecedented social, economic, and political change, inaugurating the so-called *desarrollismo* (developmentalism) and *apertura* (openness) from 1960 onward.[1] The plan, according to Galiana, "had to facilitate foreign investment, the inflow of capital, integrate the Spanish economy into international organizations, adapt the currency to the international monetary system, reduce all obstacles (not just tariffs) to trade, and encourage investment and national savings" (2017, 51). As stated in the first chapter, this plan included three phases of development, though only two of them ended up completely developed. The result, following Miguel Fernández and Sanz Rozalén, was that the economy grew "at a mean annual rate of 8 per cent from 1959 until 1972, just before the oil crisis of 1973" (2009, 193).

The origin of this openness, however, is found mainly in the injection of money coming from the United States in the period from 1953 to 1963.[2] With an estimated total of just over two billion dollars, according to the Foreign Affairs Ministry, it represented "a little less than 1 percent of the Spanish GDP" (Delgado 2003, 267, 259).[3] The aid was conducted "through three different channels: the aid itself, the funds from Public Law 480 and those from the so-called 'McCarran Amendment'" (Barciela López 2000, "La España de los años cuarenta").[4] In exchange, Spain allowed the Americans to have four military bases for the Cold War. Unlike the Marshall Plan, which involved donations with no interest charged (Delgado 2003, 239), in this case donations made up only a portion of the funds, and "a significant part ... consisted of interest-bearing loans" (Barciela López 2000, "En qué consistió la ayuda americana").[5] The other differentiation from the Marshall Plan was the requirement for "counterpart funds," which meant that Spain had to convert part of the aid into pesetas so that the American government could use it to cover its needs in Spanish territory.[6] As a result, rather than acting as an ally of the United States, Spain behaved with "a strong strategic subordination to American power" (Delgado 2003, 231). The agreements also eased the path for those American companies, such as Colgate, Palmolive, and Purina, who wanted to export to Spain (Miguel Fernández and Sanz Rozalén 2009, 192).[7] The Francoist apparatus, on the other hand, saw the relationship with the United States as an offense that would bring about social upheavals and closures of Spanish companies (Robles Piquer 2011, 181).

The arrival of John F. Kennedy in the White House in 1960 led to a noticeable distancing from the fascist state, although the agreements, above all those relating to tourism, would last until 1963. The Stabilization Plan also "grant[ed] foreigners permission to buy Spanish securities" (Solsten and Meditz 1988, "Foreign Investment"). Consequently, the country saw real estate speculation, a large influx of tourists,[8] and the rise of the advertising industry (Miguel Fernández and Sanz Rozalén 2009, 192). The result, for Spain, was more exposure to American culture, through electrical appliances, cinema, songs, television, women's clothing, and so on (Marín Silvestre and Ramírez 2004, 27).

INDIVIDUAL EMPOWERMENT THROUGH SOCIAL MOVEMENTS

Agustí Casanova identifies three great influencers of the social movement in Spain, and particularly in 1960s Catalonia: John F. Kennedy, Martin Luther King Jr., and Pope John XXIII.[9] Catalans looked up to Kennedy for his emphasis on "peaceful coexistence" and because "he guides the way of being of Americans" (2011). Indeed, Kennedy hoped to reach out to anyone living in the United States regardless of their origin or beliefs. Catalans also closely monitored the civil rights movement, and King's leadership in it, because they could see parallels between the situation of the African American community in the United States at that time and their own situation within an asphyxiating Spain.[10] Lastly, they had a great hope about the outcome of

Second Vatican Council, which had been called by Pope John XXIII, and its impact on Catalan citizenship.

THE CONSEQUENCES OF *DESARROLLISMO* FOR PUBLISHERS

The publisher's job is risky.[11] Because publishers did not have a stable income, it was almost impossible for them to get credit. The openness of Spain and competition from Argentina and Mexico in the book sector (Ferrer i Roca 2009, 300) led to the approval of the Order of November 24, 1962, "on tax relief for books, newspapers, magazines, etc."[12] Its aim was to "achieve greater cultural dissemination" through exportation to the "various Spanish or Portuguese-speaking countries," but "it is therefore independent of the tax effect on such books within Spain" (*BOE*, December 8, 1962, no. 294, 17410).

In other words, it provided a tax exemption that only benefited Spanish-language publishing houses that exported their books. According to Fernández Moya, the order provided a "refund by Public Finance [Hacienda Pública] of all or part of the indirect taxes incurred in the production and commercialization process of the book to be exported. INLE collaborated with the General Directorate of Customs to manage the collection of the deductions from its associates" (2017, 19). This tax relief was the beginning of a new era for many publishers in the Spanish language, but it was not the only incentive. The First Development Plan (1964–1967/9) considered, for the first time, the publishing industry as a "priority sector" (18), which eased the path for official credit concessions.[13]

Moreover, the scarcity and control of paper, which I mentioned in the previous chapter in relationship to the Gilian Law of 1946, remained an issue in 1960: "There was a very high barrier to foreign paper, taxed at a tariff of between 24 and 28 percent ad valorem, plus 15 percent import duty. The Act provided for the possibility for a publisher to purchase duty-free a quantity of paper equal to that previously exported through books sold to other countries" (Fernández Moya 2017, 17). This law, however, was not applied until 1961, and five years later, "Decree 784/1966 of March 31 authorized Spanish publishers to import, free of duty, the paper corresponding to the replacement of exports of books previously made" (17, 18). This law benefited not only publishers who published in Spanish, but also the Catalan book market as a whole, because part of the money from book exports was channeled to the publication of books in Catalan by such publishers as Vergara, Lumen, Grijalbo, Plaza y Janés, Polígrafa, Destino, Fontanella, Planeta, Alfaguara, Anagrama, and Bruguera, this last one with the Històries series, translated from its series in Spanish and started on November 1964.

A revolution in sales came with the introduction of American crime fiction in Spain, which featured corrupt cops and "attempted to look at criminals in their natural habitat and to hear how they spoke" (Hart 1987, 15). This influence, together with the mainstream low-cost Livre de Poche (pocket book) catalyzed the expansion of publications. The best example was the crime-genre series La Cua de Palla (Edicions 62), with seventy-one titles published from 1963 to 1969. Most books in this series were translations of works, many by famous American authors such as Raymond Chandler and Dashiell Hammett. This collection was the beginning of a very important crime fiction tradition in Catalonia.[14]

SECOND VATICAN COUNCIL

On January 25, 1959, Pope John XXIII first announced the Ecumenical Council and an Update of the Code of Canonic Law (John XXIII 1959), which would be developed in three phases, from 1962 to 1965. His aim was "the path to renewal (*aggiornamento*), the proclamation of the Gospel . . . integrating fundamental features of the paradigm of the Reformation . . . and of the paradigm of the Enlightenment and modernity" (Küng 2002, 118). The objective was to reach "not only Christians, but all people of good will" (Minobis 1963, 8) with a "spirit of dialogue and peace" (Manonelles 2005, 8) through the gospel.[15] For Minobis, the great conquest was the encyclical *Pacem in Terris*, which brought "the condemnation of atomic weapons, of colonialism, the approval of the socialization of the tripartite division of powers as sources of order and security of the freedoms proper to the regime of nations, the active intervention of citizens in the election of rulers, the establishment of the spiritual and moral background that must govern every community, respect for minority ethnic groups" (Minobis 1963, 9). Catalan publishers, the majority of whom were fervent devotees, received these words with hope and rushed to publish books, cyclostyled pamphlets, and even a daily chronicle to share the pope's statements with the rest of society.[16]

As a consequence, two publishing houses arose to "confront the ideological foundations of National Catholicism in force at that time" (Llanas 2006, 120): Estela (1958–1971) and Nova Terra (1958–1978), the latter of which was concerned about the Christian working class. Collaborations between publishers, in the form of co-editions, were not uncommon, as in the case of some issues of the magazine *Qüestions de vida cristiana* by

Estela and Publicacions de l'Abadia de Montserrat publishers (Llanas 2006, 121). Between 1964 and 1967, conciliar texts were translated and published in different collections, such as the seventeen-volume series Documents del Concili Vaticà II by Editorial Estela, presented with an introduction, Latin original, and Catalan translation (1964–1966), and the Spanish-language series Biblioteca de Autores Cristianos, translated into Catalan and published in 1967. Catalan authors and publishers found in modern-facing Rome the hope that they did not find under the retrograde Spanish regime; some, such as Josep M. Boix i Selva, even went to the Vatican on a pilgrimage.

Without even seeking it, publishers had in front of them a golden business opportunity: religious concerns had become mainstream, and religious books "often skipped the mandatory government censorship and left only with the approval of the more agile and indulgent church censorship" (Bacardí 2012, 42). This was a great step forward for Catalans considering that one of the most important nuclei of anti-Franco resistance was the Monastery of Montserrat.[17]

CHANGE OF MINISTER AND "OPENNESS"

The economic and governmental changes discussed in the previous sections contrast with the traditionalism of the Falangist Gabriel Arias-Salgado, who was still in charge of the censorship apparatus, MIT. At that time, the minister's mission was "to make the dictatorship endure . . . to achieve social support . . . and to recover foreign credibility" (Rojas Claros 2013, 38). The Council of Europe became more interested in the social situation of Spain, and the Committee on Non-represented Nations started inviting "distinguished members of the anti-Franco opposition-in-exile," along with prominent personalities of the Franco regime, such as Manuel Fraga Iribarne, who declared that "there was no 'Spanish problem,' the sole problem being that 'the rest of the world was misinformed about Spain'" (López 2016, 3). As a result, the committee issued reports about the unstable situation of the country in the 1960s. In February 1962, Spain applied, through Minister for Foreign Affairs Fernando María Castiella, to join the European Economic Community. Two months later and on the occasion of the Fourth Congress of the European International Movement in Munich, "118 representatives of Spain's internal and exiled opposition came together in rejection of the Francoist regime and called on the European Community not to admit Spain while the dictatorship remained in place" (López 2016, 3).[18]

As a result, Spain was rejected from both the Council of Europe and the European Economic Community.

Spain needed to tackle the issue of censorship to show a better image around the world. The first movement to do so occurred on July 10, 1962, when Manuel Fraga Iribarne was appointed as the new minister of MIT. Under his rule, in 1966 a new Press and Printing Law was approved, apparently fostering dialogue and "freedom of speech." The main aim of the appointment was to curtail the increase in the number of anti-Francoists who went all over the world denouncing the atrocities of the regime and thus to make sure the Spanish issue would be left aside. Herrero-Olaizola calls this renovation a "sort of a family affair" because the director general of censorship services, Carlos Robles Piquer, was Fraga's brother-in-law and also because the relations encouraged between people belonging to the book industry and the MIT were "quasi familial" (2007, 39).

In 1962, the Sixteenth Conference of the International Publishers Association (IPA) took place in Barcelona. Following the policy of not speaking about the Spanish problem—because for them there is no such problem—the officials of the regime aimed to be on good terms with Catalan publishers before the conference started. To do so, in 1961 the general chief of information and tourism, Vicente Rodríguez Casado, met the representatives of the Barcelona Book Chamber, promising a more relaxed control over the publication of books in Catalan. Following the proceedings of that meeting published by IPA, only one of the Catalan publishers, Miquel Arimany, addressed the audience. However, he presented twice: once about "contradictory trends between Spain and the rest of the world" (Arimany 1993, 327) and once about the problem in granting royalties to a region and not to a language (for example when publishers in Catalan saw their requests of royalties rejected because they had already been granted to a publisher in Spanish), and about the misconceptions between Catalan and Spanish literatures (IPA 1962, 122–23).

In order to make sure that the attendees would be aware of the differences between the two languages, Frederic-Pau Verrié gifted them *Versions de poesia catalana*, and Arimany even held a meeting with minority-language publishers, distributing about 150 pamphlets "of four pages in booklet format, two of which were in French and the other two of the same text in English. . . . I let them know in advance what Catalan culture and literature are" (Arimany 1993, 328). Although he admitted that the meeting was not very crowded, he was pleased just to have handed out the pamphlets.

Catalan Book Market Trends until the End of the Dictatorship

In the previous chapter I mentioned the difficulties that the Franco regime put on the exchange of currency and, therefore, on copyrighted work. To address this issue, one of the first measures of the Stabilization Plan was the Decree of July 17, 1959, which established the exchange of 60 pesetas to the dollar, in accordance with the gold standard (Sabín and Hernández Sandoica 1997, 130). This represented a relief for the publishers, who could sign copyright agreements more easily and more quickly. Therefore, the publishing scene in Catalonia changed completely: those publishers that had a tradition issuing books in Catalan benefited, and those who were traditionally publishing in Spanish saw a new business opportunity. Once they requested copyright for a book to be translated in Spanish, it was easier for them to do the same for Catalan. This, along with the economic privileges they enjoyed at that time, led translations into Catalan to become so popular.

In an effort to categorize this unprecedented period, Cornellà-Detrell (2013), Bacardí (2012), and Vallverdú (2013) referred to a *boom of translations*.[19] In contrast, Llanas, discussing the total number of books issued in Catalan, called it "years of moderate expansion" (2006, 74). My first objective, therefore, is to determine whether this is truly a translation boom or a boom of books in Catalan. Figure 3.1 sheds light on this question, comparing the numbers of original books in Catalan with translations.

The chart shows that in 1965 and 1966 around half of the books published in Catalan were translations. In contrast, in the rest of Spain translations made up about 26 percent of the total books published during the same period of time.[20] In Italy or Denmark, translations made up 20 percent of the total (Vallverdú 1987, 118). Iglésias stated that in Europe as a whole "at that time . . . the proportion of translations ranged from 20 percent to 30 percent at most" (2019, 99). Therefore, the fact that Catalonia had such a high number of translations might confirm the hypothesis of a translation boom. Hargrave defines booms as "often medium- to long-term periods of economic or market growth and may eventually turn into a bubble. A bubble is when the boom extends far beyond the fundamental growth trend in value where buyers become irrationally exuberant" (2019). Indeed, in 1965 translations represented more than half of the total production of books in Catalan, and I pinpoint the start of the bubble to this year, even though those who became "irrationally exuberant"

FIGURE 3.1. Comparison between the number of Catalan books produced and the number of translations into Catalan, 1962–1977. For the number of translations, data retrieved from Francesc Vallverdú 1987, 111–18. The number of publications in Catalan is the mean of the data provided by Vallverdú 1975, 106, and the sources that Llanas 2006, 77, provides (INLE, Güell-Reixach, and others).

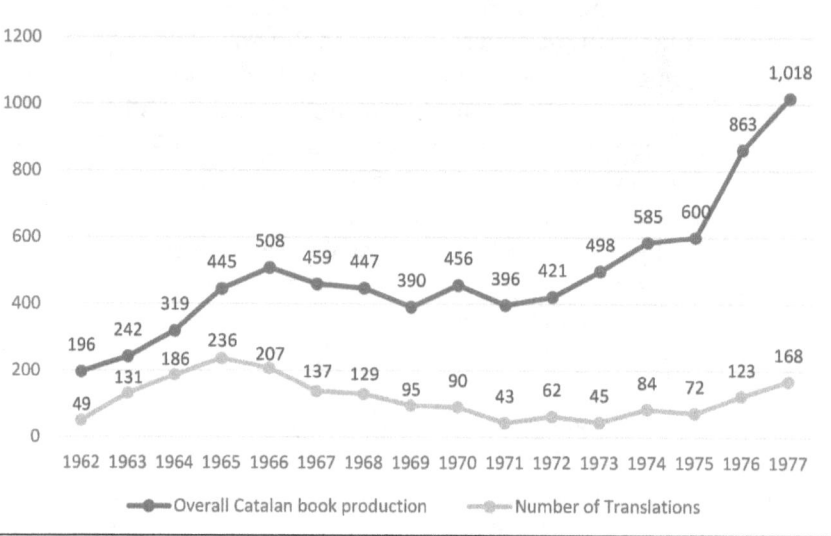

were publishers, not buyers. I totally agree with Vallverdú when he stated, "There was an excessive joy and lack of planning" (1987, 118), where the figures were lower than those from the first stage of the boom. The consequences of the bubble are visible in 1969 and the following years. In contrast, production of books in Catalan did not decline so abruptly because there was a new generation of writers in Catalan that were pushing to find a gap in the publishing sector. Thus, given the economic circumstances and the subsequent bubble, there is no doubt we should call it a *boom of translations*.

A BOOM OF TRANSLATIONS AND ITS CONSEQUENCES FOR WRITERS

While in the first decades of the dictatorship the priority for Catalan publishers was to publish translations of classics, in the 1960s publishers focused on works of contemporary interest from overseas (Bacardí 2012, 74). The professionalization of Catalan writers was difficult since the language was banned and, therefore, it was hard to earn a living from creative writing. Ferran de Pol pointed out that "the role of the Catalan narrator today is a sad one: that of a martyr" (interviewed in *Serra d'Or* 1961b, 13) and suggested that writers should add "translations, essays and articles in newspapers and magazines, radio, etc." (13) to their writing output, but without letting these activities become their priority. The reality, though, is that the boom of translations brought about a shortage of creative Catalan authors (Bacardí 2012, 41) since most writers switched to translations to put bread on the table.

As pointed out by Calders and discussed more in the next chapter, there was no connection between intellectuals and their readers, who were mostly from the generation born before or during the Spanish Civil War. Thus, Joaquim Molas identified writers as *outsiders*, since their essential characteristics were "instinct, self-education, scarce and irregular production, lack of imagination, autobiography, obsession with language and style" (1966, 55–57). In an interview conducted by *Serra d'Or* in April 1966 with the most important publishers of that time, Maria Martinell from Editorial Estela stated, "We have examined many originals with the best of intentions, and we have to recognize that they have a very low level: they are pure copies of the French without the veracity of those" (interviewed in Sales-Balmes 1966, 62). As a result, they had to resort to translations, even though they were more expensive, because "the editorial program cannot be affected by these ups and downs" (62). Publishing translations was rewarding: the adventures of James Bond, for example, were obviously much more attractive to readers than a novel written during a weekend. In contrast, as the boom subsided (1969–1975), the new readership born after the Spanish Civil War, more and more interested in Catalan literature, gave rise to a new generation of writers in Catalan. With authors such as Josep M. Benet i Jornet and Francesc Parcerisas, they became the mainstream because originals in Catalan were much cheaper—no royalties had to be paid, no translator was needed, the publishers didn't have to hire readers to find the right books to be translated, and so on.

THE BOOM EXPLAINED THROUGH ATTENTION ECONOMY THEORIES

Given the data provided by Llanas (2006), Vallverdú (1975), and Cornellà-Detrell (2013) and the figures mentioned in Figure 3.1, I identify three different stages of the boom: the gestational age (1960–1962), years of expansion (1963–1968), and years of regression (1969–1975). Although Catalan publishers were initially reluctant to advertise their books because they thought that doing so was the job of the bookseller, they soon reversed course. In the heat of the boom, Antoni Mas, publisher of the Barcelonan Editorial Labor, stated: "The book deserves to be treated with respect and demands to be treated with advertising aggressiveness. In all orders, today, it is necessary to call attention. All products do, don't they? If the book doesn't, other articles will attract the consumer and the book will continue to suffer from oblivion" (Mas and Gordon 1966, 275). In the 1960s and 1970s, consumers had a near infinite amount of information and new products at their disposal that were previously available to only the privileged few: new media, radio, television, cleaning supplies, beauty products, and the like. Suddenly, publishers had to find their niche, capturing the attention of potential readers in this avalanche. In order to do so, they first selected the products they thought would be interesting and then sought to catch the attention of consumers—in other words, attention economics in its purest form (Hendricks and Vestergaard 2019, 4).

Just as today we have personalized ads, Netflix movie recommendations, and suggested searches in Google, publishers suddenly relied on imaginative strategies that included TV advertisements, magazines, movie tie-ins, tours promoted by the publishing house, and familiar faces who persuaded consumers to buy products. Isard even promoted its translators instead of its authors. Like today, the intermediary—newspaper, radio, or television, for example—also benefited from the marketing. According to Tim Wu's *The Attention Merchants* (2017), media firms earn more from advertising than from the sale of their products. The same is true of Instagram, YouTube, Facebook, and Google.

In order to understand the phenomenon, let us first focus on *attention*, to explain the strategy of publishers to convince not only final consumers but also booksellers, who were the ones that persuaded the client to buy one book rather than another. I agree with Manuel Aguilar that the publishers and booksellers were not on the best terms:

> I, as a publisher and bookseller, experienced the good and the bad of the relationships between them. The publisher expects the book to be sold, despite the bookseller; that the bookseller does not replace the copies he sells; that when a book is ordered and he does not have it, he says that it is sold out without being sold out; that if each bookstore in Spain sold from one to three copies,

it would be enough to cover the costs of an edition; that the bookseller, without risking anything, takes 25 to 40 percent of the value of the book, etc. But what is true about all these accusations? (Aguilar 1965, 90)

One of the solutions to all of these issues was to avoid conventional booksellers and distributors and use local people to offer the product at a better price. Here Círculo de Lectores (discussed below) taught everyone a lesson. However, this was an isolated case, and publishers worked very hard to get a foothold among both consumers and booksellers; they were successful enough that their business strategies are still alive. Following Herrero-Olaizola, "in my view, the fiercely competitive publishing world of the 1960s and 1970s defined the marketing strategies that govern today's book trade" (2007, xii).

1960–1962. Gestational Age: Know-How

In 1961, Max Cahner, working together with Ramon Bastardes and advised by Albert Manent, created Edicions 62, which "acted as a wake-up call in the Catalan publishing scene due to the variety and pace of its production" (Muñoz and Branchadell 2002, 164).[21] However, their ideas were guided by their experience at the 1961 Frankfurt Book Fair, where they sought to "acquire knowledge and develop criteria on the characteristics of paperback collections . . . of the role of literary agents, of the contracts of translations and the cost of royalties, of co-publications" (Cahner 2001, 42). Thanks to the advice of Josep Benet, they also aimed to create a pocket book series inspired by the French collection "Que Sais-je?" (42). The new trend of leaving aside large formats and betting on pocket books "can be considered the most important post-war event in the publishing field" (INLE 1963, 330).

Editorial Vergara, a Spanish-language publishing house, was also finalizing details to launch Isard, its only series in Catalan, in 1962. Josep M. Boix i Selva, its literary director, sent dozens of letters to authors in 1960 and 1961, inquiring for the copyright of their books, and also to translators, asking their preferences in terms of books and source languages, which allowed him to choose the translators before the works to be published.[22]

To me, the publishers' efforts can be understood through the three approaches to catching consumers' attention suggested by Wu's *Attention Merchants* (ch. 4): desire, branding, and advertisements.

"Creating the **desire** for products that otherwise might not exist" (Wu, 2017, ch. 4): Through surveys, publishers assessed whether there was a real demand or whether they had to *create the desire*. For instance, in 1963, Vergara spent 195,000 pesetas ($3,250) for a single survey before investing in Catalan books.[23] The survey's most worrying outcome was the scarce reading habit of the Catalans, though they showed specific interest in series published in Catalan. As a result of what it learned, Vergara took two different approaches. First, it used innovative strategies *to create the habit of reading* in the lower and middle classes. Second, following Fernández de Bobadilla from "Selecciones del *Reader's Digest*," books in Spanish needed marketing campaigns to modify the concept of "books as luxury objects" (Cendán Pazos 1960, 348) and make them accessible to everyone.

"The relatively new discipline of branding . . . creat[es] the impression, valid or not, that something truly sets it apart from others like it" (Wu 2017, ch. 4): A substantial increase in book publishing was forecast for the 1960s. Thus a clear catalog, including their aims and target audience, was key for the success of publishers. Following the trend of pocket books, series tried to be as colorful and easily recognizable as possible. For example, Isard printed an image of the chamois, the characteristic animal from the Pyrenees, on its covers, reminiscent of Penguin Books. In addition to that, some of the prewar series were relaunched, as in the case of A tot vent, published by Edicions Proa, offering memories from before the war. It was a small world, and editors would meet at events and learn about each other's publishing projects, seeking ways to stand out and offer a greater variety of products to the consumer.

Advertisements. According to INLE, a book promotion campaign must have two stages: The first is the promotion of reading in general "oriented toward what the book is and represents in the abstract, familiarizing the general public with it" (Cendán Pazos 1960, 348). The second one, discussed below, focuses on the specific behavior of each publisher who directed efforts to get new clients and to maintain existing clients.

Consequently, the promotion of reading habits was crucial. Triadú observed, "There are publishers who don't believe in advertisements and there are booksellers that don't move themselves from the chair to sell and they don't even know what they sell" (1964, 38). For example, in 1962 Vergara spent 418 pesetas ($7) for marketing and advertising, whereas the publisher expended 3,883 pesetas ($64.71) for copyrights and 663 pesetas ($11.05) for unspecified material. From 1962 onward, though, magazines and newspapers started to give publishers a voice. These publications included *Serra d'Or*,

FIGURE 3.2. Translations into Catalan in 1962 and 1963, organized by categories. Data retrieved from Martí 1962 and 1963. Data has slight variation from Figure 3.1, because that chart uses the mean of all data points available.

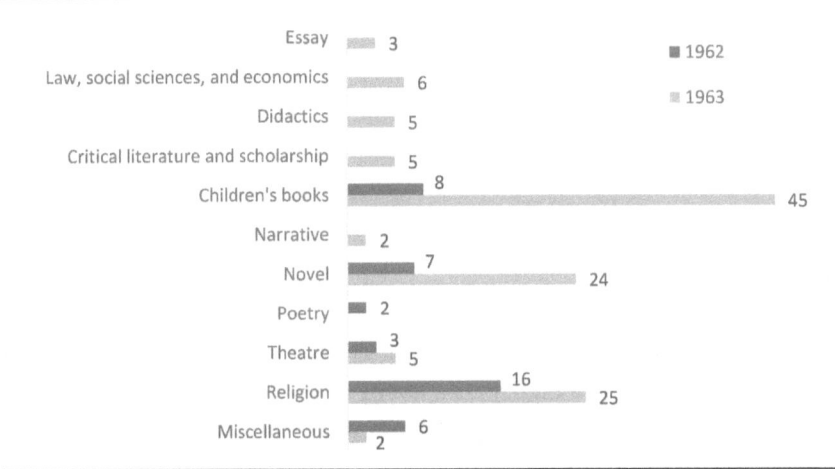

which had a section of recently published Catalan books, as well as *Diario de Barcelona*, *Destino*, *Revista Europa* (M.M. i B. 1963, 45), and *La Vanguardia Española*. The last of these even offered gifts, discounted books, and seven-day delayed payment to newspaper subscribers.

Years of Expansion of the Boom in Translations (1963–1968)

Vallverdú (2002, 2013) and Cornellà-Detrell (2013) establish the start of the golden age of translations into Catalan with the appointment of Manuel Fraga Iribarne as minister of MIT in 1962.[24] This is confirmed by Carlos Robles Piquer, "We tried (because I always had the support of the minister) to extend the opening to the different Spanish languages other than Spanish," recognizing that it was still virgin territory (2011, 202). His visit to Barcelona and the meetings he had with writers and publishers in 1962 were part of this "sweet moment of the meltdown of censorship" (Manent 1993, 143). However, according to the data provided in Figure 3.2, I consider 1962 to be the last year of the gestational age, so I establish 1963 as the inauguration of the boom.

This thesis is confirmed by Bacardí: "The breakthrough came in 1963—the year in which the last discriminatory measures against Catalan translations ceased—the number of translations almost tripled that of the previous year" (2012, 51). Furthermore, some of the books published at the end of 1962 counted, in fact, as 1963 releases, as happened with *La Pesta*, the first issue of the Isard series.[25]

Even though censorship was more relaxed, we need to bear in mind that prior censorship was still in force until 1966 and even later with exceptions. On the one hand, this greatly delayed the editions, and, on the other, publishers had to have quick alternatives in order to replace books in case they were not authorized.

Following the attention economy theory, I focus my analysis of the years of expansion on the ideas of Gabriel Tarde (1902; qtd. in Citton 2017, 5), dividing them into three branches of analysis: (a) the "exhaustion" of attention of the receiver, (b) targeted advertising, and (c) fame.

The "Exhaustion of Attention" of the Receiver. The "exhaustion of attention" was summarized by Tiphaigne de La Roche already in 1760 in this question: "'How [can one] attract attention' when 'everyone has started writing and it is easier to find an author [or translator] than a reader?'" (qtd. in Citton 2017, 12).[26] Triadú distinguished two different categories of consumers: "the reader of Catalan books, readapting incessantly, pushes the publisher's effort into new perspectives, without end. In contrast, the loyal, traditional reader needs to make, maybe, an adaptation effort" (1965, 63). Calders added one other category of consumer: "the buyer of books and printed paper who does not have time to read the product purchased, but still buys" (1964b, 50). Whatever the case, the saturation of the market caught the reader unprepared, "without the schooling base, the institutional support, or the echo of the press" (Bacardí 2012, 52; Triadú 1964, 37–39). It was also a shock for publishers, who suddenly considered their industry colleagues as their rivals, given that the reading audience was not wide enough to be able to celebrate competition. For example, Joan Sales blamed Isard (Vergara) and Ara i Ací (Alfaguara) for stealing readers from his El Club dels Novel·listes series.[27]

Publishers, in an effort to find solutions, relied on what Ann Blair calls *splitting the available information*, creating catalogs, sections, or genres "so that they could orientate themselves to the overabundance of texts" (2011; qtd. in Citton 2017, 12). In the 1960s, Catalan publishers first created the broadest possible division: literature for popular consumption and genre literature (Triadú 1964, 37–39). In this way, people who would not dare to read high literature in Catalan could read, for example, Georges Simenon in the language (Canals interviewed in Viladomat 2020, 58). The creation of collections was undoubtedly one of the most successful commercial strategies, but the collections were poorly managed, as the distribution of translations by genre was irregular and based only on consumer demand (Bacardí 2012, 52). Edicions 62, for example, was running ten series in 1966: "two for essays, three for novels, two for directly or indirectly religious themes, one for an anthology of our culture, one for research works on historical, sociological, and cultural themes, and one for complete works by our intellectuals. In addition, we have several in study: the one on medicine is also one" (Bastardes, interviewed in Sales-Balmes 1966, 62). And this does not include their collections in Spanish released in 1964 under the Ediciones Península label.

Targeted Advertising. Advertising plays a key role in shaping attention: "Interrupting attention, fixing it on the thing being proffered, is the immediate and direct effect of advertising" (Citton 2017, 5). According to INLE, the second step of a book promotion campaign needs "to make this or that book known to people who might actually be interested in it" (Cendán Pazos 1960, 348). Thus, publishers sent promotional materials to people who previously bought a book from that publisher, Catalan associations abroad, and schools and universities that might be interested in new products.[28]

Just a second of the consumer's time was enough to assess the success or defeat of a product. If within this second the consumer hesitated, there was a huge range of other available products clamoring for attention. As a result, editors gave complimentary books to people who would write a review of their work to increase its visibility (Citton 2017, 9).[29] The Spanish-language publisher Espasa-Calpe channeled its propaganda through its Austral collection as a way to gain consumers' attention. According to its publisher, Ernesto Antón, "Its price is of authentic propaganda, 30 pesetas [$.50]. The collection costs the publisher a lot of money: it is not business, it is our advertising" (Antón and Gordon 1966, 114).

Once they identified the potential consumer of their books, publishers tried to acquire new customers. The celebration of Sant Jordi, or Book Day, every April 23 was the right occasion for doing so. Publishers spent lots of money on advertisements in newspapers, magazines, cinema, records, radio, and television.[30] Publishers also sold books by phone and offered prizes for the best new releases.

Fame. Fame is "the simultaneity and convergence of attention and judgment on a man or event which then becomes well-known or famous" (Citton 2017, 5). In the case of Isard, as Pere Calders pointed out: "the criterion was to commission translations from the most prestigious Catalan writers" (1964a,

54–55), paying "the highest prices in Barcelona" (Calders and Triadú 2009, 115). He even increased their visibility by having them write prologues and footnotes, and sometimes they even proclaimed the book's success abroad.

1969–1975: Regression

According to Vallverdú (1987, 109–118) and as illustrated in Figure 3.1, from 1969 to 1975 a destabilizing period in the publication of books in Catalan began. I also set 1969 as the first year of the regression because of other events taking place at that time: a social and political crisis, student revolts, the Ifac distributor's bankruptcy, and the replacement of Manuel Fraga by Alfredo Sánchez Bella as minister of MIT.

As Catalan publishers already feared the worst, they tried to join forces and met around 1966 in Barcelona to discuss "common and specific problems of Catalan book today and here (Josep M. Boix i Selva Collection, MS9474)."[31] They tried to implement, again, the principles that were stated in the gestational age—in particular, increasing desire for products and targeting prospective audiences—because they realized that it was better to focus on security rather than greed. The document generated in this meeting focuses mainly on catching the attention of those born between 1940 and 1950 (in other words, the first generation after the Spanish Civil War), who were becoming increasingly interested in Catalan books. Indeed, the first point of the document was the lack of books for teenagers in Catalan and the strategies for bringing those readers back to Catalan once they reached adulthood. Other concerns included censorship and an education system that was not optimal for increasing the number of readers. They reached the following agreements:

1. Not to rely on readers while choosing the books for the catalog. Publishing houses had been more concerned about audience feedback than creating a homogeneous catalog. They agreed to avoid a laissez-faire approach and instead focus on their editorial aims. This conclusion is an example of classical economy, based in production and not in the reception of goods (Citton 2017, 2).
2. "Rational intervention into the problem," channeling efforts not toward "a limitation of the production, but to a promotion of sales, to a basic extension of the market, to a discovery of new markets, and to the creation of new interest centers." Basically, this is a mixture of branding and advertising, following Wu's principle of creating a need for a certain product and making the product attractive because, as Citton points out, "the product is our attention" (2017, 9).

3. "The problem of the promotion of sales of Catalan books is a problem of promotion of Catalan culture; publishers alone could not face this issue with authentic effectiveness."

Having identified the struggles, they started brainstorming solutions. One of them was to create a section of INLE focused on Catalan or, if that was not possible, to create an embryonic Catalan Book Institute or "a sort of commercial set up with exclusively economic aims." In order to do so, they agreed on the need for market surveys to confirm the viability of the project. They justified their aim because trading books is much more complex than selling other products. According to Verdura, "You can't sell books like they're shoes.... Distributors and booksellers cannot just be salesmen: the task requires an effort, a dedication that projects them beyond the purely commercial sphere. Because books today and here are perhaps the least commercial of all the products manufactured, and their sale therefore requires a concern of a higher order than the purely economic one" (interviewed in Sales-Balmes 1966, 67). However, "at the lowest point of the crisis... [Catalan book] production tripled the [number published] in 1961" (Vallverdú 1987, 118), as a new generation of writers and readers emerged. However, the increase in production was not tied to translations: in 1971 there were only forty-three translations, fewer than the forty-nine published in 1962. The end of the boom was also related to censorship. As Joan Baptista Cendrós, director of Aymà publishing, wrote in a letter of September 16, 1970, to Jordi Arbonès: "The censorship situation is worse than before. It's now more chaotic and insincere.... The situation for publishers is more and more difficult. Many publishers are closing down" (Arbonès 1995, 93).

Decisive Factors for the Fluctuation in the Number of Books Published in the 1960s and 1970s

OVERVIEW OF THE VARIABLES FOR SPANISH-LANGUAGE PUBLISHERS

Even though there are similarities between the struggles of the publishers who edit in Spanish and those who edit only in Catalan for the period 1960 to 1970, they were not the same. In this section I list the most common struggles of the Spanish-language publishers, based on the data offered by the Service of Studies of the Ministry of Commerce and published in its magazine *Información Comercial Española* (May 1960). The journal published a survey in which they asked "sixteen important publishers" about the challenges they faced, which INLE commented on (Cendán Pazos 1960, 344–49).

The first constraint was the price of books, which was too high compared to "the standard of living of individuals" (344). The reasoning behind those expensive books can be found in the print runs, which could not exceed three thousand copies because of insufficient readership. Varela Pol, from Ediciones Cid in Barcelona, stated that people read what they could according to their economic possibilities, not to their preferences (344). The other big constraint was paper, which was "expensive because its price is above the average international level—approximately double—and of poor quality" (344). Paper accounted for 15 percent of the cost of the books. Exports to Latin America (which would later be made cost effective through aid and credit advantages) and postal rates that increased by 75 percent compared to the previous years made it very difficult to print and distribute books. Speaking about distribution, Fernando Baeza of Ediciones Arión stated that in 40 percent of cities within Spain there were no fixed-stand booksellers, which is why Círculo de Lectores became so popular. The survey identified two other important economic problems: machinery renewal and taxes. Lorente Arraiza, from Ediciones Castilla, stated that for the following five years, the Spanish publishing industry had to invest $10,000,000 in imported machinery to compete with foreign publishing houses (346). Taxes were also significant: publishers had to pay a "fiscal license" as well as a "tax on expenditure and profits" that represented 30 percent "of the profits obtained by the publishing companies." These fees totaled about "15 percent of the sale of each book," and the tax on paper expenditure was equivalent to another 12 percent of each sale. The contraction of the domestic market and the purchasing power of recipients also affected book sales: "A current book of literature, which in 1936 was sold at 5 pesetas and in 1945 at 20, today [1960] is sold at 110 or 120 pesetas" (348).

OVERVIEW OF THE VARIABLES FOR CATALAN-LANGUAGE PUBLISHERS

Catalan publishers shared struggles with their Spanish-language counterparts, such as the cost of paper, taxes, and machinery renewal. However, because the audience was reduced and books were also censored, book print runs had to be lower, making it even more difficult for Catalan publishers to sell books at a price comparable to books in Spanish. In addition, the

TABLE 3.1. Incidence of book censorship in Spain as a whole

Year	Authorized with suppressions[1]	Not authorized[2]	Official silence and not authorized[3]	Total for Spain
1959–1961	4.56%	5.3%		9.86%
1962–1966	7.22%	3.1%		10.32%
1967–1975	9.12%		6.82%	15.94%

Based on Abellán 1980a. Percentages represent the average value over the chronological year range.
1. Abellán 1980a, 144–45.
2. Abellán 1980a, 148–49.
3. Abellán 1980a, 150.

distribution network in Catalan was very limited, and the domestic market faced the effects of the lower prestige of the language.

The factors influencing book sales in Catalonia from 1960 to 1975 can be divided into four groups: dictatorship-led constraints, the situation of Catalan as a language in public and in schooling, the promotion of Catalan language, and the constraints of books sales. Explaining the effects of these influences on television, theater, and music will give the reader an even better idea of the publishers' struggle to issue books in Catalan.

Dictatorship-Led Constraints

The first constraint on Catalan-language publishers was harsh censorship. In 1962, Francesc Galí in a conversation with Carlos Robles Piquer, at that time director general of censorship services, made him aware of the censorship problems publishers and authors were still facing. Robles Piquer's answer was this: "From now on, everything that can be published in Spanish can be published in Catalan" (Manent 1993, 220–21, qtd. by Cornellà-Detrell 2013, 54). Even though Cornellà-Detrell is skeptical that censorship was the only factor that led Catalan publishers to emphasize translations, after 1962 the censorship process was apparently less repressive, despite the fact that the 1938 Order was still in force. The incidence of censorship in Spain is shown in Table 3.1.

Regarding the incidence of censorship in Catalonia, Hout-Huijben writes:

> During the first half of the 1960s, the consequences of censorship affected 26.5 percent of literary production in Catalan. In the second half of the 1960s,

FIGURE 3.3. Time delay between the completion of a work in Catalan and its publication, 1950–1970. Based on Abellán 1980b, 123–32.

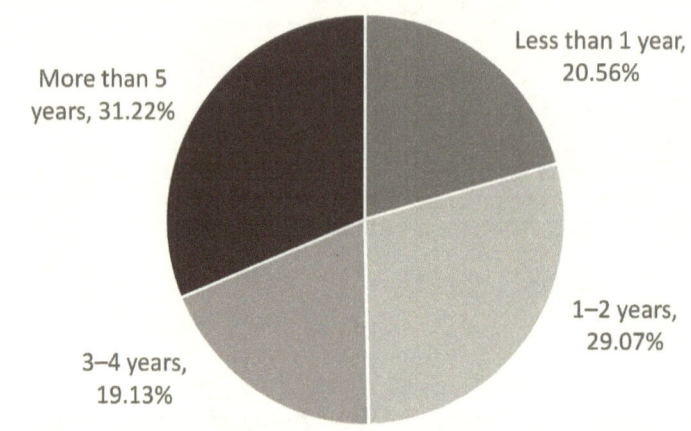

the last years of Manuel Fraga Iribarne at the Ministry of Information and Tourism, 37.1 percent suffered censorship. During the period immediately afterward, beginning at the end of 1969 . . . censorial repression reached 61.5 percent. Between 1974 and 1977, the last years of the official existence of censorship, 22.6 percent of books had problems. (2007; qtd. in Clotet and Torra 2010, 12–13)

It is interesting to note that both Table 3.1 and Hout-Huijben prove that the most repressive period was, surprisingly, when the 1966 Press and Printing Law was in force. The explanation lies in the fact that since the law aimed to establish dialogue, publishers were more confident in submitting books to the censorship services. The difference between the repression in Catalonia and the repression in Spain as a whole highlights the arbitrariness of the regime and recalls past times. The proclamation of the state of alarm in January 1969 and the entry of Alfredo Sánchez Bella into MIT strengthened censorship efforts against printed material.

Another way of viewing the repression is by measuring the delay between the completion of the drafting of an original in Catalan and the authorization by the censorship body. Abellán sheds light on this point, showing the "interval between the final editing and the publication of the work" for books published in Catalan between 1950 and 1970. Figure 3.3 shows the two big peaks: delays of between one and two years and delays of greater than five years. It is not surprising that the most repressed genre is narrative, which had been persecuted since time immemorial.

The Situation of Catalan as a Language in Public and in Schooling

Catalan Television and Theater. On October 17, 1964, Televisión Española broadcast a play, *La ferida lluminosa*, for the first time in Catalan, opening a monthly tradition of broadcasting theater in Catalan on TV (Muñoz and Branchadell 2002, 165). In 1967, *Mare nostrum*, the "first informative program in Catalan" (Morales Pérez 2018), was launched, "but it was not until 1973, with the arrival of the informative program *Giravolt* that it became a recognized space" (Muñoz and Branchadell 2002, 165). Theater was regulated by two different censor bodies: the censors for written plays (the same as the ones who controlled book publications) and the "inspectors of theater and/or provincial or counties' delegates" for performances (Gallén 2016, 58). Performing in Catalan was allowed from 1946 onward (59) and the use of Catalan was more common in plays than it was in other artistic disciplines, like in songs or poetry, though some painters were also censored.[32]

Catalan Music. In the early 1960s, a protest movement of Catalan singer-songwriters arose, who denounced through self-censorship the atrocities of the regime. Led by the group Setze Jutges it became a "mass cultural-political movement" (Eaude 2008, 150). While at the beginning it was tolerated by the regime (150), it later was highly monitored. Filled with tongue twisters and metaphors and inspired by Bob Dylan, Pete Seeger, and Joan Baez, the songs became anthems of resistance. As a strategy to resist the police, who were often present at concerts, singers would sometimes remain silent, letting the audience finish their lyrics, to avoid going to jail; when the whole audience would sing, it was impossible for the police to report every single person.[33]

Education-Related Initiatives. Because the Catalan language was not allowed in schools until the 1970s, there were no textbooks in the language, so Catalans relied on magazines as a substitute, many of which were under the protection of religious institutions (Larruela 1985). These publications provided language instruction for the new generation of readers.[34] *Cavall Fort* was first issued in December 1961 and became the most important children's magazine in Catalan.[35] It was protected legally by the bishoprics of Vic, Girona, and Solsona. Albert Jané admitted that the magazine faced major problems with censorship in the 1970s; in contrast, in the 1960s, "as the magazine had no legal status and was under the protection of the church, we were left alone" (Puigtobella 2020). However, until August 1964, the magazine could not be shown in bookstore windows (Larruela 1985, 8).

The objective of the magazine was to educate Catalan children about different areas of Catalan culture, such as theater, as issue 42 of the magazine explained: "*Cavall Fort* shows interest in informing its readers about different aspects of theatrical history, experience and practice" (Carbó 1975, 9). The magazine's interest in theater led to the creation of El teatre per a nois i noies (Theater for boys and girls) in 1967, and Catalan theater eventually became a mass phenomenon. The Romea Theatre and the Barcelona City Council were also involved, providing space to amateur groups, while Editorial Estela sponsored singers. El teatre per a nois i noies charged "pre-war prices" (Carbó 1975, 10) until 1987, the last year of the initiative, to ensure that the public could enjoy the show.

Obviously, these initiatives cannot be compared to the number of textbooks in Spanish, which made up a quarter of the total number of books issued annually (Vallverdú 1987, 114). Josep Verdura, from Edicions Nova Terra, identified education as the "fundamental problem" of the publishing market in Catalan: "Catalonia has the highest percentage of illiterates, in the sense of people who have not studied the language at school. If we consider that the problem of book distribution is essentially a cultural problem, it is clear that illiteracy [in Catalan] plays an important role" (interviewed in Sales-Balmes 1966, 67). And I would add that publishers also had the task of creating particular linguistic registers in Catalan to catch potential reader's attention and thus incentivize book sales (Coromina and Vilardell 2019, 146–47).[36] Sales explained, "The duty of writers to write in their own language is correlative to the duty of readers to read in their own language as well" (interviewed in *Serra d'Or* 1961a, 16). Boix was not optimistic about this happening: "On a European scale, people in our country [Catalonia] read as little as people in underdeveloped countries, although, on a peninsular scale, they appear to read a lot" (interviewed in Sales-Balmes 1966, 68).[37] In conclusion and quoting Ferran de Pol, "we have some authors, few publishers and very few readers" (April 1960, 19). Sales concurred: "The feeling of preaching in the desert is devastating" (interviewed in *Serra d'Or* 1961a, 16).

Promotion of Catalan Language

One of the most important events for Catalan publishers is Sant Jordi's Day, April 23, when there is a tradition of buying books and roses. Thus, publishers often reserved their best books to be sold during this time of the year. The new releases listed in *La Vanguardia Española* illustrate this point: among the new releases of April 1966 there were eleven books from Edicions 62, three from Destino, five from Proa, and three from Vergara (Recasens 1966b); in contrast, there were only four new releases from Edicions 62 and one from Vergara in January of the same year, and the rest of the publishers were not even listed (Recasens 1966a).

Other methods of promotion included literary awards, which were the only incentive for authors to write in Catalan. As Joan Oliver of Aymà Editor stated, "Most original works are written under the stimulus of a literary prize" (interviewed in Sales-Balmes 1966, 61). "Barcelona has the honor of having initiated the trend of literary prizes with a social category and of awarding . . . the most representative ones in the national sphere" (Salvador 1960). Alongside the ones already mentioned in the previous chapter (Nit de Santa Llúcia and Premi Sant Jordi), the most important ones in the 1960s were Josep M. de Sagarra for theater (initiated in 1963), Josep M. Folch i Torres for children's fiction (1963), the *Serra d'Or* Critics' Awards (1967), the Josep Pla Prize for prose (1968), and Prudenci Bertrana (1968).

But Franco's regime gave priority to Catalan poetry. Thus, in 1966 Fraga promoted the Jacinto Verdaguer National Literature Prize granted by MIT, the ceremony for which was held on December 20 (Cifra 1966).[38] The surprise winner was the avant-garde Catalan-language poet J. V. Foix, who didn't even apply for the award. Astonished, he stated, "Given my attitude or my political directives, it had an unpleasant effect on me" (interviewed in Cort 1987, 12:40–12:57). It seems that the Nauta publishing house submitted his book *Obres poètiques* without his consent. According to *La Vanguardia Española*, Foix decided to offer the amount earned to "promoting the cultivation of Catalan poetry among children and adolescents . . . creating multiple small prizes and distributing them throughout Catalonia" (Díaz-Plaja 1966).

Strategies of Catalan-Language Publishers to Increase Book Sales

In the 1960s, there was an increase in the cost of living, and publishers were afraid of losses. Thus, aligning with European trends and in order to better understand the needs of their clients, they resorted to selling by installments. This modality offered much cheaper prices and also forced readers to keep buying the installments in order to end up with a complete work. In addition to this, books sold by installment could be acquired both in street-level kiosks, where the newspaper was sold every day, and in bookstores. Given the success of the initiative, publications ranging from encyclopedias to dictionaries were offered in this format.

The price difference was dramatic. For example, in the "Novedades del mes de abril" (April book releases) section of *La Vanguardia Española*, the second installment of the *Diccionari català general*, published by Arimany, sold for 40 pesetas. On the other hand, the entire *Diccionari general de la llengua catalana*, by Pompeu Fabra, was 750 pesetas (Recasens 1966b). Normally, publishers offered the covers of the book for free, once the parts had already been purchased.

Books were also sold by subscription.[39] In 1955, Editorial Selecta founded the Central de Literatura Catalana, which, in addition to offering book subscriptions, also organized "literary trips and excursions" for its members (Subirana 1995). From the point of view of publishers, who had to pay authors, proofreaders, and staff, selling by installments fragmented their income while subscriptions allowed a more accurate forecast. Regardless the sales procedure, defaulters were very common. According to Antonio Mas Esteve, manager of Editorial Labor in Madrid, there were three types of clients: "those who pay on time, those who simply delay payment, and those who don't pay" (1971, 138). Publishers sent written reminders, made telephone calls, and even talked to subscribers in person in order to obtain payments (139). But with the really difficult ones, publishers tried a combination of "plea, disappointment, threat, option, and last chance" (140).

In order to overcome these adverse economic circumstances, many of the publishers used bills of exchange to meet their payments, a risky practice that I argue was one of the causes of the crisis in the book sector in the 1970s. This was the case for Josep Pedreira, editor of Els Llibres de l'Óssa Menor (1949–1963), which published mainly poetry. "While donations were spaced out and the number of subscribers dropped, a headache that had long preoccupied Pedreira became chronic: the defaulters" (Sopena 2011, 308).

CÍRCULO DE LECTORES

Círculo de Lectores can be considered a cross between a distribution company and a publishing house. It became a real mass phenomenon, with more than one hundred thousand members in 1966 (INLE 1966, 145). According to Raquel Jimeno Revilla, it was founded on September 11, 1962, by Editorial Vergara and Bertelsmann, though Vergara retired in 1964 (2016). The service entrusted sales to local people instead of salespeople. This commercial strategy became very effective because a friendly face was more convincing to potential clients than a stranger. Furthermore, the door-to-door approach had another advantage: books went directly from the publisher to the client, without intermediaries or worries about a sometimes-unreliable postal service. The price was also another factor. According to

INLE, "The price of the book is significantly lower than that of the same book, with similar presentation, purchased on the normal market.... The member receives the book at his home, without any inconvenience on his part, having previously been able to choose freely among the titles on offer, with greater knowledge of the situation and more accurately than he would have been able to do in a shop" (INLE 1966, 145). In 1964 Vergara decided to step aside and left the business.

Economic Struggles of Publishers Due to Distributing Companies

Llanas acknowledged the situation of distribution companies of books in Catalan in these terms: "For many years ... there was no distribution company dedicated exclusively to Catalan books, a circumstance that condemned them to being shipwrecked in the middle of the Spanish-language bibliographic sea of general distributors" (Llanas 2006, 75). In 1961, the year in which Edicions 62 was founded, Max Cahner and Ramon Bastardes created Distribuïdora Ifac, which had its origins in an initiative of Bastardes and Lluís Procel. It opened up a distribution network for books in Catalan for the first time, although the fact that the same people were in charge of both the publishing house and the distributing company had monopolizing effect, according to a letter from the writer and publisher Joan Sales to the Occitan poet and translator Bernard Lesfargues.[40] This created, according to Montserrat Casals, a "crime of conflict of interest" (Massot 2012). Although at first Edicions 62's aim was only to publish books of essays, "they soon adopted narrative as well and, logically, despite the disloyalty, they sought out the authors who were already published by Ifac's client publishers." Even though they set "a royalty rate that was much higher than the average," in 1969 Ifac had to close down. To pay for the debts, according to Casals, they used all their reserves, and "bills of exchange [were] returned, unpaid. Ifac came to owe more than a million pesetas to Joan Sales of El Club Editor," (Massot 2012) among many others.[41]

According to the data provided by the 1967 to 1970 catalogs of *Llibres en català*, an initiative of the new director of INLE, Guillermo Díaz-Plaja, and compiled by Maria Ballester, the following publishers also worked as distributors:

Barcelona
- Aymà: Distributed products from Alcides (1969–1970), Josep Pedreira (1967, 1969–1970), and Proa (1967–1970).
- Alpha: Institut d'Estudis Catalans (1967). We need to keep in mind that IEC was not fully official until the dictatorship ended, so it was semi-official at that time. However, from 1968 to 1970 it distributed its own books.

Balmes: Distributed books from Foment de Pietat (1968–1970) and Unión Musical Española (1967–1970).

Catalònia: Distributed books from López-Llausàs, Edhasa (1968–1970), and Antònia i Montserrat Raventós (1969–1970).

Joventut: Distributed books from Mentora (1968–1970).

Valencia and surrounding areas

Sercali: Distributed books from Andorranes (1969–1970).

Balearic Islands

Editorial Moll: Distributed books from Associació per la Cultura de Mallorca (1967–1970), Martínez Pavía (1967–1970), Obra Cultural Balear (1967–1970), Obra del Diccionari (1967–1970), and Oficina Romànica (1967–1970).

Considering that in 1967 there were seventy-nine publishers that issued books in Catalan (Fig. 3.7) and by 1969 Ifac already had closed down (even though they distributed at least until 1970, due to the contracts signed), I conclude that the poor book distribution network in Catalan was another cause of the sharp decline in sales during the final years of the boom. Other factors related to distribution also created pressure on booksellers, among them the following:

New book service (Servicio de novedades). This service already had an implicit right of return. Once a new book was published, the publisher or distributor sent to the bookseller the number of books agreed upon beforehand without further consultation. The books that could not be sold were sent back to the publisher, who needed to deduct those unsold and returned copies to get the total number of books sold (Arimany 1993, 179). Given the great number of new titles during the boom, this service was cancelled by many booksellers (180).

Returns (Marín Silvestre and Ramírez 2004, 71). Any kind of sale with the right of return means that when the bookseller reached the deadline and had not yet sold a certain number of books, those were returned to the publisher and the bookseller was charged only for the books sold (Arimany 1993, 179). Josep Janés's solution was to grant the distributor exclusive sales rights and "admit the return of unsold books to be compensated with new services" (179). Afterward, some of the distributors would not accept these deals. Unlike the new book service, this was not cancelled by booksellers.

Commercial margins. An article published in *La Gaceta Papelera* provides the margins generated by book sales: "the commercial margins achieved by the distributors (over 30 percent) and by the publishers themselves (under

10 percent in many cases)" (*La Gaceta Papelera* 1970, reprinted in *El Libro Español* 1971, 142).

Reduction in the number of copies distributed (Marín Silvestre and Ramírez 2004, 71). "The maximum sales figure for Catalan novels is between 4,000 and 6,000 copies; compare these figures with the 100,000 copies (sold mostly in Catalan-speaking territory) that a Catalan author can sell while writing in Spanish" (Sales, interviewed in *Serra d'Or* 1961a, 16). That also had an impact on the price of the book. For example, *Geografia de Catalunya*, written in Catalan by Dr. L. Solé Sabaris and published by Aedos, cost 65 pesetas per installment, while Salvat's *La tierra y sus límites: Gran atlas geográfico, económico e histórico (en fascículos)*, published in Spanish, was 50 pesetas.

The cost of intermediaries between the publisher and reader can be summarized using the example of Ifac's distribution of Isard's books. The print run of *La Pesta* was three thousand volumes. The price was 60 pesetas in paperback and 75 pesetas in clothbound. According to the terms of the agreement signed on September 17, 1963, Distribuïdora Ifac bought from Vergara one thousand books (they had committed themselves to always buying this number of narrative books), and they asked for a 45 percent discount "in order to distribute the series properly." Assuming that the distributor would take only the ones in paperback, as they were less expensive, the discount for the distributor would be 27,000 pesetas ($450). Assuming that the distributor would sell all the books agreed, the publisher would make 33,000 pesetas ($550) instead of 60,000 pesetas ($1,000) that could have been earned without the intermediaries. Moreover, the distributor would also have the right to return unsold books, which made the publisher's economic situation even more uncertain.

To compensate for this, Vergara used two resources: sales by subscription and order form sales for nonsubscribers. Those who were not yet subscribers also had the option of subscribing using a purchase order form. If they agreed, there were two forms of payment: in paperback, the eleven volumes already published totaled 750 pesetas ($12.50), and in clothbound the volumes totaled 930 pesetas ($15.50). The paperback volumes could be paid in seven installments, one of 150 pesetas ($2.50) and six of 100 pesetas ($1.60); the clothbound volumes could be paid in eight installments of 130 pesetas ($2.16), with "free shipping and no [additional] charges of any kind." In the case of books of essays, Ifac committed to selling only 750, with the same 45 percent discount.

As seen by this example, it was easy for publishers to face serious economic problems. The consequence was short print runs because there was insufficient demand and because publishers were afraid that books would be returned by distributors. In addition to this, publishers faced the lack of means to protect intellectual property in Catalan, the paper shortage, and the possibility of nonauthorization from the censorship services. Jaume Aymà Mayol, in a 1985 interview, summed it up as follows: "When the publisher has no money of his own, when he has to count on other people's money and, in the end, does not have a sales department but has to rely on the distributors, it is fatal when things do not go well" (Llanas 2006, 76).

Ramon Sopena, director of the eponymous publishing house, pointed out another the constraint for publishers when it came to distribution: "The economic shortage faced by public libraries for the purchase of books, is also disadvantageous, as is the small number of such institutions" (Sánchez 1963, 45). Indeed, although the subject of libraries is beyond the scope of this study, it is worth pointing out that in Catalonia in 1964 there were forty libraries in the province of Barcelona, some of which became centers of anti-Franco resistance as well as places to learn Catalan clandestinely.[42] According to Mayol, in 1968 more than thirty of those libraries offered Catalan classes. Public libraries also filled the gap of school libraries, which were practically nonexistent at that time (2005).

Case Study: Editorial Vergara

Vergara S.A. (1949–1976) was founded by Josep M. Esteve. It demonstrates what has been discussed so far for two reasons: first, because it is one of the publishers that exported to Latin America and also launched a collection in Catalan at the same time as the translation boom; second, because it illustrates the theory of attention economy. Vergara started as a distributor and bookseller, offering books for cash or by installment. Over time, it became a solid Spanish-language publishing house with offices in Spain and Latin America.[43] Starting in 1950, the manager of the company was Nicolau Surís i Palomé, and in 1954 Josep M. Boix i Selva was hired as a literary director, bringing book know-how to the administration of the firm. The company offered two different products, books and records.

Books. Vergara offered a rich catalog ranging from large-format works to encyclopedias sold in installments and pocket books. Among its publications, I would like to highlight the *Historia general de las literaturas hispánicas*, issued between 1949 and 1968, and the seven editions in three years of *Enciclopedia Vergara* (which had four reprints between 1961 and 1962). During the life of the publishing house, it launched the following series: Colección de obras de gran formato (including the history of different fields), Mitologías ilustradas, Clásicos Vergara, Colección nuevos horizontes (providing introductions to different disciplines), Colección verdad y vida (religious), Enciclopedias y diccionarios, Manuales Vergara, Velero, Abedul, Mapamundi, Isard, and Círculo de lectores (with Bertelsmann, until 1964).

Records. Vergara initiated record sales in 1961 under the name Discos Vergara, directed by Oriol Martorell; record sales continued until 1970. In 1963, Discos Vergara had two affiliated companies: Almapres, S.A., focused on recording, distributing, and selling albums, and Bibliodisc, S.A., specialized in door-to-door sales of books, albums, and record players. The series they offered included Teatrodisc, Poesia Catalana, Series 2000, Música Sacra, Discoteca Cavall Fort, Grandes Clásicos Universales, and Antologia de la Sardana; they also released recordings of monologues and much of "the pop music that was exported from Catalonia to all Latin America: Los Sirex, Los Catinos, Lita Torelló, Los Gatos Negros, Alex y Los Findes, Francisco Heredero, etc." (Shepherd, Wicke, and Wicke 2003, 686). In the 1960s Discos Vergara opened up the market with global alliances, first by adding classical music to its catalog through the German label Ariola-Eurodisc, owned by BMG Entertainment, Bertelsmann AG (686). Discos Vergara also traded in America, collaborating with American Liberty and United Artists. In 1970, Discos Vergara was acquired by Ariola (686).

ISARD SERIES

Born in 1962, Isard was the only Vergara series totally in Catalan, publishing thirty-nine volumes, all of them translations except for four original books in Catalan. Its director, Josep M. Boix i Selva, sought inspiration in the British Penguin Books and Spanish Austral (Ll.S.B. 1966). The series illustrates the evolution of the boom of translations into Catalan in 1960s, as shown in Figure 3.4. The peak for the total number of books published, all of them translations except one, was in 1965, and the decline is obvious after 1967. Even though the aim of the series was to offer books from all time periods, around 40 percent of the books issued were published

FIGURE 3.4. Number of books published in the Isard series, by year.

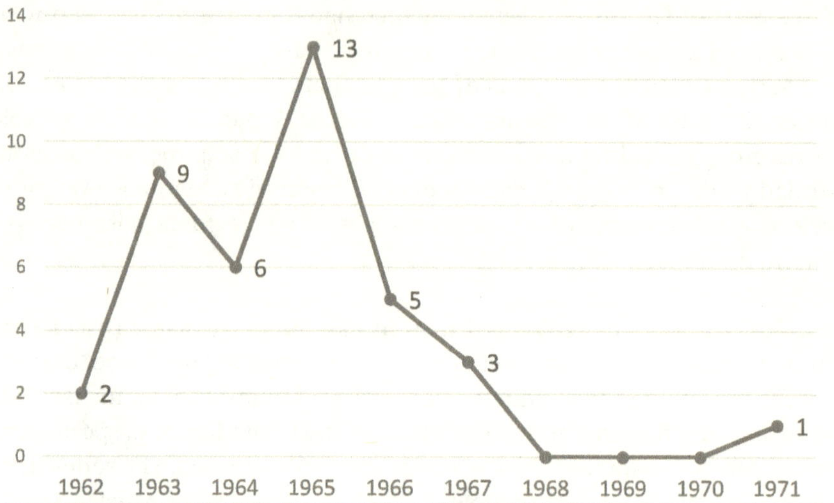

between 1950 and 1969, and more than a half belonged to the period after the Spanish Civil War. The reason for this is tied to the earlier-mentioned policy of focusing on the readership's preferences. According to Pere Calders, the choice of some titles might seem strange in isolation, but in the context of the series as a whole, there is a balance (Calders 1964a, 54–55). Following the principles of attention economy, I identify three strategies that Boix took in order to catch attention: promotion, fame and visibility, and choice of categories.

Promotion. Boix leveraged the successful promotion of the original book abroad by hiring readers in different languages to assess the quality of original works published abroad. I argue that readers based their decisions about whether to approve translations on two different factors: the success of the work overseas (Ferran de Pol, letter dated November 6, 1961, Josep M. Boix i Selva Collection, MS9480/1) and the reception of the film version of the book.[44] Of the thirty-nine volumes issued by the series, thirteen were translated into Catalan after film premieres, as in the case of *Barrabàs* (the movie premiered in 1961 and Isard issued a translation in 1963) and *El Doctor Givago*, issued the same year of its premiere (1965). This shows close attention to events in the cinematographic and literary worlds. In order to make the books more affordable, Isard offered both clothbound (around 110 pesetas, $1.83) and paperback bindings (around 125 pesetas, $2.08).[45]

Fame and Visibility. Boix used the translators' reputations as way to increase the sales of the series, because they "were widely known by the educated Catalan population" (Ribes de Dios 2003, 342–44). Indeed, Isard was one of the first series to incorporate, on the back cover of the books, a summary of the work and a short biography of both the author and the translator. Boix also asked his translators to make their role visible in the text, either through prologues, footnotes, or translator's notes.

Hiring professional writers as translators had another advantage—quality. All translations of the series were direct, and Boix was especially proud of the introduction of Greek novels in Catalan by the well-known Hellenist Jaume Berenguer Amenós (Vilardell 2011, 261) and the Russian translations done by the prestigious Slavic specialist August Vidal. Boix tried to combine hallowed prewar names, such as M. Teresa Vernet and Carles Soldevila, with new postwar figures, such as Ramon Folch i Camarasa and Jaume Berenguer Amenós. In this way, he sought to make his offerings more inclusive and approach all potential readers, whatever their age. Another decisive factor for Boix when hiring translators was the publicity they could generate as a result of awards. For example, the brief biography of Ramon Folch i Camarasa found on the back cover of paperback books he translated mentions that he won the Premi Ciutat de Barcelona in 1954, the Premi Ignasi Iglésies (Cambridge) in 1956, the Premi Joanot Martorell in 1956, and the Premi Víctor Català in 1960.

Categories. Isard was divided into eight categories: "classics," "religion," "novels, stories, and short stories," "biographies and autobiographies," "essays, articles, and reports," "history, philology, and statistics," "poetry," and "adventure, mystery, and exoticism." However, a majority of the total fell under the "novels, stories, and short stories" category. This shows the imbalance of catalogs I mentioned earlier, as publishers were more worried about feedback from readers than about creating a homogeneous catalog.

Isard is considered to have ended by 1968, coinciding with the decline of the Catalan translation boom, though the last book was technically published in 1971, due to contracts that had been signed much earlier.[46] The fact that the last book in the collection is *Introducció a l'estudi de la llengua catalana* (1971), a reference textbook of the Catalan language by Josep

Roca Pons, a professor at Indiana University, is a good metaphor of the new era for Catalan books in which a new generation of writers no longer had to resort to translation but could invent stories as interesting as those from abroad.

From the 1966 Press Law's "Voluntary Consultation" until the End of the Dictatorship

THE 1966 PRESS AND PRINTING LAW, OR CONTROLLED FREEDOM OF SPEECH

The Press and Printing Law was approved by Minister Manuel Fraga Iribarne on March 18, 1966, and came into force on April 9 of the same year.[47] Drafted by Pío Cabanillas, undersecretary of the ministry and a jurist (Chuliá 1999, 210), it included seventy-two articles, ten chapters, a prologue, and transitory final dispositions. Unlike the previous censorship law—approved in 1938 and with only twenty-three articles—it aimed to better organize the censorship apparatus and to find a balance between "a martial and obsessive censorship" (Cisquella, Erviti, and Sorolla 2002, 28) and freedom of speech. In short, the new law was a tactic to show to the world how *tolerant* the regime was. In truth, though, a closer look at the law leads to the conclusion that they created a sophisticated, more ambiguous, and discriminating monster. This Frankenstein's creature was made up of new concepts that became double-edged weapons: freedom of expression, voluntary consultation, official registration number, prior deposit, and official silence.

Freedom of speech and the right to spread information was only for printed material.[48] According to article 2, there was no limitation on what could be said, except for what was imposed by law: "Respect for the truth and morality, obey the laws, national defense, national security, public domestic order and external peace, respect for institutions and workers in politics and administration, independence of justice, and protection of intimacy and personal and familiar order."[49] In short, the limits were arbitrary. How can one justify whether a book obeys the law if the law rightly says that there is freedom of speech except when the law is not obeyed? This Kafkaesque article brought many complaints and was finally invalidated on April 13, 1977.

The *voluntary consultation* was another trick. While article 3 specified that it made prior censorship and compulsory consultation *invalid*, except in case of emergency or war, it left the door open for those responsible for the dissemination of any publication to consult *voluntarily* with the administration about its verdict on a specific book. Two typed copies had to be submitted in Spanish, although the foreign language original was also required in the case of translations. The censorship apparatus had a maximum response time of thirty working days (Sopena 2006, 70). If the administration did not contact the publisher within the established period of time, then the publisher ended up "accepting all the risks of any subsequent accusation" (Rojas Claros 2017a, 11). That was called "official silence" (*silencio administrativo*), and it was another of the newly created strategies.

When a book was subjected to voluntary censorship, the outcomes could be as follows: not recommended, authorized, suppression of some passages, obligation to present the original in case of translations, or official silence, but "a book was never prohibited . . . it was [just] not recommended" (Cisquella, Erviti, and Sorolla 2002, 56). The terminology used here is essential. For books that required the suppression of an excerpt, the letter sent to the editor said that "it is advisable to suppress the passages indicated on the pages . . . of the attached original copy." It is "advisable." This euphemism, if not fulfilled, could lead to book sequestration (*secuestro*), trial, and prison. The economic consequences of the *secuestros* were dire for publishers, who compiled, edited, and printed the volumes only for them to be taken away by the police.

Article 51 established one of the most ferocious tricks, which was the obligation for all publishers who wanted to publish in Spain to register at MIT within one year from April 9, 1966, to get an *official registration number* for publishing houses. Otherwise, "they may not pursue their publishing activity" (T. A. 1966, 287).[50] It was difficult to get a number because the government didn't want to offer carte blanche to everything published, especially by Catalan publishers, with whom they had to be very careful. If a publisher had the official number, it was good to publish as long as it deposited six copies within the required period and received either the free circulation card or official silence. Prior censorship was not abolished; it was *mandatory* for publishers who did not have the official registration number, which seems to be a common circumstance for Catalan publishers. Edicions 62, for example, did not have an official registration number from 1966 to 1973, which meant that everything that was about to be published needed to be submitted to compulsory censorship (Edicions 62 1979, LII). The reasoning behind this, according to Jesús A. Martínez, was "the political characterization of its members and the publication of books in Catalan" (2011, 138). The same was true for Publicacions de l'Abadia de Montserrat, which had to wait until Franco's death in 1975 (Massot i Muntaner 2016, 21) before obtaining the official registration number for publishing houses, even though they had one for journalistic companies for *Serra d'Or*. However, even those who had the official registration number, following the proverb once bitten, twice shy, often decided to go through *voluntary* censorship, at least until 1970.[51]

If everything looked fine after *voluntary* consultation, MIT sent a letter to the editor stating that they could proceed to comply with the prior deposit requisite before distributing it. The *prior deposit* was another trick. It was mandatory for everyone—those who passed voluntary consultation and those who didn't, as well as those who had the registration number and those who didn't—to deposit six copies of any publication, once already printed and ready to distribute, at least one day before its dissemination for every fifty pages in length (Article 12).[52] The possible scenarios resulting from the deposits were three: official silence, a free circulation card (from 1966 to 1975), or the sequestration of the edition—and this final practice was "relatively usual" (Cisquella, Erviti, and Sorolla 2002, 60). Even though a book was available for sale, anyone could report it, even years after its publication, and MIT would then proceed to sequester the edition (62). The imprint was also essential. If it did not include the place of publication, year of printing and the name and address of the printer or publisher (T. A. 1966, 285), it was considered to have been printed clandestinely.

The 1966 Press and Printing Law was very juridical (Barral, interviewed in Beneyto 1975, 189), but, ironically, the MIT did not have a legal office. It was the Servicio de Ordenación Editorial (Editorial Management Service), through either the director general of the press or the director general of information, who presented the books that the censors found to be the cause of any crime to the Tribunal de Orden Público (Public Order Court) or Fiscalía (Public Prosecutor), depending on the subject (Cisquella, Erviti, and Sorolla 2002, 62).[53] The complaints mainly revolved around the proletariat (to avoid working-class movements), political issues, or moral and religious concerns. However, it is fair to say that books about different ideologies, such as Marxism, had a better chance of being approved: "Subjects and authors that were always prohibited were authorized" (58).

Fraga was still in charge of the MIT on the night of January 18, 1969, when the regime's officers in Madrid took the university student Enrique Ruano who was "shot to death in custody" (Casanellas 2019, "excepción normativa").[54] The official cause of death, which had been manipulated by MIT, was suicide (Marfull 2009). The student protests that resulted from this event caused Spain to live in a state of emergency for six months, starting on January 25, 1969 (*BOE*, January 25, 1969, no. 2, 1175).[55] In Barcelona, "the rectorate of the central university was assaulted" (Casanellas 2019, "excepción normativa"). Fraga's response was to say that "prevention is better than cure. We are not going to wait for a journey of May so that later it will be more difficult and more expensive to repair" (*La Vanguardia Española* 1969).[56] The regime saw its end approaching and rushed to pass decree-laws in 1968 and 1969 to "organize" the country under Fraga's successor, Alfredo Sánchez Bella.

MINISTERS OF MIT FOR THE PERIOD 1969 TO 1976

In October 1969, Alfredo Sánchez Bella was appointed as the new minister of MIT, and he remained in that post until 1973. According to Payne, he was "a veteran diplomat of ultra-right-wing Catholic background, who was imposed personally by Franco" (2011, 546). Sopena acknowledges that this period was one of the toughest in terms of gaining authorization for publication. Even though prior censorship was abolished for some Catalan publishers, the repression came once books were already disseminated. Sure enough, according to my own investigations in *La Vanguardia Española*, the majority of book sequestrations took place in 1968 and 1969, likely as a consequence of the French social revolution of May 1968. Military repression was fierce. In addition, many books were seized, as in the case of *Los escritos del Che*, which was seized on March 3, 1968, by the provincial delegation and brought before a judge (*La Vanguardia Española* 1968).

At this point, it is worth stopping for a moment to explain the consequences of these sequestrations. In 1970, Joan Oliver was ready to give the fortieth performance of his Catalan-language play *Allò que tal vegada s'esdevingué*, directed by Ventura Pons and performed in the small Capsa theatre in Barcelona. The success of the play made the producers extend its run, but Minister Sanchez Bella's visit in Barcelona changed everything, as according to Oliver, the delegate of censorship services in Barcelona "called the director of the play and the owner of the place and advised them to stop the play immediately" (interviewed in Beneyto 1975, 211). After hearing about the loss of capital this decision entailed, the delegate agreed to permit them five more days of performance. The play would not be staged again until four years later when it was performed in the Barcelonan Romea Theatre.

After the state of alarm in 1969 and the repression under Sánchez Bella (1969–1973), MIT had a number of ministers with very short tenures. As a matter of fact, in 1974 there were three—Fernando de Liñán, Pío Cabanillas, and León Herrera—highlighting the internal cracks in the regime that forecast its end. This did not impact censorship, which was even tighter against anything that smacked of modernity. In 1975, the year of the dictator's death, MIT had two ministers—León Herrera and Adolfo Martín-Gamero—and then Andrés Reguera held the post until July 4, 1977.

Ricardo de la Cierva, director general of popular culture and entertainment and president of INLE between 1973 and 1974, established what his predecessor Carlos Robles Piquer had already initiated: *censura oficiosa*—that is, semi-official censorship that implied that the director himself read the books that were most controversial and established slightly more flexible criteria.[57] Many of the publications that had not been authorized before found hope in de la Cierva.[58]

In order to avoid so many sequestrations, publishers' representatives met then minister Adolfo Martín-Gamero in March 1976 to hand him a letter signed by forty-one publishers in which they asked him to lift the sequestration of those books that had been confiscated and also requested that "the inquisitorial attitudes toward book publishing should cease so that our country can enter into a situation that is comparable to that of the other European countries" (Europa Press 1976). There is no record of the minister's reply.

BOOKS IN CATALAN AVAILABLE FOR SALE (1967–1970)

As stated in Chapter 2, the appointment of Guillermo Díaz-Plaja as director of INLE in June 1966 showed once again the regime's attempt to approach Catalonia. Given the boom in publications in Catalan that occurred in the 1960s and in order to help booksellers organize themselves better, one of the first decisions of the new director was to create a catalog of books in Catalan, *Catàleg de llibres en català* (INLE 1967–1970). The catalog, available from 1967 until 1988 and compiled by Maria Ballester, provides a wealth of information about the availability of books in Catalan. It was presented by Díaz-Plaja, who emphasized the "splendid flowering of Catalan literature" within the "general Spanish" culture (Díaz-Plaja 1967, n.p.). Reading between the lines, it is clear that the new director of INLE wanted to bring the two cultures closer together, but by subordinating Catalan culture to Spanish culture. He also expressed a "gesture of cordiality for Latin America where so many colonies of Catalan residents like to cultivate their vernacular" (Díaz-Plaja 1967). He forgot to mention, though, that the majority of these colonies were made up of exiles.

FIGURE 3.5. Comparison between the number of new releases and total availability of books in Catalan, 1967–1970. Based on INLE 1967–1970 and Figure 3.1.

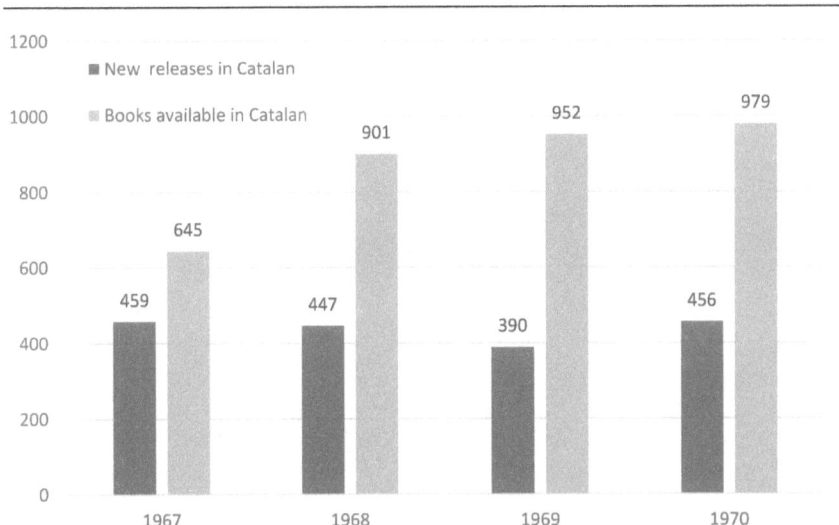

In this section, I focus my attention on the final years of the expansion of the boom in translations and the first years of the regression of the boom (1967–1970). I aim to confirm three hypotheses: (1) more than 80 percent of the books that were published at that time were not new releases (reeditions or in stock); (2) during the regression of the boom (starting in 1969) there was an increase of publishers who issued books in Catalan; and (3) the majority of publishers were located in Barcelona.

Hypothesis 1: The data I analyzed shows that from 1967 to 1970, about 50 percent of the books available in Catalan were new releases (see Figure 3.5). The reasons are varied: a) if hypothesis 2 is confirmed, the increase in the number of traditionally Spanish-language publishers who published also in Catalan; b) the time delay between the completion of a work and its publication (Figure 3.3) due to censorship restrictions; c) the contracts that were already signed and had to be executed. Also, for the last two years, when the boom in translations is in the regression stage, there is the thrust of the new generation of writers in Catalan that emerged as a result of the boom and explored new genres, such as books for children and young adults. Thus, the hypothesis that more than 80 percent of the books that were published at that time were not new releases is refuted, as seen in Figure 3.6.

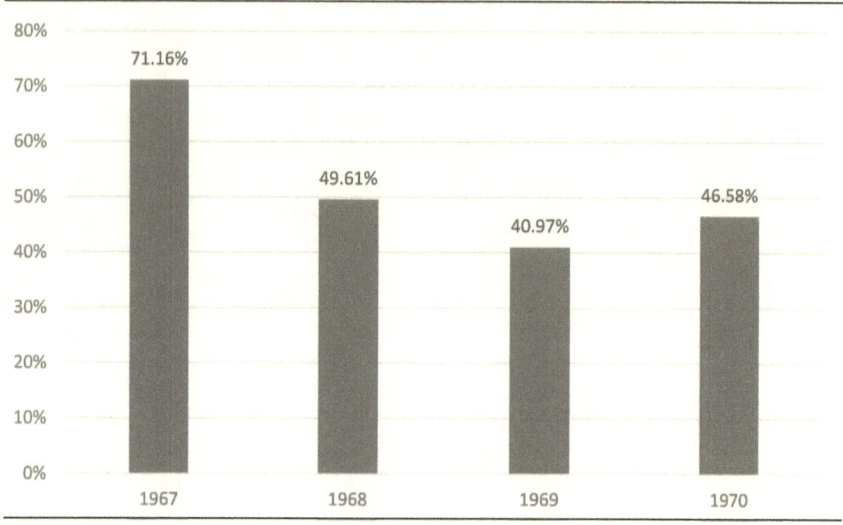

FIGURE 3.6. Books in Catalan. Percentage of new releases compared to the total books available, 1967–1970. Based on INLE 1967–1970 and Figure 3.5.

Hypothesis 2: The hypothesis that during the regression of the boom (starting in 1969) there was an increase of publishers who issued books in Catalan is confirmed in Figure 3.7. This graph points out two correlative phenomena: first, the number of Catalan book publishers increased during the crisis years of the translation boom, and, second, Spanish-language publishers jumped on the bandwagon of publications in Catalan with the advantage of tax relief, official credit for exports, and advantages in obtaining paper; these additional incentives began in 1964 and ended in 1969.[59] Even in the midst of the crisis, the number of publishers that issued books in Catalan increased (Vallverdú 1987, 118) and that correlates with the production of new books seen in Figure 3.5.

Hypothesis 3: The hypothesis that the majority of publishers publishing in Catalan were located in Barcelona is confirmed, as seen in Figure 3.8. The graph demonstrates that more than 65 percent of the publishers were located in Barcelona, making it difficult to reach a wider audience. Table 3.2 shows the availability of books in Catalan, according to the geographic zone.

When comparing the production of Andorra, the Balearic Islands, and Valencia with that of Madrid and Salamanca, you can see that production in Madrid and Salamanca was higher by 1970. There are two reasons for this:

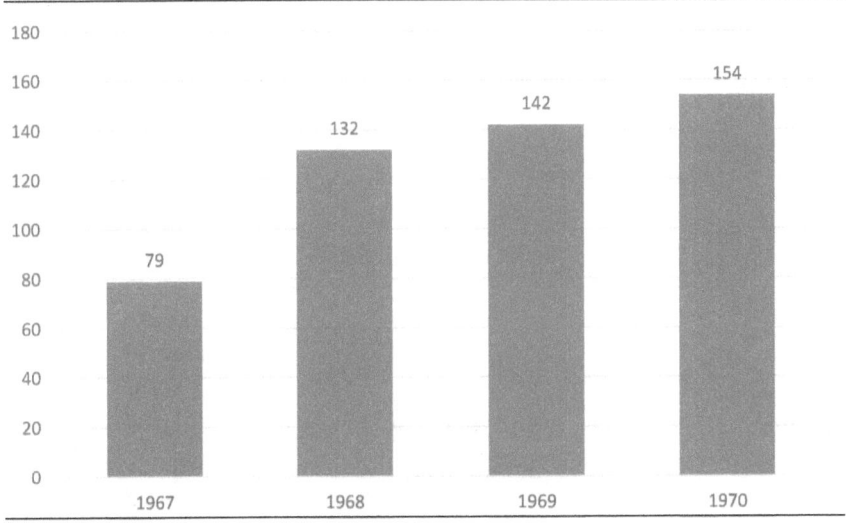

FIGURE 3.7. Number of publishers issuing books in Catalan, 1967–1970. Based on INLE 1967–1970.

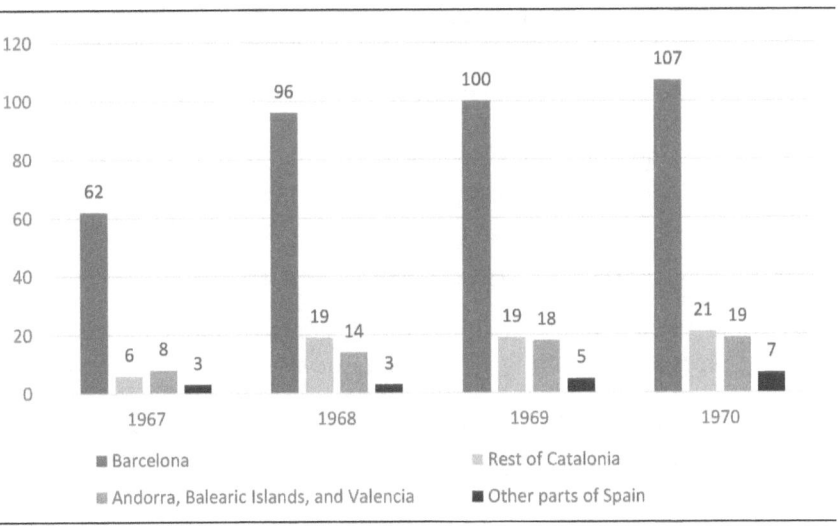

FIGURE 3.8. Number of publishers of Catalan books distributed geographically, 1967–1970. Based on INLE 1967–1970.

TABLE 3.2. Availability of books in Catalan according to the geographic location of their publishers

Year	Barcelona	Rest of Catalonia	Andorra, Balearic Islands, and Valencia	Other parts of Spain (Madrid and Salamanca)
1967	602	6	19	18
1968	840	19	24	18
1969	867	19	31	35
1970	884	21	32	42

Based on INLE 1967–1970.

censorship and purchasing power. In 1970 the Press Law of 1966 was in force, and it required an official registration number to publish legally. While for Catalan publishers, as I mentioned earlier, it was very difficult to obtain such a number, publishers based in Madrid or Salamanca seemed to be perceived as less dangerous, and authorizations of their books became a mere formality. The second reason is in line with the first one: while publishers in Andorra, the Balearic Islands, and Valencia issued books in Catalan as an act of resistance, in Madrid they did so for economic advantages. Ediciones Fax (from Madrid) published in Catalan because, according to one of their owners, José María Bernáldez, "Madrid and Barcelona undoubtedly occupy a preferential place" (Sánchez 1966, 455). Díaz-Plaja also emphasized this in the presentation of the catalog when he mentioned "publishers from Catalonia, Valencia, Mallorca, and even Madrid" (1967, "presentación").

VERGARA AND OTHER PUBLISHERS ARE SINKING: 1967–1971

Lluís Vicenç Estrada was in charge of the Vergara division in Mexico. After noticing that the publishing house had not issued even one new title, instead only reprinting commercially successful works in Spanish, he wrote a letter to Josep M. Boix in December 1967 asking about the situation in Barcelona.[60] The main cause for the focus on reprints, according to Boix, was the attitude of the manager of the company, Nicolau Surís:

> Discs and books are a screen. I have reached the sad conclusion that Vergara will never be a normal publishing house, as you and me would like to, because

TABLE 3.3. List of publishers and their companies' liabilities

Company	Liabilities
Cíclope S.A.	34 million pesetas ($566,666)
Editorial Codex	236 million pesetas ($3,933,333)
Distribuidora Europea de Publicaciones	74 million pesetas ($1,233,333)
Editorial Epos S.A.	20 million pesetas ($333,333)
Editorial Vergara	257 million pesetas ($4,283,333)
Editorial Mateu	14 million pesetas ($233,333)
Total:	635 million pesetas ($10,583,331)

Based on *La Gaceta Papelera* 1970, reprinted in *El Libro Español* 1971, 141.

its boss is not a publisher and doesn't want to be, doesn't do anything and doesn't let others do anything. . . . The publishing house has remained a minimized, marginalized, appendicular organism—almost parasitic—of Vergara. (Letter written by Boix to Lluís Vicens Estrada, December 17, 1967, Josep M. Boix i Selva Collection, MS9479/4)

However, the economic and political context also took its toll, particularly in 1969. According to INLE, the credits enjoyed by publishers who exported books were stopped in that year, which was one of the causes of the crisis in the publishing sector.[61] Feliciano Baratech ratified it in *La hoja del lunes*, stating, "With Blume, six Catalan publishers have suspended payments so far this year." He pointed to the official credit as its cause, since "not all the credits agreed upon for 1969 have yet been released," nor had the ones for 1970 (Baratech 1970). In March 1971, INLE listed the publishers and the company's liabilities, as shown in Table 3.3. *La Gaceta Papelera* points out that one of the main causes was a credit restriction for publishers but also highlights the real issue: "purchases of books by Spaniards are very low" (1970, 141). This means that "the average print run of the Spanish title does not currently exceed 6,500 copies, compared with the print runs of other countries, such as France, which exceed 10,000 copies" (reprinted in *El Libro Español* 1971, 142). In Catalan, print runs were even lower, ranging between fifteen hundred and three thousand copies.

Indeed, the book sector was going through the worst times of its existence. In the case of Vergara, the toughest moment was when Boix saw his family stability endangered by the nonpayment of his July, August, and September salaries, for which Vergara owed him 80,000 pesetas (around $1,350). Boix communicated this situation to Nicolau Surís by letter (October 10, 1970), hoping that it would be fixed quickly, but the manager left the letter unanswered.

Surís was in conversations with Banco Catalán de Desarrollo (Catalan Development Bank), a powerful financial group, about acquiring Vergara. However, in order to make the contract valid, Surís needed the signature of Boix, who asked for five or six hours to examine the document. Once he had done so, Boix called Lluís Serra Pujol to suggest some changes. Serra forgot to tell Surís, and on October 15, Vergara's stocks were purchased by Banco Catalán de Desarrollo without any opposition. That was the company's last breath, announced as a ray of hope to Estrada: "The true current situation: Vergara signed a contract with a powerful financial group, that acquires the main part of the stocks and amplifies its capital. Then, the 'suspension [of payments]' will be lifted. I think that now we can see the future with hope" (October 30, 1970, Josep M. Boix i Selva Collection, MS9479/4). Jaume Castell, director general and managing director of Banco Catalán de Desarrollo, was also the founder of the Spanish-language newspaper *Tele/eXpres* (1964–1980) and the Catalan weekly publication *Tele/Estel* (1966–1970) (*El País* 1984a). The financial group controlled a total of eighty-four companies (letter from Boix to Vicenç, December, 10, 1970, Josep M. Boix i Selva Collection, MS9479/4).

Ignasi Agustí, who had been Boix's friend before the war, took ownership of Librería Editorial Argos in 1958, as a result of the sale of shares of the magazine *Destino* and funding from Jaume Castell. From then on, the bookstore had good sales until 1970, when Agustí had to retire due to health problems. Consequently, the firm was transferred to Banco de Madrid, which was controlled by Jaume Castell, the same person who helped Agustí to acquire Argos. In 1976, Castell decided to merge Argos and Vergara to create a new firm: Argos-Vergara, with Mario Lacruz as a manager.[62]

When Banco Catalán de Desarrollo purchased a great part of the stocks of Vergara, in 1970, Vergara moved their Barcelona offices from Aragó Street to the *Tele/Exprés* building on Roger de Llúria. Boix did not have any energy for a new battle, and he decided to retire officially in 1978 (Flotats i Crispi 1997, n.p.). According to Adelina Plana, Boix's secretary for six years (1964–1970), whereas dealing with translators, authors, and editors had taken place in a close and friendly atmosphere at Vergara, at Argos everything was colder and very "impersonal" (personal conversation, December 29, 2018). Once the merger had been finalized, in 1976, the staff was reorganized and there were many layoffs. This change also affected Adelina Plana, who became general secretary to the detriment of Boix, who was left without a secretary for the first time. To illustrate that moment, Adelina Plana told me that Boix gifted her the *Diccionari general de la llengua catalana* by Fabra, and asked that she "remember it as a memory," because he was sure he would never need it again in the publishing house: Argos was only interested in encyclopedias and big formats, and Boix's ideas didn't fit in there. Neither did the Isard series, which had already been ended by that time.

It is easy to extrapolate this circumstance to other publishers. As Joan Triadú reported, in October 1970 there were only *two* publishing houses that still issued translations and current Catalan novels: Editorial Aymà (which offered two series, Biblioteca A tot vent by Proa and Col·lecció Tròpics) and Edicions 62 (which offered the El Balancí series). He no longer counted Vergara (1970a, 61–66). Here, Catalan-language publishers and Spanish-language ones found themselves in a struggle for survival (Triadú 1970b, 47). It was the end that brought about a new generation.

How is it possible that the number of publishers in Catalan increased in 1970 in the midst of this crisis that forced many publishers to close? In this case, two realities must be differentiated: those who published translations and those who began to publish literature originally in Catalan. As stated before, the translation boom ended in 1969, and it dragged many publishing houses down with it. This is scarcely visible in the data shown in Figure 3.7 because there were contracts signed prior to the decline that had yet to be fulfilled. The withdrawal of subsidies for exporting Spanish-language books to Latin America had a big impact on Spanish-language publishers. Catalan publishers tried to target a new generation of adults by producing new creative works and exploring other genres, such as juvenile literature, which is why publications in this language— both those written by local authors and those written by foreign authors— never stopped.

STRATEGIES TO OVERCOME CENSORSHIP

Through research at Archivo General de la Administración and analysis of accounts from different Catalan publishers, I have classified the strategies taken by Catalan publishers to overcome censorship in thirteen points:[63]

> 1. *Oral agreements*. In reviewing all of the Isard censorship files, I found that during the gestational age, oral agreements had been made with the censorship apparatus:

In an interview with the then Head of Section Mr. Hierro, to whom we explained our editorial plans and very specifically the reasons that encouraged us to publish a few titles in this language, we received his agreement subject to his personal visa, . . . being nevertheless warned that each and every one of the works that VERGARA would publish in the future with these special characteristics, should be submitted for a visa to the Head of the Book Inspection Section, who would decide on behalf of your honor, whether or not it should be published. (Letter of May 29, 1962, signed by Nicolau Surís. Censorship file of *Déu ha nascut a l'exili*, file 3250-61)

Despite these agreements, however, the censors retained the right to approve or reject a book.[64] For example, *Déu ha nascut a l'exili* was published in 1963, and reprinted in 1965, but the prologue, written by its author especially for the Catalan version, never came out (Pinyol i Torrents and Vilardell 2018, 172n23).

2. *Self-censorship*. Self-censorship was common in many publications, both before and after the 1966 Press and Printing Law. For *Serra d'Or*, for instance, it was necessary to consider not only the censor on duty but also the critical gazes of readers, who could also denounce content. The same was true for other journals and even nonperiodical publications. Massot i Muntaner recounts that in some cases the scandal even reached the Vatican (2016, 20).

3. *Making changes after submitting manuscripts to censorship*. Before the 1966 Press and Printing Law, publishers sometimes submitted copies to censorship and then emended them if necessary afterward (letter from Joan Sales to Mercè Rodoreda, May 17, 1961, in Sánchez Gordaliza 2012, 2:46).

4. *Submitting translations only in the original language*. In the case of translations, publishers sometimes submitted only the original in the original language and not the translation in the target language, in this case Catalan. It seems that the censors who could read languages other than the languages of Spain were a little more broad-minded. The 1966 Press and Printing Law made it compulsory to submit both versions (Cisquella, Erviti, and Sorolla 2002, 56), but because the law encouraged dialogue, many publishers reached out to the minister to discuss publishing constraints. Boix, for example, sent a letter to Minister Fraga saying,

This way of censoring is really harmful to publishers because we contract a work, we pay the copyright, we send it to you, and you say we cannot publish it; or we send it to you and you cross out so much that the work has no sense and we cannot publish it. We suggest that, if you don't have any objection, we will send the entire books in English, French, Italian, German, the four languages ... and tell us if that can be published or not or this can be published but with few changes. ... They said yes, OK. (Flotats i Crispi and Boix i Selva 1994)

5. *Not mentioning the target language in the censorship file.* This was a common practice: if it was not stated that the book was to be published in Catalan, the reader/censor inferred that it would be in Spanish. Boix stated that "the censorship files included 'work ... ; translator.' ... It was not even specified if it was translated into Catalan or Spanish. Because it was known that Catalan was impossible, we played with that" (Flotats i Crispi and Boix i Selva 1994). However, prologues and any other additional pages had to be submitted.
6. *Not mentioning the series.* In many cases of Catalan series, publishers did not mention the name of the series. This tactic goes hand in hand with the previous one: if publishers did not include the series or the target language, readers/censors usually believed the books were in Spanish.
7. *Using initials for author or translator.* Often publishers used initials instead of the full names of the authors or translators as a way to hide whether the people had Catalan or Spanish names. For example, "J. Fuster" appears instead of "Joan Fuster," as "Joan" rather than "Juan" indicates Catalan heritage.
8. *Short print runs.* As in the previous years, censors were more likely to accept a work with a short print run than one with a longer run. It is for this reason that Vergara initially asked for permission to publish only fifteen hundred volumes at a time, although after 1965 they changed the print run length to three thousand. Although in some cases they did not specify the name of the series, we can deduce that the shortest print-run volumes were those of the Catalan collection.
9. *International pressure.* When publishers were unsure about the authorization of a book, they had their arsenal ready to denounce the nonauthorization across Europe. This is how Boix explained it:

> Then, one filled the form and wrote: "Work: La Pesta, Author: Camus; Translator: J. Fuster."[65] This was the first one we issued—and they thought it was in Spanish. We printed it in Catalan, and we sent it to them. Then, they lasted three weeks or a month without any answer, not even yes or no. But meanwhile we had already written letters to the most important

publishers in Europe saying, "We don't know if Camus would be allowed to publish"; we didn't say anything about Catalan, we were in the know and thought that if they denied it, in Europe they would know "Camus prohibited in Spain." And then it was authorized. (Flotats i Crispi and Boix i Selva 1994)

10. *Hiring a representative in Madrid.* One of the best-known tactics was to hire a representative of the publishing house to handle censorship in Madrid. This person was in charge of either sending the works to voluntary consultation or to prior deposit, depending on the case, and also retrieved the copies once they had a verdict from the censorship services. The representative also processed notices and cards of free circulation and arranged meetings with the head of the censorship services and the publisher. Bernardo Crespo, who was indispensable to Catalan publishers, earned 35 pesetas [$0.58] in 1963 and 75 pesetas [$1.25] in 1967 for managing the censorship process for one book cover. For the management of a whole book, representatives received between 100 and 275 pesetas [$1.66–4.58] in 1967 and 600 pesetas [$10] per book in 1975 (Sopena 2006, 77). Unlike other publishers, Vergara hired J. Gómez Torrano as its representative.[66]

11. *Offering gifts.* It is an open secret that publishers often sent gifts to MIT so that the censors would make exceptions. Thus, especially during the Christmas season, "Christmas baskets were sent to the readers and chocolates to the readers" (Cisquella, Erviti, and Sorolla 2002, 51). According to Adelina Plana, Boix even sent an antique chest of drawers to Madrid (personal conversation, December 29, 2018), and Sopena mentions that Josep Fornàs sent a tenth share of a Christmas lottery ticket at the end of every year to Bernardo Crespo (2006, 77).

12. *Asking for authorization of Spanish version first.* Publishers sometimes asked for authorization once the Spanish version was already issued in Spain or, in the case of Vergara, asked first for the authorization in Spanish and then submitted the Catalan version for authorization (Plana, personal conversation, December 29, 2018). While in the majority of cases having already been published in Spanish was a reason for authorization,[67] sometimes, because the copyrights for the Spanish version were granted to Latin America and books issued abroad were hard to send to Spain, the first publication of the book in the Iberian Peninsula was in Catalan.[68] There are other curious cases, such as the one noted by Xavier Ayén speaking about George Orwell's *1984*: "In Spain it was published in 1952 but with many suppressions. The first full version did not arrive until 1963 . . . in Catalan, by Editorial Vergara.

In Spanish, the censored version continued to be reissued... curiously enough, according to the records, until 1984" (2010).

13. *Skipping voluntary consultation.* Some publishers skipped voluntary consultation, but then were attentive to the feedback the book received after publication. This was the practice, according to Francisco Candel, of Ariel publishing house, which had "the criterion of not going to *prior consultation* or censorship but did carry out a kind of test at the level of the ministerial corridor, with which the confidential approval was never found, but warnings were given on this or that point of the book so that the book was read by jurists and other specialists. There were adjustments and suppressions, but that we made ourselves" (emphasis in original, interviewed in Beneyto 1975, 35–36).

As can be inferred, after the entry of Fraga and also Carlos Robles Piquer at MIT, censorship was opened up a little and dialogue was encouraged. Fornàs, from Editorial Pòrtic, and Boix i Selva spoke about Ricardo de la Cierva as one of the saviors of those times. However, censorship was certainly not eliminated, and Isard left more than thirty books in preparation. The substantial changes in the 1966 Press and Printing Law caused publishers to change strategies: on the one hand, much more could be published, but, on the other hand, there was greater risk and "discomfort" (Gomis, interviewed in Beneyto 1975, 63). The dialogue that Fraga and his allies fostered at MIT was received as a ray of hope, but with the understanding that an offhand comment could have a negative effect on the authorization of other publications (63).

Conclusions

In the 1960s there was an evident social, political, and economic opening up. The Second Vatican Council, together with the injection of international money, the Stabilization Plan, and Spain's admission into more and more international organizations, led publishers in Catalan to invest in publishing originals and translations. After examining the data, mostly based on unpublished documents, I've separated two different variables—translations into Catalan and book production in Catalan. I argue that there is a boom in translations that moves through three stages: gestation, golden age, and regression. The growth trend in the publication of books in Catalan, however, is constant. Indeed, the rebirth of fictional literature in Catalan needs to be understood as a consequence of the decline in translations. This had positive economic implications for publishers because issuing original books in Catalan was much cheaper for them.

In this chapter I used the theory of attention economy to examine this unprecedented moment in Catalan publishing history, explaining the commercial tactics that most publishers used during the boom to find a niche in the publishing market. Looking at history from the point of view of attention highlights the way focus was placed on catching the attention of booksellers and consumers, sometimes to the detriment of the quality of the product. This became the seed for a new generation of writers in the Catalan language. Indeed, even though publishers had an unmeasured moment of euphoria in 1965 that soon dissipated, this boom left a developed model of the Catalan language, a foundation on which new generations of publishers and writers have continued to build (Iglésias 2019, 100).

The 1966 Press and Printing Law was a rule of contrasts and euphemisms that maintained voracious control over anything and everything that touched on social, political, historical, moral, or religious concerns. Beginning in the 1970s, many priests began their fight against repression, so it is not surprising that religious works were also sequestered, even some written by bishops.[69] The Press and Printing Law may have appeared to foster dialogue and conciliation, but it eventually showed its uncomfortable and repressive face. It was a tool to keep the publishers' and writers' eyes open because once a work had been published, it was not exempt from retaliation. The replacement of Manuel Fraga by Alfredo Sánchez Bella in 1969 was difficult for Catalan publishers, who had hoped that the censorial system would become a little more permissive. Later, under Ricardo de la Cierva, it seemed that censorship was a little friendlier, although I found books that had been sequestered until 1977.[70]

Toward the end, the dictatorship was not able to evolve, as evidenced by the succession of ministers who headed MIT in 1974. In 1975, with Franco's death, censorship did not end, but it had lost its power.

We have to consider publishers, writers, journalists, and anyone related to the world of cultural dissemination of that time as heroes. They sacrificed themselves, experiencing misery, hunger, and even arrest so that people could have access to books, ideologies, and thoughts that made the regime uncomfortable. Their struggle has often been overshadowed by other cultural disseminators, although the consequences of the censorship apparatus, the repression of Catalan in public, and the poor distribution network, together with economic problems and the burden of debt, show the suffering experienced by those participating in what was an initiative of goodwill. The difficulties of this period have been illustrated through a case study of the Vergara publishing house from Barcelona, one of the most prolific houses that went out of business due to economic problems. This example is not unique and exemplifies the situation faced by the majority of Catalan-language (and Spanish-language) publishers at that time.

CHAPTER 4

Writers Speak Up about Censorship

"There is no doubt that some time ago I had a moment of downfall. I published little or nothing.... But how could you want me to publish if all the books were banned, <u>one after another</u>? And publishers accepted my works, but of course, conditioned to see what would happen <u>with the censorship</u>." (Manuel de Pedrolo interviewed in Torres 1995, 42).

As can be inferred from this excerpt of a conversation between Manuel de Pedrolo and Estanislau Torres in 1973, writers normally did not receive remuneration until the publisher received a thumbs up from the censorship facility. If authors were lucky enough to have the regime's authorization for a book, their text was sure to be mutilated, and they faced, from within their own circle, criticism that "if it overcame censorship it is not impartial" (Torres 1995, 24). Therefore, writers had to constantly break down walls in order to raise their voices. That is why in this last chapter I give them a voice by collecting their accounts and discussing their concept of censorship, the strategies they used to circumvent it, and their experiences with the two censorship laws; by doing so, I seek to determine if they faced the same sort of repression as the publishers.

Censorship from the Writers' Perspective

The concept of censorship itself has been mutating over time. Censorship can be defined as the suppression, modification, repression, or distortion of ideas, thoughts, writings, or messages that may be found to be improper, offensive, or harmful by the rulers of a society. Today, one can think about whether laws restricting the use of social media are effective, and whether hate speech should be allowed on the Internet. Before, it was about freedom of speech.

In order to dive deep into the time period studied and its protagonists, I use the definition of censorship given by Salvador Espriu, one of the most celebrated Catalan poets of the twentieth century. Although the field of censorship was less strict in the case of poetry in Catalan,[1] this definition allows me to establish links with the experiences of over a dozen writers. Espriu said that censorship "is one of the many weapons that those who 'hold' power use to keep themselves in it. 'Ideological principles' are, in general, accessory, opportunistic and fluctuating" (interviewed in Beneyto 1975, 234). The analysis of this sentence leads me to divide the concept in the following way:

> **Holds power.** According to Griffin, Spain and Portugal were "para-fascist" regimes—that is, authoritarian and totalitarian regimes whose objective was to remain in power indefinitely, even if this required altering the forms of repression or the criteria of censorship (1993, qtd. in Rundle 2018, 31). I already mentioned in previous chapters that the Francoist regime did not have an ideology of its own; it acted by deconstructing ideology rather than building a unifying one.
>
> **Opportunistic.** Franco joined the cause of fascism when it was convenient for him—for example, when being interviewed with Hitler and Mussolini—but he disassociated himself from those leaders after the defeat of the Axis Powers in World War II. Suddenly, he became a staunch anticommunist, a successful gateway to acceptance in international bodies such as the United Nations and the Organisation for Economic Co-operation and Development (OECD).
>
> **Fluctuating.** The consequence of Franco being opportunistic is that the censorship apparatus did not follow homogeneous guidelines. That is especially relevant during the first years of the dictatorship, where the name of the author or the language in which a book was written determined its fate. The reasoning behind that, according to Joan Fuster, was that "the intellectual-policeman, the inquisitor, is a ferocious beast" and their verdicts were unpredictable (interviewed in Beneyto 1975, 223).

CENSORSHIP AND REPRESSION

While Josep Pla considered censorship as an organizational measure for all governments, Joan Oliver relied on laws, rather than impositions, to rule a country (interviewed in Beneyto 1975, 209). Joan Brossa, discussing the origin of censorship, found it important to identify those who held power and their motivations to censor (interviewed in Beneyto 1975, 79), while Joan Fuster looked at the consequences: "the more censorship, the less culture" (interviewed in Beneyto 1975, 223).

Never Surrender

At the end of the day, writers had to do their job, and if they wanted to earn money from publishing, they had to obey the laws. To do so, some of them used their own strategy: self-censorship. As Calders explained, "There is no longer any need for an official to tell you that you cannot do this, that you cannot do that: it is you yourself who is self-censoring" (interviewed in Torres 1995, 39). Writers used ingenious metaphors to talk about its impact: it was "like wearing an orthopedic shoe with a healthy foot" that "harms your work and deceives your readers" (Brossa, interviewed in Beneyto 1975, 78), a brake, a mutilation, or a "muzzle" (Fuster, interviewed in Beneyto 1975, 223).

One of the best examples of the use of self-censorship was Josep Pla, considered by many to be a well of political contradictions because he had switched to the Franco side in 1939, after his stay in Italy. The intellectual, who wanted to make a career as a writer, accepted self-censorship as a seasoning for all his books. All he cared about was writing and getting paid for it (Josep Pla, interviewed in Beneyto 1975, 183). Probably for this reason, in 1975 he told his interviewer, Antonio Beneyto: "At this moment, I don't know if one can say what I am telling you." Beneyto answered, "Of course it can be said, why not?" Pla replied, "But, be careful, another issue is that you don't have difficulties afterwards" (183). This testifies to Pla's fear of what could and could not be said.

The Methodology

Pla noted the various methods by which censorship can take place: "There are many ways to do censorship.... Here in Spain ... there is a man who says this cannot 'be authorized.' However, the manager of a newspaper has a journalist, a secretary, or whatever, and then he talks to the person who wants to do the suppression—he invites him to eat, gives him money and all set" (Pla, interviewed in Beneyto 1975, 181–82). The key was influence, as Víctor Mora related: "If you don't know the right people and you're not 'in' there's no need to fight. It's like you don't write, my dear. As if you didn't exist" (interviewed in Torres 1995, 44).

Manuel de Pedrolo even commented, "There are works, right here, published, that are more up-tempo than mine and with rude vocabulary to no avail" (interviewed in Torres 1995, 42). He was referring to *San Camilo, 1936*, by Camilo José Cela, which was published by Editorial Alfaguara, "directed by Cela's brothers" (Larraz 2014, 152), and was finally authorized in 1969 due to Fraga's friendship with Cela and also with some of the regime's censors.[2]

Repression

In times of censorship, repression becomes a double-sided sword. On the one hand there is the "psychosis of censorship" (Porcel, interviewed in Beneyto 1975, 100): authors are always concerned about whether their publication will be accepted by the censorship services. Then, once it has been approved by the administration and seems all set, the judgments of the author's peers start. In this last case, according to Joan Oliver, "the unfavorable verdict that a work of a *cofrade* deserves is in danger of being attributed to envy, resentment or pedantry" (1964, 82). Oliver even detailed different critic profiles: those offering indirect criticism, the treacherous ones, those that praise somebody to be praised one day, and "those that feel wounded by the spectacle of the unhappiness of others" (82). To illustrate this point, I cite the case of Pere Calders, who had to go into exile in Mexico for a good part of his life for fear of Franco's repression. In an article published in *Fascicles Literaris* in September 1958, he wrote, "That forces me to reflect on the fact that censorship, being so meticulous in matters of morality, has let slip a novel like *El mar* (Joanot Martorell Prize, 1957), published by Editorial Aymà in 1958, in which the characters seem to have no other obsession than to button and unbutton their pants, raise their hair to the category of a lyrical image and urinate to celebrate any occasion" (Calders 2019, "una indústria que no prospera a Catalunya"). Obviously, Blai Bonet's novel sparked a great deal of controversy because of its content, but recently Xavier Pla discovered, in reviewing the files in the Archivo General de la Administración (AGA), that the novel had nine censored chapters. The version that was published, compared to that submitted to AGA, "simplifies the voices and condenses several characters into one for narrative economy, shortens the stories and restrains the excess and savagery of some characters and passages in search of a greater balance" (Massot 2017). On this point, it is interesting to note Jordi Cornellà-Detrell's statement: "Censorship is one of the most invisible bequests of the dictatorship, not only because it has survived but because it has gone on transforming and reproducing itself far beyond the end of the regime" (Cornellà-Detrell 2010, 47, qtd. by Iglésias 2019, 99).

Salvador Pàniker, discussing the ways to defend a system, described the whole strategy of the Francoist dictatorship toward censorship over time: (1) "prohibiting criticism of the system," which Franco did during the first

Francoism with the Order of 1938 in force; (2) "allowing criticism of the system, but in such a way that the criticism cannot in any case modify it essentially," as in the case of the 1966 Press and Printing Law, which punished, but with a kinder face; and (3) "criticism should be allowed as a margin such that the system can really change" (interviewed in Beneyto 1975, 275), which was the transition to democracy.

THE WRITER'S ROLE IN SOCIETY

The purpose of most authoritarian governments is to make the society believe that it is self-sufficient and there is no need to bring goods from outside the borders. In Spain, the same applied to culture and to any manifestation contrary to the Spanish ideal of "one, great and free Spain," with no room for regional manifestations whatsoever.

For this reason, at the beginning of the dictatorship, Catalan literature evolved more slowly when compared to Spanish literature, since the first was considered a threat to the integrity of the regime. Thus, while in the beginning (1939–1959) the symbolist and academic literature of Carles Riba was the one that inspired Catalan writers (Porcel, interviewed in Beneyto 1975, 103), in 1959, with the start of Second Francoism, that allowed more books in this language, Catalan literature could abandon its earlier sophistication and focus on the everyday life of the writer, as Spanish literature was already doing. However, there was room for another expansion, from 1969 to 1971,[3] showing that different genres could coexist harmoniously, thanks to the new generation of writers who, under the guidance of Joan Brossa and J. V. Foix, recovered archaic forms of writing. However, Porcel denounced the fact that young novelists, instead of writing about contemporary events, told stories of their youth (around 1955 to 1960) without taking into account the social reality of the 1970s (interviewed in Beneyto 1975, 104).

Ramon Planas described two ways of understanding the writer's role in society: "The Catalan narrator of today, like that of anywhere and always, has two paths at his feet: to be a witness of his time, in an impassive way, we would say; or to look inside himself (a man like so many others) putting his present, his circumstance as a backdrop. I am inclined, categorically, towards the latter tendency" (interviewed in *Serra d'Or* 1961a, 17–18). The first option was supported by Foix, who said "the established Power always takes advantage, for its own benefit, of the silence of the writer" (interviewed in Beneyto 1975, 111). In between the two options there was Josep M. Espinàs, who did not believe that the writer had more power than an ordinary citizen, stating, "The writer does not exist. There are different writers, and each of them has to fulfill the function that is proper to him and is given by his personality and his means of expression" (interviewed in *Serra d'Or* 1961b, 14). A majority of the authors, though, supported the second option, as Planas himself did. Candel added that the role of the writer had to be combined with "a critical and denouncing work of the situation" (interviewed in Beneyto 1975, 29), and for Manuel de Pedrolo the narrator "needs to confront—and the good novelist always has done so—his reader with living and painful problems—of a personal, social, political nature, etc." (interviewed in *Serra d'Or* 1961a, 16).

Candel, however, warned the fact that literature could not be "to the service of a movement, revolution, or regime" (interviewed in Beneyto 1975, 29). In practice, it was not that easy. The reality was that writers had to compromise in order to survive. Choosing one publisher or another determined their political positions as well, but their hands were tied because without these channels, they would not have been able to make a living from writing. The publisher was key to negotiations and authorizations in Madrid, as in the case of Pla, whose "publisher [Mr. Vergés] has so much power" (interviewed in Beneyto 1975, 183, see also Vergés 2017).

Writing for a politically committed publisher and also doing it in Catalan was deadly: "Here there has been normal censorship and censorship for being Catalan" and also for Catalanism, because "being Catalan has meant being, in principle, a suspicious citizen (Porcel, interviewed in Beneyto 1975, 101). Foix emphasized the contrast between those who thought of Spain as a great country in the past and those who considered Spain a European country (interviewed in Beneyto 1975, 112).

Whether because of the old-fashioned ideas of the Franco regime or because of the repression, for many years mass media in Catalan was prohibited; after Franco's death in 1975, mass media outlets remained insufficient. Teaching in Catalan was not allowed during the regime, and even at the end of the dictatorship it was monitored heavily. Some writers like Pedrolo argued that if the Catalan language had the same level of freedom as the Spanish one, writers would not have had to assume roles that did not apply to them as intellectuals. This idea is also shared by Josep M. Castellet, who witnessed the lack of good novelists because "an original thought is missing, a thought that translates the historical-political-cultural Catalan moment" (Muñoz i Lloret 2006, "Els anys d'aprenentatge"). The reasoning behind that can be found in the lack of communication between intellectuals and their society, because "daily, weekly, monthly press (as there was)"

was inexistent in Catalan (Calders, interviewed in Torres 1995, 40). But why wasn't there a press in Catalan? Jordi Maluquer aimed to become a professional journalist and gathered capital to buy three weekly newspapers in Catalan, but he never received authorization from MIT. The most disastrous case was the purchase in the 1960s of the weekly *Tele/Estel*, mentioned in the previous chapter. It seems that once Maluquer gathered the required money, "they had a permit [that had] expired three years ago and the name [was] not registered" (interviewed in Torres 1995, 43). And when he went to renew the permit, he was told verbally that there would be no problem, but "at the moment of truth" (43) he was never granted permission to publish.

THE ECONOMIC SITUATION OF THE CATALAN WRITER

Although all agree that writers are a key element of a society, unfortunately at that time it was impossible to make a living writing Catalan literature. According to Candel, "I live in the same economic-social insecurity that the worker lives in" (interviewed in Beneyto 1975, 32). Following the analogy of the worker and the writer, Fuster compared their situation in these terms: while "workers can gain part of their rights through a strike that leads to chaos, writers and intellectuals would surely not be as effective if they went on strike" (Beneyto 1975, 224).

Apart from this, there was another factor for Catalan writers that I briefly mentioned at the beginning of this chapter: they usually did not get paid until their text was approved by the censors. In a letter dated August 4, 1970, Albert Manent described the situation to Jordi Arbonès. He stated that the publishing house Pòrtic "issues a book every fifteen days" and pays "ten thousand pesetas, when the book is approved by censorship. I think this is the best solution" (Arbonès and Manent 2011, 80), referring to a book that Arbonès had in preparation. Even though Arbonès followed his advice, the whole book ended up being suppressed (88). Therefore, economic insecurity was a permanent feature for writers beginning with the triumph of Franco's forces in 1939 and lasting until the end of the dictatorship. "All of us, as Catalan writers, are Sunday afternoon writers. Some are good, others not so good. Until we have a country we won't do more than we do." (de Pol, interviewed in Torres 1995, 41).

TOWARD A MODEL OF LANGUAGE DESPITE THE DIFFICULTIES

With a forbidden language as their tool, Catalan writers had a duty to leave a standard linguistic register for the generations to come. Given the situation of the language, the standardization came from translations and, to a lesser extent, original works of fiction rather than textbooks.

More than a note from the translator, Joan Fuster's prologue to Albert Camus's *La Pesta* (Fuster 1962) is a true manifesto that definitively shaped this standard of language.[4] In 1961 Josep Maria Espinàs explained two innovations in Catalan narrative: "the adoption of a more sober and functional language" to get many more readers and "the more accentuated professional character of some writers" to maintain a faithful audience (interviewed in *Serra d'Or* 1961b, 14). This is how Joan Sales summarized it to Mercè Rodoreda: the "hard battle of CONVINCING OUR PEOPLE TO READ CATALAN BOOKS" (letter of May 12, 1961, in Sánchez Gordaliza 2012, 2:42). As mentioned in the previous chapter, one of the greatest limitations from the editor's point of view was precisely the small number of Catalan readers (Pol, interviewed in Torres 1995, 40)—when this was added to the linguistic and cultural repression, turning things around became even more difficult.

PROCESS BEHIND SELF-CENSORSHIP

The act of self-censorship is itself a response to the repression.[5] Following Víctor Gómez Pin, it can be defined as "the process by which certain representations are rejected from consciousness and held in the unconscious" (1981, 32). In this section, I focus my attention on the psychological process undergone by the authors and the ethical-social constraints they faced in achieving a final product (Zamora, interviewed in Beneyto 1975, 116).

As I noted in the previous chapters, I disagree with scholars who define publishers as censors. Instead, I argue that both writers and publishers exercise self-censorship, as the publisher Esther Tusquets confirmed: "Francoism dragged us all—writers, journalists, publishers—into the sordid perversion of self-censorship" (Tusquets 2020).

According to INLE, the goal of a publisher was "to multiply the fruit of the author's creative imagination and to take the risk of spreading it in the internal and external market" (Editorial 1970, 653). As a result, for the sake of their business, publishers could suggest or modify passages to avoid nonauthorization from the censorship services (Ricardo de la Cierva, interviewed in Beneyto 1975, 92). Therefore, they can never be considered censors, a term intended only for government officials who exercise censorship.

Self-censorship brings its own risks; according to Ricardo de la Cierva, director general of popular culture and entertainment (1973–1974), "it is much more dangerous than censorship itself" (interviewed in Beneyto 1975, 92). The types of self-censorship, according to Manuel Abellán, are as follows:

Explicit self-censorship refers to "the changes made by writers in order to publish the text *once they receive it back from the Censorship Services*" (my emphasis, Abellán 1987, 18). Julián Marías is a good example of this behavior, since he argued that he preferred to write without restrictions and then, having received the verdict, suppress accordingly. Usually those changes would undermine the text, which is why some authors preferred to publish abroad. However, the case of *Cinco horas con Mario* provides a counterpoint, since the author, Miguel Delibes, after receiving the verdict from censorship services decided to turn "Mario into a deceased person" (Abellán 1987, 20), which ended up making the novel better.

Implicit conscious self-censorship refers to the "measures taken by the writer *before writing the work*, as he or she writes or after writing the manuscript, as a last revision" (my emphasis, Abellán 1987, 20). In this case, it happens when the author uses linguistic strategies to avoid censorship but maintains the core idea (Francisco Umbral, interviewed in Beneyto 1975, 40–45) or changes topics to avoid conflicting issues (Aranguren, interviewed in Beneyto 1975, 46–53). As an illustrative example, Buero Vallejo made up the euphemism "expressive limitations" or "limitations of expression" (interviewed in Beneyto 1975, 24) to speak about censorship. As a result, he could discuss an illegal term without being punished, since there was no explicit reference.

Implicit unconscious self-censorship refers to *acquired censorship*, or ideas of the regime's doctrine that penetrated the layer of consciousness. Consequently, the subject cannot determine whether a thought is part of her or his thinking or if it was learned from outside. Salvador Pàniker called it the "socialization of our conscience" (interviewed in Beneyto 1975, 278). About the same topic, Francisco Umbral declared: "There will undoubtedly be historical, psychological, national conditioning that will influence all of us; one no longer perceives them, since unfortunately one has been raised with them" (interviewed in Beneyto 1975, 43).

I argue that self-censorship can also be explicit before submitting one's work to the censorship services, in order to prevent any change afterward. Thus, I suggest another way of classifying based on consciousness of one's actions and also on Blas (2007): *conscious self-censorship* and *unconscious self-censorship* rather than *implicit* and *explicit self-censorship*. In the first one, the author explicitly makes changes, either before or after submitting their work to the censorship services, in order to be able to publish it; in the second, acquired doctrines lead the author to choose subjects or words according to the principles of the regime. Buero Vallejo argued for the validity of this approach: "Self-censorship can only act in the domain or in the sphere of the unconscious. In the sphere of the conscious the author chooses, determines, and fixes the theme and the dramatic structure without stopping at details" (Abellán 1987, 21).

In the sphere of consciousness, according to Francisco Umbral, in literature what is not said is more important than what is said. "Censorship stimulates metaphor," said the attorney Vilamitjana (Puigtobella 2020).[6] This practice was called "writing in situation" by Buero Vallejo, who argued that it did not mean "necessarily mutilating" the text (interviewed in Beneyto 1975, 24). Instead, following Porcel, the author would create a "spiral" language with allusions and illusions (interviewed in Beneyto 1975, 99) to reach the final target: readers. Salvador Pàniker's strategy of using "redundancies" became a very popular trend. The result was a camouflaged literature or "metaphorical poetry" (Carlos Edmundo de Ory, interviewed in Beneyto 1975, 287). Joan Oliver considered his journalistic self-censorship "subtle. [He] often resorted to euphemisms or unusual synonyms in passages that [he] considered 'dangerous' to avoid 'other censorship'" (interviewed in Beneyto 1975, 210).

Although it is a little more unusual, I also wish to point out self-censorship in a translation that actually came from the original work. This is the case explained by the translator Jordi Arbonès. In *For Whom the Bell Tolls*, first published in 1940 (though Arbonès was working from the 1955 edition by Penguin Books) Hemingway practiced two different types of censorship: sometimes he used untranslated Spanish swear words italicized in the text, at other times he simply used the term "obscenity" or "unprintable."[7] In the Catalan edition, for the first case Arbonès decided to keep the Spanish words even though the publisher, self-censoring, replaced some of the Spanish terms with the first letter followed by suspension points (for example *cojones*, a vulgar term that refers to testicles, was replaced with "c . . ."). For the second case, Arbonès replaced "obscenity" with a very general Catalan hyperonym, *dallonses*, meaning "so and so" (Arbonès 1995, 89).

Self-Censorship: Conclusions

According to Joan Oliver, there are positive aspects of self-censorship, since it "enriches the lexicon and develops mental agility" (interviewed in Beneyto 1975, 210). Salvador Pàniker saw it as having "therapeutic and creative value" (interviewed in Beneyto 1975, 277), but for Ramon Nieto, camouflaged language has no positive contribution. It is evident that working with the handbrake on is a challenge, but most authors in Catalan had a readership that could understand their cryptic messages and figure out what the author really meant. It required an extra effort from the audience that taught them to be skeptical about what they read and at the same time enhanced mental agility. However, that was definitely not ideal, and many foreign authors did not consent to that for their works. That is the case for Aldous Huxley, who "had made it very clear that they preferred to publish in Argentine publishing houses precisely to avoid the mutilations of censorship or self-censored translations" (Mengual Català 2013, "Janés y la literatura española").

THE TWO LAWS OF CENSORSHIP ANALYZED BY THE WRITERS

In the previous chapters I pointed out the arbitrariness and rigidity in censoring what Kate Edwards calls the "'big three': sex, violence and profanity" (2015, 22). Such censorship was ultimately focused on the continuity of the regime, which could lead to differences in criteria, as for example in the tolerance toward texts written in Catalan. According to Baltasar Porcel, it was "the censorship of a country at war" (interviewed in Beneyto 1975, 97). He warned that what must be taken into account were not the laws (which are more or less enforced) but those who are in power and who helped them in their enforcement.

Order of April 29, 1938

The first stage of censorship, from 1938 to 1966, has a common denominator: Gabriel Arias-Salgado, considered "the black beast of censorship" (Candel, interviewed in Beneyto 1975, 33). Baltasar Porcel outlined Arias-Salgado's character even more: "This gentleman, about literature, about society, about religion, about sexual morality, about any form of expression that man has had on Earth in the course of his entire history, had absolutely primitive ideas that had been displaced from his time" (interviewed in Beneyto 1975, 97). Porcel himself added his judgment about those who were in charge of censoring Catalan books at the beginning: they were "from the right-wing ideological branch, old monarchic lords, Catholics. They applied much more censorship to sexual and religious matters, etc. than in Spanish, where they were also there, but there were many more people" (102).

Paco Candel, a portraitist of the country's social reality and defender of the workers' movement in his writing, described the difference between the two types of censorship: "At that time censorship of a 'moral type' or 'anti-erotic type' was prevalent above all," but "for me, censorship during this period has been more benevolent or, perhaps, less complicated than . . . that of Fraga Iribarne, the liberalizer" (interviewed in Beneyto 1975, 33–34). As mentioned in the first chapter, censors scanned texts in search of specific bad or "harmful" words, such as the term "fascist." Estanislau Torres argued: "It is undeniable that it was a great contradiction that, while in *Els ulls i la cendra* the presence of this term did not have any kind of incidence, they forced [me] to eliminate it, systematically, from *La derrota*" (1995, 18). The two novels are only one year apart, but they were governed by two different laws: the first one by the 1938 Order and the second one by the 1966 Press and Printing Law. Therefore, Torres agreed with Candel's point of view. The red mark from the censorship services was also always on the word "Civil War," which had to be referred to as "War of Liberation" or simply "war" (Candel, interviewed in Beneyto 1975, 39), and also on the word "communist," which had to be referred to as "socialist."

In contrast, Mercè Rodoreda, author of the best-selling novel *La plaça del diamant*, which is set in Barcelona during the time of the Republic and the Spanish Civil War and recounts the atrocities of living at that time, stated that she never noticed censorship nor did she ever censor herself, although she defined censorship as "useless" (interviewed in Beneyto 1975, 163).

This is not the case with Manuel de Pedrolo, who in his interview with Antonio Beneyto listed his struggles with censorship, which were greater in number from 1966 onward than before. Santiago Albertí, who was one of Manuel de Pedrolo's publishers during the first censorship, highlighted the repercussions of "the usual procedure in absolute prohibitions" (1994, 227). The publisher would receive a printed notice (in the case of *Un món per a tothom*, the notice was provided on April 9, 1956), which referred to an "Enclosed Record." This "Enclosed Record," according to Albertí, was one tracing-paper without any sign of identification, where someone had typed: "SUSPENDED ITS PUBLICATION" (227). This was the only thing the author and publisher got back. Not knowing the cause of the nonauthorization forced the author to keep the book in a drawer, lost in oblivion. In the case of *Un món per a tothom*, though, having a good network was crucial: Ferran Canyameres had a liaison within the censorship services who could explain to them the reasons for the nonauthorization. Thus, after asking their contact, they discovered that the second of the three stories in the work "has only a few things crossed out" (Albertí 1994, 227), and their contact also recommended that they change the title. Once the changes were made, the text was submitted again. According to the files that I have been able to consult, it was submitted to censorship as a new book on June 14, 1956 (Censorship File of *Un món per a tothom*, file 3080–56), and delivered to reader number 15. In the resolution section, it says that there are two authorizations, one on July 30, 1956, and the other on October 15, 1956, this last one the date of the deposit. A print run of eighteen hundred copies was requested with a selling price of twenty pesetas per copy. The verdict of the reader, whom I would venture to say was José de Pablo Muñoz, although the signature is not very legible, was dated July 20, 1956:

> It is a collection of literary stories of little value and anecdotal nature. In the first one, Miguel flees from his world and embarks for America but finds the surprise at high seas that a man appears in his cabin to avenge old grievances. In a short distance streetcar we see the scene of the fat lady who is disturbed by smoking in her presence: She is getting up, fighting and coming back. — A beggar approaches the country house and asks for bread, but he doesn't want it, he wants love; she defends herself and is saved by the dogs of the house that chase and attack him. — Office scenes with Mr. Baró and the employees Perramon, Agustí, etc. — Jok tells Roberto, Ernesto and others about his adventurous life. . . . IT CAN BE PUBLISHED.

Thus, on July 30, 1956, the book *Un món per a tothom* was authorized, and it was printed in August 1956. This example highlights two ideas: the lack of definition and the delay in the verdict. If the publisher hadn't had a person in Madrid that could tell them which fragments could be published and which were not allowed, they would have forced Pedrolo to leave the work in the drawer for fear of reprisals. The other issue was the delayed verdict, which often made writers and publishers give up and leave the work in "pending publication" mode, waiting for better times.[8] In other words, there was little dialogue and much ambiguity, few explanations (as in the case of the "Enclosed Record" Albertí received) and much motivation to abandon publication. Nevertheless, Catalans were a difficult nut to crack. Joan Sales, in a letter to Mercè Rodoreda, dated May 17, 1961, told of the strategies they used to get around this first censorship: "Censorship is eminently bureaucratic, and it never takes the trouble to check whether the edition that appears in print is exactly the same as the copy they approved, so you can correct it quite calmly" (Sánchez Gordaliza 2012, 2:46). However, with the Fraga Law of March 1966, the censorship apparatus filled this legal gap, since once the book had been distributed, anyone could denounce it if it failed to comply with any of the censorship rules. Fraga and his allies were ready to whip things into shape, though with a kinder face.

CASE STUDY: *INCERTA GLÒRIA*

Incerta glòria is, according to many scholars, the first novel about the Spanish Civil War that focuses on the losing side "from a Catalan Nationalist, Republican, but at the same time Catholic perspective, and that denounces with virulence both Fascism and Anarchism" (Pla 2011, 10).[9] Lisa Russ Spaar considers it a symbolic novel "full of philosophical, religious and literary meditations" (2018). Its author, the publisher Joan Sales, was not a controversial author, but rather a solitary, fervent Catholic who wanted to denounce some facts that he lived in the flesh. When asked about the reasons that led him to write the novel, he answered, "I would say that my obsession both when I wrote *Incerta glòria* [Uncertain glory] and now that I have decided to publish the letters to Màrius Torres has been this: to contribute to give a testimony of the truth, at least of that truth that I have been able to see with my eyes and feel with my ears" (Canosa 2013, 1:30–1:59). The novel, considered by Xavier Vall to have introduced existentialism to Catalonia (1994, 70), deals with the love triangle between a powerful woman and two brothers, who were on opposing sides of the war, and the book also includes the shooting of the president of Catalonia, Lluís Companys, by the regime in 1940. It won the Joanot Martorell Prize, one of the most prestigious awards in Catalan literature, on December 13, 1955.

The brief summary here attests to the complexity of the novel and foresees the reaction of Gabriel Arias-Salgado, at that time in charge of Ministry of Information and Tourism (MIT). Studying the censorship process of *Incerta glòria* illustrates the vicissitudes of the period and puts to an end to one of the greatest enigmas of Catalan literature. This case study is based on letters from both Sales and his editor to MIT—unpublished until today and kept in the Joan Sales Collection (referred to hereafter as FS), together with the censorship file of the book (Censorship file of *Incerta glòria*, file 1059-56), published in Clotet and Torra (2010, 68–80).

The novel was registered by MIT on February 25, 1956, a couple of months after it won the Joanot Martorell Prize. The first piece of documentation I found in the censorship file (Censorship file of *Incerta glòria*, file 1059-56)[10] was a single letter, written by the publisher, where he summarized the plot of the novel and the reasons he thought it should be authorized. Among the reasons were the Joanot Martorell Prize of 25,000 pesetas ($410) and the interest that French publisher Galimard had in publishing it in France. The latter was taken by the publisher as a golden opportunity to push for its authorization: "It will be perplexing if a book appears in a French version before the Spanish original (Catalan)."[11] After alleging that the author does not want to create a scandal and would accept "all the phrases that the censorship indicates to him," the letter ends with a warning: "If the censorship approves the book with such amendments, it will give to 'Galimard' the original as amended and without any comment to its expurgation; if the censorship insists on banning it, it will give to 'Galimard' the original as a whole and without amendments. (The ban will increase 'Galimard's' interest in publishing it, of course)" (FS). However, the outcome was not as expected, and the process took eight months, six files, and seven letters. Manuel Sancho Millán, a reader/censor since February 19, 1946 (Clotet and Torra 2010, 18), was the first to write a report about the book; the report was submitted on March 16, 1956. The verdict was to delete what was crossed out on only twenty-six pages of the book. About the rest, "we have no problem in proposing its publication" (69). This "generous" authorization was not shared by his colleagues.

José de Pablo Muñoz, the "Falangist, lawyer and schoolteacher" (Rojas Claros 2017b, 105), read and strongly censored the work on three occasions (March 22, June 22, and October 18). On March 22, the outcome was twenty-four pages with deletions and a final verdict that reads, "The word war is the most frequent word when talking about the times that are told, and to know the diary of a militiaman it is not necessary to write a work in Catalan, with philosophical pushes at every step and with mumbo-jumbo" (Clotet and Torra 2010, 70). Reading between the lines of this quotation, one realizes that speaking in Catalan is a provocation in itself. Surely, as I discussed in Chapter 2, there was an unwritten law about the need to harshly censor publications in languages other than Spanish, and this could not be an exception. In view of the disagreements between Millán's report and the first report from José de Pablo Muñoz, the censorship body requested the report of a religious advisor, the Franciscan philosopher Fr. Miguel Oromí Inglés (Godayol 2016, 145). He was so well regarded by the regime that they sometimes trusted his verdict alone (Sopena 2013, 154). The outcome of his report was the same as that of de Pablo Muñoz. He had no hesitation in calling the work "a very dirty and macabre existentialist type of novel" (Clotet and Torra 2010, 71).

Once de la Madrid, the representative of Editorial Aymà in the censorship services, was notified verbally of the verdict of *Incerta glòria*, he rushed to let the publisher know the outcome. In order to clarify the issue, on April 4, 1956, Aymà sent a letter directly to Florentino Pérez Embid, director general of information (1952–1957), requesting the exact reasoning behind this decision so as to communicate it to the author, a "practicing Catholic," who "is willing to introduce into the book the amendments and deletions deemed fair and indispensable by that Direction." Beyond the economic losses that would follow, Aymà argued that the decision would bring "disenchantment and perplexity" (FS) among those who were informed about the result of the Joanot Martorell Prize of 1955, in addition to all the celebrities that attended the event. The very next day, Pérez Embid answered the letter, stating that he would request more information about this particular issue and would reach out to the publishing house shortly. The resulting document was called "Work History," and it summarized the verdicts of the three censors who had reviewed the work so far. This document, along with the galley proofs, was sent to the publisher. On May 22, 1956, the publisher stated that the author had already "thoroughly redone" the text, helped by another writer and a priest (FS). In order to speed up the process—using Galimard as an excuse—the publisher asked Domingo Casanovas, a friend of the author who lived in Madrid, to have a conversation with Pérez Embid before submitting it through the representative they had in Madrid, at that time Federico Martínez. On June 8, 1956, the manuscript was again submitted to censorship services. Pérez Embid sent a letter to the head of the Book Inspection Services in which he stated that they would need to speed up the process and let him know the verdict before communicating with the publisher. The reaction of censorship services was to make the same censor, José de Pablo Muñoz, read it again, which caught the attention of Sales, who wrote directly to Pérez Embid on June 27, 1956. In this letter, the author expressed his surprise after noticing that the same censor issued another negative report, mentioning passages that did not exist anymore in the new version of the book.

Pérez Embid found the letter from Sales very reasonable and asked a different reader to censor the book. The fifth censor, Miguel Piernavieja, stated in his report of July 19 and the note of July 27, 1956, that the book was not authorizable. Pérez Embid sent a letter to Joan Sales on August 29, 1956, and one day later to the publisher to let them know about the decision. On October 11, 1956, Aymà sent over a letter to Pérez Embid that included the fact that the boss of the company, Aymà Ayala, went to Madrid to speak to the director general of information, but he was out of his office. In the same letter, the publishing house let Pérez Embid know that the novel had been modified following the criteria of Dr. Juan Roig Gironella, who stated that he would give the *nihil obstat* for the book. The publisher also stated that they were submitting it once again to be authorized by the civil censorship, but Sales had already reached out to Maur M. Boix to share his concern and ask for advice from the Abbot of Montserrat. Luckily, on October 18, 1956, the same José de Pablo Muñoz agreed that if the book had the *nihil obstat* of the Bishopric of Barcelona, "it can be published," even though "the nature of the work persists in all its parts" (Clotet and Torra 2010, 79). The Catalan version was finally published in December 1956, and the French translation by Bernard Lesfargues was issued in 1962, thanks to the help of Juan Goytisolo, who was working "as a reader of original works for Galimard" (Pla 2007).

The chronology of the correspondence with MIT by the publisher and also by the writer himself can be seen in Table 4.1. In May 2020, Club Editor reissued *Incerta glòria*. On the credits page there is this chronology: First edition: 1956; First complete edition: 1971; First digital edition: May 2020.

The 1966 Press and Printing Law

The 1966 Press and Printing Law brought changes in repression, including much more uncertainty for writers. The transition between the two censorship laws, according to Manuel Vázquez Montalbán, meant a movement from the "war situation to the post-war situation," but never from war to peace (interviewed in Beneyto 1975, 215). Even Salvador Pàniker called the law "the only real milestone in the democratization of the regime" (interviewed in Beneyto 1975, 276).

Although "it is true that from Fraga's time onwards you get a little more wide-sleeved, especially in the erotic or sexual area" (Pedrolo, interviewed in Beneyto 1975, 261), that loosening was not accompanied by other expected changes.[12] Pàniker noted, "When a crack is opened, as was the case with the Press and Printing Law, others must be opened as well" (interviewed in Beneyto 1975, 276). According to Pedrolo, "a door is not open until you can enter and exit through it, moving freely; if it is opened by two fingers, with a guard behind you, you cannot say that it is an open door" (interviewed in Beneyto 1975, 261). In a letter dated February 9, 1972, Pedrolo explained to Jordi Arbonès, "As far as censorship is concerned, don't be surprised if they put obstacles in the way of the publication of the book [*Teatre català de postguerra*]; they are very hard right now. Now there is no longer any talk concerning 'openness.' It's sad, infinitely sad" (Arbonès and Pedrolo 2011, 78, letter 30).

Candel concluded that, in the sexual aspect, censorship was quite arbitrary and "continues to cross out whenever it feels good to do so in a prudish way" (interviewed in Beneyto 1975, 39). As for the religious aspect, Candel noted that even after 1966, "they still defended a religion that was old fashioned and orthodoxly traditional" (39). Pàniker explained that as an editor in 1975 he still had a "retained" book entitled *El matrimonio*

TABLE 4.1. Documentation of the censorship process of *Incerta glòria*

Date	Type of Document	People Involved	Verdict
February 25, 1956	Entry file*		
February 1956	Background†		
March 16, 1956	First report*	Manuel Sancho Millán	Suppressions
March 22, 1956	Second report*	José de Pablo Muñoz	Nonauthorization
March 28, 1956	Third report*	Fray Miguel Oromí	Nonauthorization
April 4, 1956	Letter†	Aymà to Florentino Pérez Embid	
April 5, 1956	Letter†	Florentino Pérez Embid to Aymà	Aymà asks for the verdict of the novel; Embid does not know yet
n.d.	Work history†		Summary of reports and verdicts and galley proofs sent to the publisher
May 22, 1956	Letter†	Aymà to Florentino Pérez Embid	They have the galley proofs of the new version
n.d.	Notes about *Incerta Glòria*†		
June 8, 1956	Internal service note 253-56*	Florentino Pérez Embid to head of the Book Inspection Services	Review the new version of the work
June 22, 1956	Letter from J. Úbeda and report by José de Pablo Muñoz*	F. Úbeda and José de Pablo Muñoz	Nonauthorization

TABLE 4.1. Documentation of the censorship process of *Incerta glòria* (cont'd.)

Date	Type of Document	People Involved	Verdict
June 27, 1956	Letter*	Joan Sales to Florentino Pérez Embid	Joan Sales complains about having the same reader as for the previous report
July 6, 1956	Letter*	Florentino Pérez Embid to Joan Sales	Pérez Embid stated he would answer once he knew what happened
July 6, 1956	Internal service note 295-56*	Florentino Pérez Embid to head of the Book Inspection Services	Florentino Pérez Embid admits that Sales is right
July 10, 1956	Internal note*	Head of the Book Inspection Services to Rumeu	Send this novel back to someone who can read Catalan
July, 19 1956	Report*	Miguel Piernavieja	Nonauthorization
July, 27 1956	Handwritten note in the same report (July 19)*	Miguel Piernavieja	Nonauthorization
August, 29 1956	Letter†	Director General of Information (Florentino Pérez Embid) to Joan Sales	Denial of authorization
August, 30 1956	Correspondence with the publishing house*	Director General of Information (Florentino Pérez Embid)	Denial of authorization
October, 11 1956	Letter*	Aymà to Florentino Pérez Embid	They want to resort to religious censorship

TABLE 4.1. Documentation of the censorship process of *Incerta glòria* (cont'd.)

Date	Type of Document	People Involved	Verdict
October 17, 1956	Letter†	Maur M. Boix to Joan Sales	Boix is going to speak about the case to the Abbot of Montserrat. He asks Sales to send over the proofs
October, 18 1956	Report*	José de Pablo Muñoz	It cannot be authorized, but if you have the *nihil obstat*, it can be published
October, 19 1956	Letter†	Florentino Pérez Embid to Joan Sales	Pérez Embid lets Sales know that he spoke to the head of the Book Inspection Services to "activate" the process
November 1, 1956	Letter†	Maur M. Boix to Joan Sales	The recommendation for the *nihil obstat* has already been made

* Clotet and Torra 2010, 68–79.
† Joan Sales Collection, Institut d'Estudis Catalans.

y sus alternativas (Marriage and its alternatives), "but it is known that in Madrid they consider that marriage has no alternatives" (interviewed in Beneyto 1975, 277). But if someone criticized the progressive church, "they will not say anything and will consent to it" (Candel, interviewed in Beneyto 1975, 39).

Regarding politics, Candel indicated that "the fundamental or elemental principles, as they say, of the Movement, and the personalities of the Regime, continue to be taboo" (interviewed in Beneyto 1975, 39). Pàniker remembered that when he began to write for the newspaper *La Vanguardia Española* he was told, "No, you do not inhibit yourself when you write and do it as if you were in an Anglo-Saxon community and then, if anything, we will review your texts here" (interviewed in Beneyto 1975, 276).

CASE STUDY: UN AMOR FORA CIUTAT

Manuel de Pedrolo was one of the most affected by the arbitrary sexual censorship.[13] *Un amor fora ciutat*, one of his novels that addressed the issue of homosexuality, was released by Editorial Aymà on Sant Jordi's Day (April 23) in 1970. Aymà printed fifteen hundred copies and planned to distribute the work without going through voluntary censorship, according to Aymà's literary editor, Joan Oliver.[14] All publications had to have six copies deposited before publication, even if they had not passed through voluntary censorship, and this deposit was completed by Fernando Moreno Sánchez, the Aymà representative in Madrid, on April 16, 1970. The following day a report was written that stated, "The deposit should not be accepted, and the work should be made available to the Public Prosecutor's Office" (Censorship file of *Un amor fora ciutat*, file 3960–70). The reasons were as follows:

> This novel, if on the one hand it offers the literary merit of being well constructed and better written, on the other hand it offers a serious aspect of social danger inasmuch as it not only excuses or, better, exculpates homosexuality, but far from presenting us with a sin against nature as an object of horror and execration, homosexuality comes to be affirmed by the protagonist, who is the homosexual, that such abnormality responds to an irrepressible tendency from which it is almost impossible to escape, and that therefore the true homosexual, who cannot be confused with the "faggot," since on the contrary he always affirms his virility, is more worthy of merciful compassion than of execration.
>
> The novel, like almost all of this author's, contains scenes that, while not bordering on pornography, are nevertheless sometimes of a great and sometimes repugnant eroticism.
>
> For all these reasons, and above all for the excellent literary quality of the work, we consider it to be seriously dangerous and in any case as an attack on public morality, in accordance with the reiterated jurisprudence of the Supreme Court on homosexuality. Consequently, the deposit should not be accepted and the work should be made available to the public prosecutor. Madrid, 17 April 1970.

On April 20, 1970, there was another report:

> This is a novel in which the Protagonist tries to prove his wife right about what happens to a homosexual (since he has been surprised by her).

In reality, the novel does not explain anything, but is a simple pornographic narrative, not only pitying the homosexual, but also highlighting his vice as if it were a great virtue. The woman, in the novel, doesn't believe it and abandons him—the readers can't swallow such pornography either. I think IT CANNOT BE PUBLISHED. Madrid 20-IV-70

On April 21, 1970, there was an "official complaint to the Magistrate Judge of the Public Order Court, with notification to the Supreme Court Prosecutor, and to the Publishing House itself." On April 25, 1970, "a summary proceeding was initiated by the Court of Public Order, having ordered the judicial confiscation of the edition." On April 28, the Supreme Court prosecutor passed the proceedings on to the prosecutor of the Audiencia Territorial de Barcelona (Barcelona Territorial Court), and after ensuring that the prior deposit had been made correctly, on May 30 "the Public Order Court ... has issued a writ against the author Manuel de Pedrolo Molina." It is interesting to note that in this case the author of the work is the one who assumes the consequences, and not the publisher, who deposited the copies as requested. "The author was charged of the crime of Public Scandal and the investigating judge ordered the abduction of the work. And the prosecutor requested that the accused would be sentenced to six months of major arrest, a fine of 25,000 pesetas ($416.6), special disqualification for 9 years, legal bonds and additional costs and the confiscation of the copies of the book" (Oliver, interviewed in Beneyto 1975, 211).[15]

This sentence indicates that articles 431 and 432 of the criminal code, which deal with public morals, modesty, and good manners, were violated. After two years, Pedrolo, with the Catalan writer Maurici Serrahima as his lawyer, was acquitted (*La Vanguardia Española* 1972). On May 2, 1972, Jordi Camañes, from the publishing house, wrote a letter to the director general of popular culture and entertainment, attaching a copy of the acquittal for Manuel de Pedrolo, dated March 27, 1972. On May 19, 1972, Aymà asked for a second edition of the book, with a print run of two thousand copies and with a new censorship file (Censorship file of *Un amor fora ciutat*, file 6106–72). On February 5, 1974, Aymà asked for a third edition of the book with a print run of two thousand copies as well (Censorship file of *Un amor fora ciutat*, file 1561–74), as part of the Tròpics series. The resolution of February 6, 1974, was "silence."

Summary of Writers' and Publishers' Censorship Strategies

The strategies for circumventing censorship from the writer's point of view focused on the text as an element of resistance. Thus, self-censorship was the key to success, as was writing to capture the attention of the publisher, the censor, the bookseller, and the reader.

When I speak of the text as an element of resistance, I mean that writers, publishers, and readers shared a kind of cryptic language—self-censored, of course—that only they understood and that, therefore, went unnoticed by the censors, who normally scanned the text for offensive words. This was the case for the already famous song and album by Quico Pi de la Serra issued in 1974, "Fills de Buda" (Sons of Buddha), an expression that, when pronounced in Catalan, suggests that they are not from Buddha but from a bad mother. The use of repetitions was also another resource for misleading the censor. Thus, writers could refer to and criticize the regime, but subtly.

Another strategy was to fill the text with footnotes. Josep Massot i Muntaner noticed that when a book or an article was returned, there were practically no deletions in the footnotes. His response, in his book *Aproximació a la història religiosa de la Catalunya contemporània*, published in 1973, was "to fill it with notes, where, through mentions in French, English or German, I could point out or at least suggest what in no way would have been authorized within the text of the book" (Massot i Muntaner 2016, 24).

I have previously talked about the fact that when a writer chose a publisher, at that very moment the writer was already committed not only to the ideology but also to a particular audience and level of self-censorship. In the different layers between author and authorization, one can find three filters: the author's, the publisher's (to determine if the work is in line with their catalog), and the censor's.

However, normally the author did not get involved in censorship issues unless asked to do so by the publisher. Exceptions can be found in the case of *Incerta glòria* or the previously mentioned example of Estanislau Torres, with more or less successful outcomes. If the publisher followed the law, the first person condemned in the case of denunciation after publication was the author, although the publisher could also be fined. That was the case of Manuel de Pedrolo's *Un amor fora ciutat*.

The task of publishers was to administer the censorship of the work, often from Madrid, through a representative who worked at censorship services. In this way, it was possible to have firsthand information about

TABLE 4.2. Contrasting publishers' and authors' strategies to overcome censorship

Publishers	Authors
Make oral agreements	Normally make agreements by letter if the publisher asked them to do so (Estanislau Torres or Joan Sales)
Self-censorship on top of writer's self-censorship	Self-censorship, unconscious or conscious
Submit the original in case of translations	If it was a creative work, try to find a title that could be read both in Catalan and Spanish
Do not mention the target language in the censorship file	Use repetitions in the text and be creative with wording, to make sure it was authorized
Do not mention the name of the series	Find an editor who could handle the censorship apparatus effectively and who was not in danger
Use initials for the name of the author or translator	Use a great number of footnotes
Print short runs; sell for a cheaper price; produce collector's editions	—
Bring international pressure to bear	Publish abroad
Hire a person to handle the censorship process in Madrid	—
Give gifts to censors	—
Ask for authorization after the Spanish version was already out	Many times publish in Spanish first and then try to publish the same book in Catalan
Do not go to voluntary censorship but be aware of the feedback about the book	—

the censorship process. The other option was to send letters to the director general of information or even to the minister. Table 4.2 contrasts these strategies.

While the editor's task of resistance was based on administrative and bureaucratic negotiations, the writer's was to offer a product that was well written in a language that had no official status and whose normalization seemed a utopia. Thus, editors and writers collaborated with each other so that new generations of writers would find a literature of resistance at a time when many decided to give up and move on by writing in another language or even by switching political sides. Although the translation boom in Catalonia was unmeasured, this splendor gave birth to quality literature in a language that at that time was forbidden. The work of these heroes must be recognized and their voice must be heard because they have left us an invaluable heritage.

NOTES

INTRODUCTION

1. The referendum was not recognized as legal by the Spanish prime minister, Partido Popular leader Mariano Rajoy. Its consequences are still visible today, with Catalan politicians living away from the country and others spent time in prison.
2. All translations from Spanish and Catalan sources are mine. Valle de los Caídos is a monument located on the outskirts of Madrid, specifically in the town of El Escorial. Franco ordered its construction after the end of the Spanish Civil War (1936–1939) to honor all those who died during the conflict. It is considered a controversial monument because it included the mortal remains of Spain's two dictators: Miguel Primo de Rivera and Francisco Franco. On September 24, 2019, the Spanish Supreme Court, at the request of the Spanish prime minister Pedro Sánchez, asked to exhume Franco's remains. On October 24 of the same year, the remains were moved to the Mingorrubio cemetery in El Pardo, Madrid.
3. The Provincial Electoral Board is in charge of "transparency and objectivity of the electoral processes" (Junta Electoral Central, 2014).
4. He is the author of the seven-volume history of publishing in Catalonia, *L'edició a Catalunya* (2001–2007), covering the Middle Ages until the twentieth century.
5. More information is provided in Chapter 4.

CHAPTER 1

1. When discussing the Spanish Civil War, the terminology used can sometimes be confusing. The term *rebel* refers to Franco's allies, those who won the war. They also used the self-denomination *Nacionales* (Nationals) to refer to themselves. They used the derogatory term *Reds* (the color related to communism) to refer to their enemies, those who defended the Second Republic. Once the war was over, the rebels were configured into subgroups

and ideologies, such as fascists, monarchists, Catholics, conservatives, and Falangists (Larraz 2014, 47).
2. However, as soon as the Francoist troops put their feet in Catalonia in 1938, they immediately derogated the Estatut de Núria, the regional law. The regime never considered the Basque and Galician regional laws to be valid, as they were approved after Franco's coup d'état in the Republican zone.
3. More information about the Spanish Second Republic is provided by Preston and Mackenzie 1996; Álvarez Tardío and del Rey Reguillo 2013; Chislett 2013; Preston 1971.
4. Serrano Suñer acknowledges, "Military, Falangists, Carlists, Catholics disillusioned with parliamentary strategy, oligarchs of the economy, clergy, etc." (1978, 196–97).
5. Translated as "movement," but related to the mission of Franco's regime.
6. All BOE are published on the webpage of Agencia Estatal Boletín Oficial del Estado. For gazettes published between 1661 and 1959, please visit: https://www.boe.es/buscar/gazeta.php. For gazettes published between 1960 and 2022, see: https://www.boe.es/buscar/boe.php.
7. As Joan Samsó explains, at the beginning of 1930s Catalan culture had a strong social and political base (1994, 13).
8. In Spanish, Álvarez Arenas's title is General de Brigada del Ejército Español, Subsecretario de Orden Público. *La Vanguardia* changed its name to *La Vanguardia Española* once Franco's troops entered Barcelona in 1939. On August 16, 1978, the paper's name changed back to *La Vanguardia*.
9. González Oliveros also added, "Those entities which could prove, by means of documentation, that they have tried in a timely manner but without success, due to a shortage of paper, to replace their documents and printed papers not written in the national language, may print the back or spare pages, crossing the non-Spanish text with the phrase 'Arriba España!' which shall be printed in red ink and in thick characters, without prejudice to the urgent replacement of such printed papers" (Martín de Pozuelo and Ellakuría 2008, 79).
10. According to Montserrat Duch Plana, "at the turn of the 20th to 21st century, 42% of Spanish citizens still lived in municipalities that retained Franco's toponymy" (2017, 52). Although this phenomenon is more common in rural areas, we still see cases where Catalan municipalities have recently stopped using the names of generals or other military leaders who were important during the dictatorship. The same happens with individuals' names. There are still cases of people whose identification shows the Spanish spelling of their first or last names.

11. For a deeper approach to Falange Española, see Slaven 2018. Ruiz explains the composition of the Tribunal de Responsabilidades Políticas; they were "composed of two generals, two Falangist national councilors, and two professional magistrates" (2005, 143). According to Cano Bueso, from 1939 to 1945 Franco counted on two different types of tribunals: "the special ones (for ideological cleansing and political accountability) and ordinary (for economic restoration)" (1985, 178). This one, considered a special one, was to apply the Ley de Responsabilidades Políticas (Law of Political Responsibilities). The offices of the Tribunal of Political Responsibilities existed at both national and regional levels.

    The term *revolutionary insurrection* refers to the events that happened in October 1934, during the Second Republic, when there was a general strike from October 5 to October 16, 1934. Catalonia declared the Catalan State of the Spanish Republic (October 6, 1934), and in Asturias there were revolts of miners. Some scholars refer to this event as the origin of the Spanish civil war. See also Payne 2011, 43.

12. However, Paul H. Lewis, following the classification of Hugh Trevor-Roper, concluded that Franco's regime should be considered "clerical fascism," against the "radicalized industrial middle classes ('dynamic fascism')" (2002, 11).

13. "The amount allocated for economic, technical and military assistance was . . . $465 million, to be implemented over a four-year period. Of this, $350 million would be allocated to military aid, and the other $115 million to economic aid" (Delgado 2003, 243).

14. The airbases, Naval Station Rota, Morón Air Base, Torrejón Air Base, and Zaragoza Air Base, "are prepared for joint utilization, will remain under Spanish flag and command, and Spain will assume the obligation of adopting the necessary measures for the external security. However, the United States may, in all cases, exercise the necessary supervision of United States personnel, facilities, and equipment" (US Department of State 1953). In general, the agreements consisted of three conventions: defensive, mutual defense assistance, and economic assistance (Delgado 2003, 246).

15. Opus Dei is a "Roman Catholic lay and clerical organization whose members seek personal Christian perfection and strive to implement Christian ideals and values in their occupations and in society as a whole. Theologically conservative, Opus Dei accepts the teaching authority of the church without question and has long been the subject of controversy; it has been accused of secrecy, cultlike practices, and political ambitions" (Encyclopedia Britannica. 2019. "Opus Dei." https://www.britannica.com/topic/Opus-Dei.)

16. The Stabilization Plan, approved in 1959, was the beginning of the openness in Spain. The three Development Plans started in 1964 as a consequence of the Stabilization Plan. According to Fabián Estapé (2000, 197; qtd. in Sánchez Sánchez 2004n9), they were asked to copy the French system word by word.
17. The First Development Plan was scheduled to end in 1967, but given the crisis in the "international monetary system" the Council of Ministers approved the extension of the First Development Plan until the start of the second one, February 12, 1969. This second one was scheduled to end on December 31, 1971 (*BOE*, February 12, 1969, no. 37, 2137).
18. "It was a name derived from a Catalan tongue-twister [*setze jutges d'un jutjat mengen fetge d'un penjat* (sixteen judges from a court eat liver of a hanged man)], containing sounds difficult for a Castilian speaker to pronounce correctly" (Eaude 2008, 149).]
19. For more on Mussolini's system, see Fabre 2018, specifically "Parte Prima, il censore," 29–256.
20. This is a phrase from the reader of *San Camilo, 1936*, written by Camilo José Cela and published in 1936. I will refer to the same book in Chapter 4.
21. See Godayol and Taronna 2018, 169–94.
22. Readers/censors were alarmed when they saw words that could "harm" the general audience. Thus, Manuel de Pedrolo shared the example of the volume of poems *Ésser en el món*, first submitted in 1948. The verdict was that the book was authorized, but they "simply took away the word 'virgin,' which forced me to suppress a whole verse" (interviewed in Beneyto 1975, 256). Twenty-five years after this submission, when another publisher wanted to issue the same book, the "little word fell out again" (256).
23. In my experience consulting more than one hundred censorship files, there was not even one that had answers to all the questions included.
24. As an example, Censorship file of *Barrabàs*, file 3309–63 was submitted in 1963 and had antecedent file 3483–58, submitted in 1958 (Censorship file of *Barrabàs*).
25. Beevor (2006, 284) states that Dionisio Ridruejo was minister of propaganda.
26. *Nihil obstat* is a Latin expression used by ecclesiastics; see O'Connor 2001, 1147.
27. "Maximiano García Venero, Falangist writer, defined the concept of 'red' in these terms: 'Reds' are the anarchists and the Marxists and even their Republican supporters" (Benet 1973, 91).
28. According to Molas, "the most implacable desert in Catalan print" (2010, 185).

CHAPTER 2

1. Even though there are, according to Blas (2007), two different types of repression—physical and cultural—for the purposes of this book I focus my attention on the cultural one.
2. More information about self-censorship can be found in Chapter 4 of this book.
3. For example, *Black Spring* by Henry Miller, which was supposed to be translated by Jordi Arbonès and published by Aymà in 1966, was nonauthorized three times (Arbonès 1995, 92). Finally, in 1970, Aymà decided to publish it without submitting it to voluntary censorship and it was finally "tolerated" (92).
4. As Carlos Barral points out, the misnamed "law" of 1938 was in fact an order "of emergency, that is, the current censorship but in time of war" (interviewed in Beneyto 1975, 198). The Order of April 29, 1938, is the one I am always referring to when I use the terms "1938 Order" or the "first censorship law," and unless noted otherwise, it is the source of all quotations in this section (*BOE*, April 30, 1938, no. 556, 7035–36).
5. Note that many Spanish exiles aimed to publish their works in Spanish territory.
6. The criteria, as discussed later in the chapter, were more restrictive for new editions than for reprints, even though in both cases they had to submit a new request form.
7. The type of paper was extremely important and sometimes the cause for the nonauthorization of books.
8. The import request for a certain book could range from one thousand copies down to just one or two, as Gargatagli (2016) relates in her article on Jorge Luis Borges's book imports.
9. "In the case of consignments of a small number of books or leaflets cosigned to individuals, as well as in the case of printed matter carried by hand by travelers" (*BOE*, June 24, 1938, no. 610, 8002).
10. Maximiano García Venero, a Falangist writer, was the first one using the term *red-separatist*, which went viral during the entire dictatorship. On April 8, 1937, he said, "We have given existence to such a word perhaps because we have suffered, more directly than other comrades, the vital influence of Catalan and Basque separatism." (qtd. in Benet 1973, 91)
11. This is another of those "black lists" I mentioned in the previous chapter. More information about black lists is provided by Casas Codinach 2012.
12. This is related to the black market of other goods, known as *estraperlo*. See the law inspired by Gustau Gili in the section on INLE.

13. "Although the April 23, 1941 Ministerial order proclaiming that fact "was never published . . ., as required, in the *Boletín Oficial del Estado*," it instead appeared in the "Falangist film magazine *Primer Plano*." The ban on non-Spanish-language movies was in force until 1967, "when the establishment of small urban art cinemas (*salas de arte y ensayo*) opened the door to the showing of films in their original languages" (Gubern and Vernon 2016, 377).
14. On March 1, 1940, the government approved the Law for the Repression of Freemasonry and Communism to control and punish communist and Masonic organizations; Julius Ruiz devotes an entire chapter to the law and its application in Madrid from 1940 to 1945 (2005, 192–232).
15. As Josep M. de Casacuberta, head of Editorial Barcino, did. His receipt can be seen in Gallofré 1991, 37. As Clotet and Torra rightly point out, the subways where the prohibited books were archived were well-known (2010, 8). As an example to illustrate the "destruction of several books," the Sindicato Español Universitario (Spanish University Union) celebrated the Book Fest on May 2, 1939, by burning "titles by Voltaire, Lamartine, Karl Marx, Freud or Rousseau; an act loaded with symbolism reminiscent of the Nazi book burnings" (Aróstegui and Álvaro Dueñas 2012, 367; Lima Grecco 2014, 365–66).
16. It is worth noting here the special dichotomy in which the Barcelona Book Chamber found itself. This is how Clotet and Torra judge it: "It is especially pathetic that it was the Chamber itself that pursued what, theoretically, had to be the object of its promotion and dissemination" (2010, 8).
17. The famous publisher Gustau Gili noted that "the book is one of the most powerful instruments and undoubtedly the most effective for the projection of Spain in America" (Llanas 2006, 51).
18. This was not the first time this topic was discussed among publishers. At the Book Festival Conference on June 17, 1938, Víctor Colomer, councilor of culture of the Barcelona City Council, said that "we must seek solutions to the issue of the paper, to the incorporation of women in the workplace, credit, energy for the machines. We must even study what refers to the markets of America, because, besides having a great economic importance and cultural irradiation of Catalonia, it has the advantage of being able to sell at a lower price the copies in these lands, as large print runs will be done" (*La Vanguardia* 1938). However, this remained only as an idea because, seven months later, Franco's troops entered Barcelona to stay. The Book Chamber and the publishers of Barcelona, annoyed by the obstacles to the export of books to America, the paper crisis, the exile of publishers and authors, and also the purging of their funds (Abellán 1980a, 17), wrote

a memorandum titled "The Current Situation of the Spanish Publishing Industry" to the head of censorship services in Burgos to ask him to reconsider the censorship of books in relation to exports to America and the great advantages that this initiative could bring (Abellán 1980a, 17).
19. Between 1931 and 1935 the figures fluctuated between nine and fifteen million pesetas (Baró Llambias 2005, 54).
20. The difference with the book censorship note published on March 5, 1939, that I previously referred to is that the latter refers not only to 1936 but to the entire Republican period, starting as far back as 1931. Moreover, for those who decided not to submit their inventories, an even more fierce repression was awaiting them, with more traps for the publication of undeclared books.
21. Even though Sebastià Sánchez-Juan published poetry in Catalan before the war, afterward he decided to collaborate with the regime. He attended some of the clandestine meetings from 1942 to 1944, reading his poems. However, at Casa Vicenç on Christmas day 1942, Sánchez Juan was asked to read a poem and, as he didn't want to read in Catalan or Spanish (for obvious reasons), he ended up reading it in French (Arimany 1993, 152).
22. It was divided into three sections: cultural policy, bibliographic management, and trade policy (*BOE*, May 22, 1941, no. 142, 3638).
23. Even though the Barcelona Book Chamber was legally dissolved, according to Llanas, it continued operating until 1942 "because of the difficulties in the functioning of INLE" (2006, 42).
24. The first book fair, celebrated in Madrid in 1943, included book burning. According to Eduardo Ruiz Bautista, "at the entrance of the promenade a couple of Falangists offered fuel to the attendees" (2005, qtd. in Llanas 2006, 43).
25. Robles Piquer was also director of censorship services (1962–1967) and director general of popular culture and entertainment (1967–1969). When Fraga's team left power, Alfredo Sánchez Bella, the new minister of MIT, offered Robles Piquer the opportunity to remain president of INLE. In the end he declined the offer because he realized that there were people in the ministry that criticized his brother-in-law's legacy, in particular Emilio Romero (Robles Piquer 2011, 214).
26. However, the complaint of publishers is that over the years the compensation became static: "When Gustau Gili asked for two pesetas per kilo, this reduced the cost of paper by 33%, which was 6 pesetas. Now we receive two pesetas to fund the cost of paper that is worth, first class, between 130 and 150 pesetas per kilogram" (Arimany 1993, 250).
27. Even though the measure was implemented in 1961 (Fernández Moya 2017, 17).

28. Gustau Gili complained about integrating different organisms into a one single body: "It is not strange that the action of each of these entities loses a lot of effectiveness due to lack of coordination" (Llanas 2006, 46). However, Beneyto reminds us that "it is not about winning, but convincing" (1987, 35).
29. Further information about the case against Giménez Siles is provided by Álvaro Dueñas 1997, 593 and Martínez Rus 2014, 113–37.
30. Enciclopèdia Catalana. N.d. "Camil Geis i Parragueras." Enciclopedia.cat. https://www.enciclopedia.cat/ec-dlc-29571.xml.
31. In fact, in *Pas i repàs* Geis explains that "it is important to know that the bishopric was reluctant and did not give me permission until after I had shown the state authorization" (*Revista de Girona* 2000, 6). Without *nihil obstat* or religious censorship, a churchman could not publish.
32. Manent precisely speaks about this unwritten guideline in these terms: "From the time of the Civil War there is an (unpublished) provision . . . that speaks explicitly of the restrictions that should be applied to the so-called regional languages" (2011, 287).
33. Even though Josep M. Cruzet decided to obey the laws and publish the complete works of Verdaguer in a nonnormalized spelling, Moll decided to use the normalized spelling starting at day one (Bacardí 2012, 16). See also Moll 1975.
34. Josep Zendrera was head of Editorial Juventud and "representative of the publishing industry in the Commission for the study of the arrangement of paper mills in Spain" (Report from the Comisión para el Estudio de la Ordenación de las Fábricas de Papel en España, 1944, qtd. by Baró Llambias 2005, 53n138).
35. Herrero-Olaizola stated that even though "the 1946 Book Law (which remained 'on the books' until 1975) foresaw a possible refund to publishers, . . . according to the publishers' accounts [it] had never really been put into effect" (2007, 179).
36. One of the regime's strategies was precisely this one: it could be published but never shown in a shop window.
37. In the case of Lajos Zilahy's royalties (Arimany 1993, 204).
38. For example, José María Gironella, in a letter dated January 19, 1963, to Josep M. Boix i Selva, defined Catalan as a dialect in these terms: "I will be so happy to be included in your Catalan series and I'll try, while reading in Catalan my own works, to learn enough the language to, from now on, be able to write the postcards in our native DIALECT" (Josep M. Boix i Selva Collection, MS9480/1).
39. More information can be found in Larios 2013.

40. Toward the end of this chapter, I refer to the ideological evolution of the magazine after 1939.
41. This was the reason why the magazine was not well received by all. Eugeni Xammar, for example, stated that it was "outside the Catalan community" because "the only publications published in Catalonia are those without an imprint"—that is, those that were clandestine (Manent 2010, "Polèmica a l'exili").
42. Ignasi Agustí first collaborated in the publication with number 5, April 3, 1937, and he assumed the role of director beginning with number 35, October 30, 1937.
43. In the correspondence of Carles Pi i Sunyer, another paradigmatic figure of the Catalan exile, who was "mayor of Barcelona, minister of Labor of the Republican Government and Minister of Culture of the Generalitat de Catalunya" (Capdevila Candell 2009, 16), we find a letter that he wrote to Antoni M. Sbert in April 1940 in which he stated: "in exile, Catalonia is above all the language" (4).
44. The ranking begins with France with 190; Mexico with 175; between 30 and 50 in Venezuela, Chile, and Argentina; 16 in Cuba; 11 in England; and in the 16 remaining countries, "we find symbolic figures" (Manent 2010, "Polèmica a l'exili").
45. Teresa Ferriz Roure ends the first stage in 1947, and starts the second one in 1948 (2001).
46. The writer Mercè Rodoreda stated, "The war ended, and we had to leave Spain. Not for nothing, because I had never been involved in politics, but because I had written in Catalan, and because I had collaborated in magazines, let's say 'left-wing,' etc., etc. And on the advice of my mother, I left thinking that after three, four, or five months I would return home, but then it went on forever" (Rodoreda interviewed in Soler Serrano 1980, 28:00–28:42). Josep Palau i Fabre recalls that in the 1940s, they believed in the "provisional nature of the Franco regime, which we assumed was linked to the fate of Italian fascism" (interviewed in Gabancho 2005, 252).
47. This dichotomy is described by Fernando Larraz in these terms: "lost fatherland versus found fatherland" (qtd. in Mengual Català 2019).
48. Josep Palau i Fabre criticized this attitude and stated that all modern cultures had overcome the cultural movements that were alive before the war except for Catalonia (interviewed in Cormand 1999, 15:40–17:00).
49. The regime authorized the festival, whose name was translated into Spanish, in 1946 under two conditions: that the eglantine prize of patriotic topic must be written in Spanish and that it must be celebrated outside Barcelona (Manent 2010, "Patricipació als Jocs Florals").

50. This is the complete list of locations: "Buenos Aires (1941), Mexico (1942), Santiago de Chile (1943), La Havana (1944), Bogotá (1945), Montpellier (1946), London (1947), Paris (1948), Montevideo (1949), Perpignan (1950), New York (1951), Toulouse of Lenguadoc (1952), Caracas (1953), Sao Paulo (1954), San José de Costa Rica (1955), Cambridge (1956), Mexico City (1957), Mendoza (1958), Paris (1959), Buenos Aires (1960), Alghero (1961), Santiago de Chile (1962), Montevideo (1963), Perpignan (1964), Paris (1965), Caracas (1966), Marseille (1967), Zurich (1968), Guadalajara (1969), Tübingen (1970), Brussels (1971), Geneva (1972), Mexico City (1973), Amsterdam (1974), Caracas (1975), Lausanne (1976) and Munich (1977)" (CRAI 2009).
51. Because the post office was controlled by the regime, legal imports of books to Spain were practically nonexistent, especially for those packages suspected of bringing books from abroad (Baró Llambias 2005, 54).
52. Even though Gili cannot be considered an exile since he left the country before the Spanish Civil War, he helped some exiled Catalan intellectuals and contributed to keeping the Catalan culture alive by publishing translations of repressed authors at the Dolphin Book Publishing Company.
53. He was held in concentration camps in Saint-Cyprien and Argelès-sur-Mer (Camps i Arbós 2019). Güell Ampuero provides more information about the camps in the south of France: "there were five main camps: Argelès-sur-Mer, Saint Cyprien, Carcarès, Arles-sur-Tech and Prats de Molló. . . The French government feared the avalanches of refugees and left them in miserable and humiliating conditions" (2006, 70).
54. In 1950, Queralt asked his subscribers to advance "the amount of the six volumes" (Camps i Arbós 2004, 51). In order to further solve the economic problems, it was decided to create the Board of Trustees of Edicions Proa in 1951, which would be presided over by the famous violoncellist Pau Casals, exiled in Prada de Conflent, in order to "provide the necessary economic support to ensure the planned publications" (57). However, economic problems interrupted the board, and from 1952 onward it was no longer a topic of discussion.
55. As stated before, 175 books were published in Mexico, according to Manent 2010, "Polèmica a l'exili."
56. In order to define clandestine meeting, Arimany acknowledged: "A meeting of a literary but clandestine nature, as was any meeting of up to twelve people that did not have the authorization of the civil government and forget about asking for it at that time for anything in Catalan" (1993, 140).
57. In these same gatherings, they sometimes celebrated the Jocs Florals: "since the forties . . . the literary festival was celebrated in a private house, without

permission, but with the three ritual speeches" (Manent 2010, "Participació als Jocs Florals").
58. According to Frederic-Pau Verrié, "what counted was that we were all there, alive and determined to do something" (interviewed in Gabancho 2005, 129).
59. Article 16 stated, "Spaniards will be able to meet and associate freely for lawful purposes and in accordance with the provisions of laws" (*BOE*, July 18, 1945, no. 199, 358). The law was ambiguous enough that people held sessions secretly, just in case the regime thought they were not *lawful*.
60. Although a majority of the initiatives that began before 1945 are listed, others of later date are also mentioned, so as not to break the discourse.
61. Amics de la Poesia was an association created originally in 1921 by Josep Carner. After the Spanish Civil War, Josep Palau i Fabre made the first attempt to revive the association. The Agrupació Benèfica Minerva, of Fèlix Millet i Maristany, "had subsidized with 5,000 pesetas the Amics de la Poesia during the course of 1943 and '44" (Samsó 1994, 192). More details about this clandestine association will be provided toward the end of this section.
62. There is a discrepancy in the number of attendees, since Arimany defended the idea that the regime prohibited meetings of more than twelve people without prior permission (1993, 140), while Palau i Fabre was certain that the limit was ten (interviewed in Gabancho 2005, 258).
63. Joan Samsó counts twelve undated pamphlets and fourteen dated ones from 1942 to 1945. See the list at Samsó 1994, 194.
64. While Manent said they "were tolerated by the police" (Manent 2010, "Participació als Jocs Florals"), Arimany stated they were kept secretly (1993, 250).
65. "Likewise, the academic and university sector was practically empty since a large part of the teaching staff had taken the path of exile; and also a large majority of the liberal professionals—doctors, journalists, economists, etc. The conclusion is clear, the first Catalan exile was a national exile since it affected all sectors of the country" (Capdevila Candell 2009, 4). "The dreadful void they left was filled by several packages of immigrant officials who, with rare and brilliant exceptions, practiced the most narrow-minded *caciquismo*" (Molas 1978).
66. Joan Triadú shared his experience, "In my time there were all sorts. There were the really bad ones and there were the good ones" (interviewed in Gabancho 2005, 38). He also said that the strategy of the regime was "to drive them away, and then they had to get closer to Catalonia by striving to be deserving" (41).
67. Albert Manent stated, "It was the first one we saw and it had a luxurious paper and presentation, an impeccable and enviable typography and a tone of

normality, without any shouts of defeat. We had the feeling that we had a European-style magazine" (2010, "L'escletxa").
68. As an anecdote, Miquel Arimany explained the process needed to edit one of the issues of his thirty-two-page magazine *El Pont*: he used two paper providers, three linotypes, two printers, an engraver, and a bookbinder (Arimany 1993, 178).
69. Verrié already had publishing experience, since "in 1942 I had clandestinely published the *Elegies de Bierveille*, by Carles Riba" at the Sallent printing house in Sabadell, although in the end he did it with a printer from Igualada (interviewed in Gabancho 2005, 132). It is important to note that the two printers were not physically located in Barcelona. Josep Palau i Fabre, once already in France, did not like knowing that they were continuing with a magazine very similar to his, because he had the impression "that they wanted to erase me from the map" (132).
70. Albert Manent in his book *La represa* (2010) stated it was issued in 1948, but Coll i Alentorn points out that although it was dated 1947–1948, it was printed in 1949 (1992, 504).
71. I make this distinction because Massot i Muntaner gives an account of the authorization of the journal *Analecta Montserratensia*, "addressed to a literate audience" (2016, 17). Three issues were published: one in 1955, another in 1962, and the last one in 1964. Also, the magazine *El Pont* was issued starting in 1952, with some interruptions, but passed censorship as if it were a book, not a magazine. It was entitled, with very prominent letters, *ENTREACTE* (Intermission) and, in more discreet but quite large letters, "i altres narracions" (and other narrations). Around the drawing of a bridge, it read Col·lecció El Pont" (Collection El Pont; Arimany 1993, 264). The publisher waited until 1956 for the second issue to pass censorship so that the regime would not relate the issue to the previous one.
72. From 1959 to 1964, *Serra d'Or* was protected by the Abbot of Montserrat, Aureli M. Escarré. Maur M. Boix became the first editor-in-chief from 1964 to 1995. He explained that "during the long years of Franco's regime, when it went out month after month, with different vicissitudes (1959–1975), 'Serra d'Or' avoided at all times mentioning the name of the dictator and publishing any photographs of him, while newspapers and magazines of the time, disaffected with the regime, did not spare them. Our magazine was not of opposition but of resistance" (Boix 2001, 188).
73. According to Tomàs Tebé, "Editorial Selecta recreated, so to speak, the 'Joanot Martorell' novel prize, which, founded by the Aymà publishers three years earlier, had been practically abandoned. That was in the year 1950.

From that moment on, it was launched by our publishing house, alternating with the above-mentioned Aymà publishers, but maintaining the Selecta continuously and always publishing the award-winning work. When the 'Sant Jordi' Prize came out we considered that both awards could not coexist, for many reasons, and therefore we agreed not to organize the 'Joanot Martorell' with the condition that we would be compensated with the edition every year of the winning work of the 'Sant Jordi' award" (interviewed in Sales-Balmes 1966, 62). The Joanot Martorell Prize was awarded from 1947 until 1959 and then replaced by the Sant Jordi Prize, which was awarded from 1960 until the present.

74. According to Miquel Coll i Alentorn, even though IEC was not recognized as an "academic corporation" (1992, 503), contacts established with Union Académique Internationale (International Academic Union) helped the institution to stay alive. Thanks to the patronage of Fèlix Millet, IEC was, in 1943 and 1944, "the first academic course with a budget" (503). When IEC in 1948 published an already printed "sign of prizes," the regime fined the printer, Altés. However, IEC paid the fine (503).

75. Not only the members of the institution were invited to these parties, but also "the subsidiaries, friends and protectors" (Coll i Alentorn 1992, 504; also see the complete list of participants there).

76. Publisher Miquel Arimany, in his memoirs, relates his experience in the 1946–1947 and 1947–1948 academic years. He took a course in the history of Catalonia conducted by Ferran Soldevila (actually taught by Miquel Coll i Alentorn, his disciple), and a course in Catalan literature by Jordi Rubió i Balaguer (Arimany 1993, 213).

77. This clandestine association would be very important and in charge of subsidizing the translations of great classics in book publishing, such as the publications of *La Divina Comèdia* (*The Divine Comedy*), translated by Josep M. de Sagarra, or *L'Odissea* (*The Odyssey*), translated by Carles Riba and now considered a classic in itself. Also, through Pere Puig Quintana, these grants were extended to the IEC and also to the Associació Protectora de l'Ensenyança Catalana (Manent 2010, "L'escletxa"). I've already referred to those while speaking about Amics de la Poesia.

78. Although Samsó assures us that it started in 1946 (1994, 93), both Biblioteca de Catalunya (2008) and Enciclopèdia Catalana (Enciclopèdia Catalana. N.d. "Esbart Verdaguer." Enciclopedia.cat. https://www.enciclopedia.cat/ec-gec-0024475.xml) state it was founded in 1945.

79. According to Joan Triadú, in November 1948, "the magazine was suspended due to governmental intervention and one of its founders, Josep Romeu,

prosecuted as the man responsible." Thus, they decided to publish some issues abroad, thanks to Josep Palau, who was in Paris, and Joan Triadú and Joan Gili, both in England. This continued until number 23, when the "terrible inspector" Pedro Polo "told me [Joan Triadú] that the solution we had adopted, to make it look like it was published in Paris with the warehouse in Oxford, was a clever solution, but that he didn't buy it and that if it didn't finish it would be to the detriment of the printer" (Triadú 2008, "Supressió i represa d'Ariel").

80. As Miquel Arimany illustrated, "One could say [in Catalan] 'Oh, Tibidabo, this mountain that acts as a beautiful head of Barcelona,' but one could not say 'Tibidabo is six hundred meters high.' This last one was science, and could not be said in Catalan" (Arimany 1993, 263).

81. Note the Spanish translation of both Carles Riba's first name and the title of the book.

82. Riba met the poet Vicente Aleixandre in Madrid. Aleixandre introduced Riba to his circle of antiregime intellectuals, which led to more ties of friendship and complicity between Catalan and Spanish intellectuals. Riba's idea was to give value to the new generations of poets who were far from the doctrine of Franco's regime (Manent 2010, "Remitent: Vicente Aleixandre"). The aim of the Bernat Metge Foundation was "to raise everyone's interest" (Miralles 1967, 52). This translation was also part of the earlier mentioned Fundació Benèfica Minerva, by Fèlix Millet i Maristany.

83. This is how the famous publisher Josep Janés rejected the offer given by the head of censorship services to run a legal magazine in Catalan in 1945 if "he took responsibility for ensuring that the collaborators did not exceed their limits" (Arimany 1993, 215). According to Albert Manent, Sagarra said "this would be like celebrating mass in a brothel" (qtd. in Gabancho 2005, 70). The magazine was never released.

84. From *Orientacions*, May 1945, qtd. in Manent 2010, "Polèmica a l'exili."

85. Even though the number of books published for the period 1946–1951 is far from the 865 books issued in 1936 (Clotet and Torra 2010, 11; Llanas 2006, 77), it is significant if we compare it with the 99 books published from 1939 to 1943.

86. The last volume of this Bible, no. 15, was published in 1948 (Bacardí 2012, 42).

87. Further information is provided toward the end of this chapter and also by Samsó 1995, 373.

88. Manent states that the Aymà publishing house "was born" in 1947 (2010, "Més editorials en català"). However, it was founded in 1944 and began its publishing activity in Catalan in 1947 (Enciclopèdia Catalana. N.d. "Societat

Anònima Editora Aymà." Enciclopedia.cat. https://www.enciclopedia.cat/ec-gec-0006357.xml.)

89. However, they were not the first books of youth literature in Catalan after the Spanish Civil War, since from 1949 to 1952 Joan Sales published "an informative adaptation of a sample of *rondalles* (tales) by Ramon Llull, Mistral, Verdaguer, Guimerà, Casaponce, and Alcover, and popular narrations from all the Catalan-speaking lands and from different time periods" (Bacardí 2012, 64).

90. According to Sopena, "In 1963 he charged 35 pesetas for the management of a cover and in 1967 he charged 75; the cost of the management for each work went from 100–275 pesetas/book in 1967 to almost 600 pesetas/book in 1975" (2006, 77).

91. Publicacions de l'Abadia de Montserrat, Dalmau, Nova Terra, Estela, Edicions 62, and Pòrtic were some of them (Sopena 2006, 76).

92. Abroad, this kind of edition also became popular, the most outstanding being B. Costa-Amic from Mexico and the Albor publishing house from Paris.

93. She did not have her books censored "because of laziness" (Manent 2010, "Més editorials").

94. Earlier it has been mentioned that in 1943 Verdaguer's complete works were authorized but in nonstandardized spelling.

95. It makes me think of what Maur M. Boix said in his *Cops d'ull al retrovisor*, when he explained that after the war, in 1939, the regime officials took many young Catalans and brought them to different parts of Spain. He explained that he was going peacefully when they were told as soon as they arrived that "if there was an incident and the perpetrator was Catalan, the punishment was double" (2001, 222).

96. These were not all publishers, but those who had "an impact beyond a limited scope" and "had behind them programs for the recovery of classical authors and for the moderate dissemination of younger ones" (Gallofré 1991, 304).

97. Gallén 1985, 249, qtd. in Bacardí 2012, 43.

98. Regarding religion, the law states that the "the Spanish Nation considers as a stamp of honor, the obedience to the law of God, according to the doctrine of Holy Catholic, Apostolic and Roman Church, the only true and inseparable faith in the national conscience, which will inspire its legislation" (Servicio Informativo Español 1967). Religion "reinforced the theoretical body" (Sopena 2006, 69) of the movement.

99. Enciclopèdia Catalana. N.d. "Edicions Destino." Enciclopedia.cat. https://www.enciclopedia.cat/ec-gec-0022209.xml.

100. This new era was considered by Molas and Castellet to be "historic realism" (1963, 177–80) and covers the broad variety of ideologies and movements of that time. However, it was a controversial term since some authors thought that it was too close to Soviet social realism. See the details in Cornellà-Detrell 2011, 29–30.
101. According to Hilari Raguer, monk of Montserrat, "We at that time [before the 1950s] believed in the United States. We thought that they were defenders of democracy and that they would help us get Franco out" (qtd. in Gabancho 2005, 75).
102. See the details and their full names in *Sàpiens* 2017.
103. Some scholars, among them Vallverdú (2013) and Rojas Claros (2013), set the start of the openness in 1962, when Manuel Fraga Iribarne became minister of MIT. Some others, such as Cisquella, Erviti, and Sorolla (2002), would set it in 1966, when the Press and Printing Law was approved. However, given the economic revolution that brought the Stabilization Plan, I consider, along with other scholars such as Valencia-García 2018, that the starting point for Second Francoism is 1959.
104. According to Montserrat Bacardí in personal conversation (July 31, 2020), this topic "has not yet been studied empirically, so we are uncertain if all religious books had to undergo religious censorship only or were subject to both civil and religious." Mireia Sopena stated that Publicacions de l'Abadia de Montserrat and Balmes "did not pass through Madrid . . . it will be necessary to know which works from other publishers censored by the curia were judged by MIT" (2016, 38).

CHAPTER 3

1. The National Stabilization Plan was created mostly by Joan Sardà, Gabriel Ferras (the representative for the International Monetary Fund in Europe), Enrique Fuentes Quintana (Vega 2019), and representatives of the Organisation for Economic Co-operation and Development (Sabín and Hernández Sandoica 1997, 130). "The ministerial renewal was promoted by Carrero Blanco: the most reactionary sectors of Franco's regime were losing influence in the key positions of the administration" (Vogel 2017, ch. 2).
2. Mutual Defense Assistance Agreement: "The three agreements were: Defense Agreement (the permission to create American air bases), Economic Aid Agreement, and the Mutual Defense Assistance Agreement" (Vogel 2017, ch. 2).
3. "The distribution of this amount would be as follows: 504.5 million from Defense Support; 17.1 million from the Development Loan Fund; 506.5 mil-

lion from Law 480; 174 million from Caritas donations plus 3.8 million from other donations; 297.5 million from Eximbank loans, together with 20 million from a 1953 wheat purchase operation" (Delgado 2003, 257).
4. Regarding Public Law 480, "its distribution was approximately equal and the part corresponding to our country also had the character of a loan." The McCarran Amendment was distributed as follows: "80 percent to the Spanish government and 20 percent to the Americans. However, unlike aid, only 43.63 percent of the amount allocated to Spain was a donation, with the remaining 36.36 percent being a loan" (Barciela López 2000, "En qué consistió la ayuda americana").
5. Spain was not part of the Marshall Plan Program. However, in Spain there was a popular belief that it was the case. Luis García Berlanga's *Bienvenido Mr. Marshall* (1953) was a parodic movie based in this new era of American assistance, portraying Americans as saviors of their country. Carlos Robles Piquer, who was director of censorship services from 1962 to 1967, stated, "A serious and responsible historian undoubtedly states with little objectivity, in my opinion, that the Marshall Plan was not applied to Spain and could not benefit it because of 'autarchy and monetary and trade policies'; when I think it is clear that the cause of this exclusion was exclusively political in nature" (Robles Piquer 2011, 180).
6. According to Barciela López, 60 percent went to military bases, 10 percent was used for administrative costs in the Spanish government, and 30 percent was given as a donation to the government to be used for transport and communications (2000, "En qué consistió la ayuda americana"). Once the US military bases began to operate in 1959, "90% [of the money] was granted to the Spanish Government to finance economic development projects" (Delgado 2003, 247).
7. Even though "a number of major American companies had already been operating... in high-technology sectors [in Spain] for quite some time" (Miguel Fernández and Sanz Rozalén 2009, 192).
8. Although the first tourist trips to Spain started in the last third of the nineteenth century (Sánchez Sánchez 2001, 201), according to Marín Silvestre and Ramírez in 1960s there was a boom of visitors: "In 1961, 7,500,000 travelers arrive, in 1970, 23,000,000 tourists arrived in Spain, that is, 1,680 million dollars" (2004, 27).
9. The identification of many Catalans with the social movement led by King is still alive. On January 14, 2019, the president of Catalonia at that time, Quim Torra, went to the Martin Luther King Jr. Institute at Stanford University to give a lecture on Catalan political prisoners and the influence of

King's civil rights movement. Many columnists gave their opinion, not always favorable (ACN 2019).
10. As early as 1967 Aymà published King's book *Strength to Love*, translated by Francesc Vallverdú. *Serra d'Or* published a two-page extract (King 1968, 15–16).
11. According to Ernesto Antón, general manager of Espasa-Calpe, "It's the toughest business. The most random. The riskiest. In other businesses you tend to sell your production within the year, not here. A book of about four thousand copies, the usual print runs in our country, sells in five and seven years. It's a disproportionate investment" (Antón and Gordon 1966, 114). He was speaking about books in Spanish. Those figures (4,000) are too far away from the Catalan reality.
12. *BOE*, December 8, 1962, no. 294, 17410, was signed by Finance Minister Mariano Navarro Rubio. It is also mentioned in Cornellà-Detrell 2013, 55.
13. *BOE*, December 30, 1963, no. 312, 18190–18198, established the benefits for priority sectors. According to Fernández Moya, the Tax Reform Act of June 11, 1964, article 202, stated that "sales of books, magazines, newspapers and journals were exempt from taxation by the new general tax on business traffic" (2017, 19). Information about the dates of this First Development Plan is found in Chapter 1.
14. Further information regarding the influence of La Cua de Palla on the crime fiction genre in Catalan is found in Canal i Artigas and Martín Escribà 2011 and also Martín Escribà 2020.
15. Statement qtd. by Planellas i Barnosell (2016, 352).
16. The daily chronicle, offered by the Lliga Espiritual de la Mare de Déu de Montserrat between 1962 and 1966, had problems with censorship because of its regularity.
17. This is the case of the famous "Tancada d'intel·lectuals i artistes a Montserrat" (Enclosure of intellectuals and artists in Montserrat) that took place from December 12 to 14, 1970, to show the discontent with the death penalty that the regime wanted to exercise against militants from ETA (Euskadi Ta Askatasuna, a terrorist group from the Basque Country) in the so-called El Proceso de Burgos. The imprisonment even included two Nobel Prize winners, Mario Vargas Llosa and Gabriel García Márquez. However, it was not the first time that Montserrat showed its anti-Francoist nature. As Ferran Sánchez Agustí relates, the abbot of Montserrat was forced into exile in 1963 for having made anti-Franco statements in the French newspaper *Le Monde* (2009). See also Batista 2019.
18. "The regime decried this 'Munich conspiracy' and, in retaliation, Franco condemned to exile or forced residence several of the delegates attempting to return to Spain" (López 2016, 3).

19. It should not be confused with the Latin American boom, even though some of the publishers who launched that boom were from Barcelona (Herrero-Olaizola 2007, xxi). The big difference between the two is that the American continent was celebrating the triumph of the original work of great writers such as Gabriel García Márquez, Mario Vargas Llosa, and Julio Cortázar, while Catalonia was celebrating the expansion of the entry of foreign literature through translations.
20. According to data provided by *El Libro Español: Revista Mensual del Instituto Nacional del Libro Español*, January 1959 to January 1969. Mean prepared by the author.
21. Martínez (2011, 138) stated that it was constituted in 1963, but Cahner (2001, 42) confirmed it was in 1961. Also, according to Cahner, Castellet was key to the firm's success: "Its development was marked by the decisive contribution of Josep M. Castellet, whom I appointed as literary editor in 1964, shortly before the Franco government expelled me from the Spanish state" (42). The first book published by Edicions 62, *Nosaltres els valencians*, by Joan Fuster, influenced an entire generation.
22. Some of the authors were Simone de Beauvoir, Max Brod, Pierre Benoît, and Cecil Roberts (Josep M. Boix i Selva Collection, MS9479); some of the translators were Ramon Folch i Camarasa, April 14, 1961; Joan Oliver, May 1961; and Ferran de Pol, April 26, 1961 (Josep M. Boix i Selva Collection, MS9480/1).
23. The survey, which took place on January 9, 1963, was created by C. R. Ibáñez, who explained, "We conclude that the Catalan literary public is truly looking for works translated into its language, which currently does not exist. In our opinion, these translations could be a great sales success" (Josep M. Boix i Selva Collection, MS9479).
24. Fraga's appointment was key to the recovery of the Catalan language and culture (Vallverdú 2013; Manent 1999, 20; Llobet 2012, 403).
25. *La Pesta* has a legal deposit date of 1962. *La Vanguardia Española* announced its publication on January 3, 1963, as a new book published in December 1962, and *Serra d'Or* announced it in its bibliographic section in January 1963. See Vilardell 2015, 100.
26. Discussing the same topic, Lera acknowledged, "The first thing that stands out . . . is the enormous disproportion between editorial production and the market's capacity to consume. Obviously, supply in this case far exceeds demand" (1971, 7).
27. Letter from Joan Sales to Mercè Rodoreda, December 21, 1974 (Rodoreda and Sales 2008, 595).
28. As an example, here is an excerpt of the letter that Josep M. Boix sent to the writer Joan Fuster: "We would like to make a great campaign of Isard in the

Valencian Country. How can we have access to some addresses of members of athenaeums or literary societies? I will be grateful if you orient me" (May 4, 1964, Josep M. Boix i Selva Collection, MS9480/1, box 16).

29. For example, Miquel Arimany sent a letter to Joan Fuster on January 19, 1957, in which he wrote, "I have sent you the volume of my latest publication 'Los Grandes del Mundo' so that you can give me a complimentary review as the book deserves in one of your journalistic forums (the one with the most subscribers who buy high-priced books)" (Joan Fuster Collection, id. 1237). Fuster agreed on February 16, 1957, to comment on "the appearance of such a memorable bibliographic-educational jewel" (id. 1238).

30. Cinema was also a reason for authorization from the censorship services, as in the case of *Barrabàs* in which the censor, Saturnino Álvarez Turienzo, begins the report by writing, "The work is known among us because of the film version that has been made of it" (Censorship file of *Barrabàs*, file 3309-63). And according to *Serra d'Or*, "The public favorably welcomes the Catalan records dedicated to our poets" (1963, 44).

31. Even though the document is not dated, I have some hypotheses that suggest that 1966 would be the year they met. This statement of Josep Verdura seems to confirm it, "As we said not long ago at a meeting of Catalan publishers, Catalonia has the highest percentage of illiterates" (interviewed in Sales-Balmes 1966, 67). Given the Catalan book market situation, it seems feasible to point toward this direction. Dr. Manuel Llanas agreed in a personal conversation with me on June 6, 2020. The quotations in this section refer to Josep M. Boix i Selva Collection, MS9474, unless noted otherwise.

32. For translations of plays, see Gallén 2016, 59–60.

33. Ringo Starr, a member of The Beatles, who performed in Madrid and Barcelona on July 1 and 2, 1965, spoke about the violence of the police in these terms: "It was the first time I'd really seen police beating kids up" (Beatles and Roylance 2000, 186).

34. There were also language courses offered by private organizations, such as Òmnium Cultural, Lo Rat Penat, and Obra Cultural Balear. According to Muñoz and Branchadell, in 1967 "private schools were authorized to schedule up to three hours a week of Catalan" and from 1970 onward, they were authorized to teach subjects in the so-called regional languages (2002, 165).

35. More information about this magazine and its translations can be found in Girons 2011, 135–40. The children's magazines were regulated by a different section of censorship services, the Advisory Board of the Children's Press (Sopena and Gassol Bellet 2017, 119).

36. Even though I have already mentioned in the previous chapters the aim of Catalan writers at that time to leave a standard for the language for generations to come, they also focused on different linguistic registers, from the most informal to the most formal. That brought more authenticity in translations and in books in Catalan.
37. According to Tomás Salvador, "Barcelona places, consumes or buys almost two thirds of Spanish books" (1960, 5).
38. Order of July 14, 1966, signed by Manuel Fraga, "for which the National Literature Awards 'Francisco Franco,' 'José Antonio Primo de Rivera,' 'Miguel de Cervantes,' 'Miguel de Unamuno,' 'Calderón de la Barca,' 'Emilia Pardo Bazán' and 'Jacinto Verdaguer' are announced" (*BOE*, August 22, 1966, no. 200, 11046).
39. Here's an example of the rhetoric in the Isard series' pamphlet: "The study of the published titles and the ones that are under preparation (a dozen titles will be issued every year), along with the offer in the attached pamphlet Payment Facilities, without any charge of any nature, we believe that it may deserve your attention, and we will be able to count you among our friend readers. VERGARA DISTRIBUTION" (Josep M. Boix i Selva Collection, MS9479).
40. As stated in the letter from Joan Sales to Bernard Lesfargues, dated December 17, 1969, "The two companies were in reality only one" (Bernard Lesfargues Correspondence).
41. This is how Sales expressed the terrible situation that affected him and other publishers due to the Ifac bankruptcy: "At the time of the fatality Ifac owed us 1,765,000 pesetas; if we had paid all our debts, we would have had almost one million pesetas left as a reserve, which would have given the Club [Editor] a well-deserved economic solidity. . . . Alas, instead of having one million pesetas we owe it . . . and we are still happy because it was the Banca Catalana that lent it to us to pull us out of the depths of the abyss" (Bernard Lesfargues Correspondence).
42. Bibliographical resources on libraries can be found in Estivill 2013, Valverde Ogallar 2015, and Ruiz Bautista, 2015. On school libraries, see Puelles Benítez 1998, 49–71.
43. In 1955, Vergara started combining its distribution services with the publication of its own books (Vergara company report, November 8, 1963, Josep M. Boix i Selva Collection, MS9476/1–2). In 1962 Vergara had headquarters in Barcelona (central office), Madrid, Bilbao, Valencia, Sevilla, Zaragoza, Las Palmas, Argentina, Uruguay, Venezuela, Colombia, and Mexico. To open the offices in Latin America, Vergara partnered with the following companies,

who added capital: on December, 19, 1952, with Vicens Mestre; on July 10, 1954, with CALVE; on October 7, 1954, with Interlibros Uruguay; on April 10, 1959, with Interlibros México; and on July, 27, 1961, with Interlibros Argentina. It also wanted to include Almapres, S.A., and Bibliodisc, S.A., to their offices in Latin America (Ms. 9476/1-2). It is not surprising that from 1964 to 1969 Vergara took advantage of the lines of credit proposed in the Plan for Social Economic Development, since it had a great deal of business in Latin America.

44. There are Nobel Prize authors in the series, such as Albert Camus (1957), François Mauriac (1952), Pär Lagervist (1951), and Father Dominique Pire (1958), along with bestsellers, such as *Grand Hotel* by Vicky Baum and *Barrabàs* by Pär Lagervist. Regarding film, Manuel Llanas says, "The echo of the cinema, which has become a mass spectacle, conditions the editorial policy. Thus, titles are selected that, adapted to the cinema, at that time were on everyone's lips" (2011, 187n7).

45. The advertising narrative was as follows: "The series in paperback is cheap and well printed, impeccably presented and practical. The clothbound volumes are a wonderful present, honoring the giver and flattering the good taste of the receiver" (Boix interviewed in Sales-Balmes 1966, 61).

46. In the April 27, 1967, issue of *La Vanguardia Española*, Ll.S.B. announced three titles in preparation: *Molts estius després*, *Correu sud*, and *La bona terra*. Sadly, they were never published under this label.

47. Unless noted otherwise, in this section I will be referring to the text of the law, which can be found at *BOE*, March 19, 1966, no. 67, 3310–3315.

48. They considered books to have at least fifty pages, and *hoja suelta* (separate sheet) to have four pages.

49. More information about this issue can be found in Beneyto 1975, 18. In 1967, the regime made these limitations offences under the criminal code (Sopena 2006, 70).

50. Article 52 gave more details: "First: Name and company name, nationality and address of the natural or legal person who owns the company. Second: Company's Regulations or Statute of the Company. Third: Name of the founder or founders and of the persons entrusted with the management and administration of the company. Fourth: Description of the Company's assets and, if applicable, its subscribed and paid-up share capital. Fifth: General lines of the editorial and financial plan and the means to carry it out" (*BOE*, March 19, 1966, no. 67, 3313–3314).

51. According to Cisquella, Erviti, and Sorolla, the publisher Lumen no longer submitted its works for voluntary consultation beginning in 1971, and Ana-

grama stopped in 1970, so four or five years after the implementation of the Press and Printing Law (2002, 57).
52. Technical or local publications, books of Spanish literature prior to 1900, pamphlets and loose sheets other than children's and young people's literature, and "posters, postcards, calendars and record folders that do not contain human figures" could be deposited at the Provincial Delegations of MIT (T. A. 1966, 285). For everything else and also for these publications, it was possible to deposit them at the General Directorate of Information of MIT. We will see that Catalan publishers found it easier to have a person assigned at MIT to manage their works.
53. "The Director General of Press or the Director General of Information, as the case may be, has the power to impose penalties for minor offences; the Minister of Information and Tourism for serious offences and the Council of Ministers for very serious offences" (T.A. 1966, 289).
54. More information can be found in Lorente Fuentes 2006.
55. "During the six months in which the country lived under the state of emergency, 2,066 people were arrested and, of these, 228 were still in detention in June 1971" (Casanellas 2019, "excepción normativa," n27).
56. "Journey of May" refers to the May 1968 protests in France.
57. Carlos Robles Piquer remembered it in these terms: "It was inevitable that quite a few books, which increased in number as society demanded more freedom and the publishers became more confident, would come to my table and require personal reading, which could lead to friendly solutions, sometimes in dialogue with the author, the publisher or both; sometimes adverse and, in these cases, possibly mistaken. More than once I had to dedicate to those readings, not always enjoyable, that time of the weekend that was theoretically reserved to the family" (2011, 189).
58. Francisco Candel, for example, thanked him for authorizing *Carta abierta a un empresario* (interviewed in Beneyto 1975, 33).
59. I shall emphasize that the effects of the crisis were not felt immediately, but that many times, as I have cited in the case of Isard, there were contracts that delayed the deficit by a year or two.
60. According to Adelina Plana, in personal conversation, she considered 1967 to be the end of Isard, although it continued until 1971 because they had editorial contracts they needed to fulfill.
61. An excerpt of the text reads as follow: "The credits in the priority sector, allocated in June 1969, have not been effective to date for any publisher, and those agreed in 1970, a fortiori, have not even been studied" (Editorial 1970, 657).

62. Lacruz became manager on January 21, 1976. The absorption of Vergara by Inmuebles e Industrias S.A. took place on June 20, 1976. The dissolution of Vergara took place in two steps, on October 4, 1977, and January 20, 1978 (Registre Mercantil de Barcelona).
63. Some of the strategies are inherited from previous periods but are still in use.
64. Other books announced by Isard, such as *Eyeless in Gaza*, *Point Counterpoint*, and *After Many a Summer*, all by Aldous Huxley, were also nonauthorized by the censorship body. The vicissitudes of censorship relating to *After Many a Summer* can be found in Vilardell 2016, 175–76.
65. *La Pesta* was published in 1962 by Isard series. For the publication of Camus in Spain, see Vilardell 2015.
66. Adelina Plana stated, "He was the one who did the censorship paperwork for us in Madrid because he worked at the Ministry. We couldn't publish anything without authorization and he expedited the procedures for us" (personal communication, December 29, 2018).
67. According to Arbonès, "In the case of translations, many books were unable to obtain authorization from the censor until they had first been published in Spanish" (1995, 88). This was the case for *La història de San Michele*, in which Fr. Francisco Aguirre stated, "This work has already been authorized by this censorship and published in Spanish so I think it can be allowed to be published" (Censorship file of *La història de San Michele*, file 7682–64).
68. Vallverdú noted that this led one journalist of *Le Figaro* to say that the censorship was more repressive in Spanish than in Catalan, because they already had Camus and Sartre in Catalan but not in Spanish. What the journalist did not know was that these works had been published in Argentina or Mexico before (2013, 13).
69. For example, *La iglesia en España: Ayer y mañana*, written by Fr. Víctor Manuel Arbeloa with a prologue by the bishop of Salamanca, Rt. Rev. Mauro Rubio, "had been submitted for pre-deposit at the MIT" (Europa Press 1968).
70. When asked about the reports to the Public Prosecutor's Office on the book sequestrations, Pío Cabanillas declared, on December 1, 1977, "Only the duty assigned by law is fulfilled when there is an abusive exercise of freedom of expression" (*La Vanguardia Española* 1977).

CHAPTER 4

Epigraph: The book was originally published in 1973, although it was censored. In 1995, Torres decided to publish some excerpts of the book that were not allowed in the first edition. The underlined text was not authorized in 1973, but was included in the 1995 edition.

1. However, Joan Brossa explains that he had more difficulties with his poems than with his work as a playwright (interviewed in Beneyto 1975, 80), probably because he published more poems than plays.
2. Larraz explains the genesis of the book in these terms: "Cela knew well that the criteria were capricious and that the opinion depended largely on who read the text. For this reason, he did not hesitate to suggest three names that he thought would be appropriate: the psychiatrist and essayist Juan Rof Carballo, a personal friend of Cela's, whose status as a censor is not known to us; Luis Díez Alegría, a military man, former combatant of the Blue Division, who had just been appointed director of the Guardia Civil; and the priest Saturnino Álvarez Turienzo" (2014, 151–52).
3. This coincides with the same years of the translation boom crisis, which made way for the new generation of writers.
4. It is not the only case. Bacardí reproduced the most important prologues during the Francoist dictatorship in Catalan (2012).
5. Because self-censorship is a universal subject, in this section I also quote authors who wrote in Spanish in order to contrast them with those who wrote in Catalan.
6. The attorney Vilamitjana is a character that the writer, translator and philologist Albert Jané created to express his own thoughts, but without taking full responsibility for them (Puigtobella 2020).
7. According to Majzoub and Doyle, there is a third type of self-censorship in this book. They state that Hemingway selected words that rhyme with the censored ones (2020, 17). Arbonès does not mention this third type.
8. This is exactly what Josep M. Castellet, publisher of Edicions 62, told Estanislau Torres after the nonauthorization of *Els ulls i la cendra*: "We need to wait for better times—he told me—minimum one year" (Torres 1995, 8). However, there was another solution: that the author himself would reach out to the head of censorship services. This is what Torres did on November 8, 1965, stating that his novel was nonauthorized two times. He got the authorization at the end of that same month (Torres 1995, 9–11).
9. In the United States, *Incerta glòria* is still in the news because it was translated into English by a specialist in Catalan literature, Peter Bush, in 2014, and also because the film version by Agustí Villaronga can still be found on Netflix.
10. First Clotet and Torra wrote "1079–56," but in the subsequent paragraph they corrected the number (2010, 68).
11. On May 20, 1957, the French publisher contacted Bernard Lesfargues, saying that they already had the rights to publish the work and inviting him to be the translator (Pla 2011, 12).

12. Some called it sarcastically "La Primavera Fraga" (Fraga Spring), parodying the Prague Spring (Candel interviewed in Beneyto 1975, 38), the brief reformist period from January 5 to August 21, 1968. Among those using this term are Salvador Pàniker (interviewed in Beneyto 1975, 277), Francisco Candel (interviewed in Beneyto 1975, 38) and Estanislau Torres (1995, 29).
13. About Manuel de Pedrolo's struggle against censorship, see Hout-Huijben 2007.
14. The quotations of this and the following paragraphs refer to Censorship file of *Un amor fora ciutat*, file 3960–70, unless noted otherwise.
15. *La Vanguardia Española* says he paid 30,000 pesetas ($500) (*La Vanguardia Española* 1970).

BIBLIOGRAPHY

Abellán, Manuel. 1980a. *Censura y creación literaria en España, 1939–1976*. Barcelona: Ediciones Península.
Abellán, Manuel. 1980b. "Apunts sobre la censura literària a Catalunya." *Revista de Catalunya*, no. 27 (1980): 123–32. http://www.represura.es/represura_6_marzo_2009_articulo7.pdf.
Abellán, Manuel. 1987. "Fenómeno censorio y represión literaria." *Diálogos Hispánicos de Amsterdam*, no. 5, 5–27.
ACN [Agència Catalana de Notícies]. 2019. "'West Cannot Allow Forceful Suppression' of Independence Movement, Says President in US." *Catalan News*, January 15, 2019. https://www.catalannews.com/politics/item/west-cannot-allow-forceful-suppression-of-independence-movement-says-president-in-us.
Agencia Estatal Boletín Oficial del Estado. Ministerio de la Presidencia, Relaciones con las Cortes y Memoria Democrática (MPR). Gazettes published from 1661 to 1959 are available here: https://www.boe.es/buscar/gazeta.php. Gazettes published from 1960 to 2022 are available here: https://www.boe.es/buscar/boe.php.
Agencias. 1984. "Suspende pagos la distribuidora Hogar del Libro." *El País*, September 5, 1984.
Aguilar, Manuel. 1965. "Coloquio en la escuela de librería de Madrid." *El Libro Español: Revista Mensual del Instituto Nacional del Libro Español* 8 (86): 83–94.
Agustí, Lluís. 2018. "L'edició espanyola a l'exili de Mèxic: 1936–1956: Inventari i propostes de significat." PhD diss., Universitat de Barcelona. http://hdl.handle.net/10803/667483.
Albertí, Santiago. 1994. "Una incidència de censura de Manuel de Pedrolo." *Urtx: Revista Cultural de l'Urgell*, no. 6, 223–39.
Allott, Anna. 1994. *Inked Over, Ripped Out: Burmese Storytellers and the Censors*. Chiang Mai: Silkworm Books.
Alonso, Miguel. 2020. "Civil War, Total War, Fascist War: Rebel Violence and Occupation Policies in the Spanish Civil War (1936–1939)." In *Fascist Warfare,*

1922–1945: Aggression, Occupation, Annihilation, edited by Miguel Alonso, Alan Kramer, and Javier Rodrigo, 73–96. Cham: Palgrave Macmillan US.

Álvarez Arenas, Eliseo. 1939. "Cataluña siente a España y a la unidad española, pese a la maldad de algunos y a los errores de muchos." *La Vanguardia Española*, January 28, 1939.

Álvarez Tardío, Manuel, and Fernando del Rey Reguillo. 2013. *The Spanish Second Republic Revisited: From Democratic Hopes to Civil War (1931–1936)*. Brighton: Sussex Academic.

Álvaro Dueñas, Manuel. 1997. "Por ministerio de la ley y voluntad del Caudillo: La jurisdicción especial de responsabilidades políticas (1939–1945)." PhD diss., Universidad Autónoma de Madrid. https://repositorio.uam.es/handle/10486/12266.

Antón, Ernesto, and Mercedes Gordon. 1966. "Entrevista con Don Ernesto Antón, Director General de Espasa-Calpe." *El Libro Español: Revista Mensual del Instituto Nacional del Libro Español* 9 (98): 113–14.

Aracil, Rafael, Joan Oliver i Puigdomènech, and Antoni Segura. 1998. *El mundo actual: De la segunda guerra mundial a nuestros días*. Barcelona: Edicions Universitat Barcelona.

Arasa, Daniel. 2008. *Historias curiosas del franquismo*. Teià: Robinbook.

Arbonès, Jordi. 1995. "La censura sobre les traduccions a l'època Franquista." *Revista de Catalunya*, no. 97, 87–96.

Arbonès, Jordi, and Albert Manent. 2011. *Epistolari Jordi Arbonès & Albert Manent*, edited by Ramon Farrés. Lleida: Punctum.

Arbonès, Jordi, and Manuel de Pedrolo. 2011. *Epistolari*, edited by M. Elena Carné. Lleida: Punctum and GETCC.

Arimany, Miquel. 1993. *Memòria de mi i de molts altres*. Barcelona: Columna.

Aróstegui, Julio, and Manuel Álvaro Dueñas. 2012. *Franco la represión como sistema*. Barcelona: Flor del Viento Ediciones.

Arroyo-Stephens, Manuel. 2015. *Pisando ceniza*. Madrid: Turner Libros.

Ayén, Xavier. 2010. "El censor que leía novelas." *La Vanguardia*, June 13, 2010.

Azagra Ros, Joaquín, and Pilar Chorén Rodriguez. 2007. *Actividad y territorio: Un siglo de cambios*. Directed by Francisco J. Goerlich Gisbert and Matilde Mas. Bilbao: Fundación BBVA.

Bacardí, Montserrat. 2012. *La traducció catalana sota el franquisme*. Lleida: Punctum.

Bacardí, Montserrat. 2013. "Clandestine Translations during Franco's Dictatorship: *Poesia* (1944–1945) and *Ariel* (1946–1951)." *MonTI*, no. 5, 241–56. https://doi.org/10.6035/MonTI.2013.5.9.

Balcells Albert. 2012. *L'Institut d'Estudis Catalans: Una síntesi històrica*. Barcelona: Institut d'Estudis Catalans.

Baratech, Feliciano. 1970. "Editorial crisis." *La Hoja del Lunes*, October 26, 1970.
Barciela López, Carlos. 2000. *La ayuda americana a España*. Alicante: Universidad de Alicante. http://www.cervantesvirtual.com/obra/la-ayuda-americana-a-espana-19531963--0/.
Baró Llambias, Mònica. 2005. "Les Edicions infantils i juvenils de l'Editorial Joventut (1923–1969)." PhD diss., Universitat de Barcelona. https://www.tdx.cat/handle/10803/761.
Batista, Antoni. 2019. "La tancada de Montserrat segons un confident." *Ara.cat*, October 3, 2019. https://www.ara.cat/suplements/diumenge/tancada-Montserrat-segons-confident_0_2320567926.html.
Beatles (band), and Brian Roylance. 2000. *The Beatles Anthology*. San Francisco: Chronicle Books.
Beevor, Antony. 2006. *The Spanish Civil War 1936–1939*. London: Weidenfeld and Nicolson.
Benet, Josep. 1973. *Catalunya sota el règim franquista: Informe sobre la persecució de la llengua i la cultura de Catalunya pel règim del General Franco*. Vol. 1. Paris: Edicions Catalanes de París.
Beneyto, Antonio. 1975. *Censura y política en los escritores españoles*. Barcelona: Euros.
Beneyto, Juan. 1987. "La censura literaria en los primeros años del franquismo." *Diálogos Hispánicos de Amsterdam*, no. 5, 27–40.
Bernard Lesfargues Correspondence. Dipòsit Digital de Documents, Universitat Autònoma de Barcelona, Barcelona. https://ddd.uab.cat/collection/blesfargues.
Bhabha, Homi K. 1994. *The Location of Culture*. New York: Routledge.
Biblioteca de Catalunya. 2008. Description of Esbart Verdaguer Collection. https://www.bnc.cat/Fons-i-col-leccions/Cerca-Fons-i-col-leccions/Esbart-Verdaguer.
Blair, Ann. 2011. *Too Much to Know: Managing Scholarly Information before the Modern Age*. New Haven, CT: Yale University Press.
Blas, José Andrés de. 2007. "Censura y Represión." *Represura*, no. 3, May 2007. http://www.represura.es/represura_3_mayo_2007_articulo7.html.
Boer, Josephine de. 1952. "Els jocs florals de la llengua catalana." *Books Abroad* 26 (3): 250–52. https://doi.org/10.2307/40038826.
Boix, Maur M. 2001. *Cops d'ull al retrovisor*, edited by Josep Massot i Muntaner. Barcelona: Publicacions de l'Abadia de Montserrat.
Brenneis, Sara J. 2018. *Spaniards in Mauthausen: Representations of a Nazi Concentration Camp, 1940-2015*. Toronto, Buffalo, London: University of Toronto Press.

Bru de Sala, Xavier, and Carme Dropez, eds. 2003. *Exili interior, represa i transició*. Barcelona: Proa; INEHCA.

Cahner, Max. 2001. "Albert Manent, amic i mestre: Notes autobiogràfiques." In *Records d'ahir i d'avui: Homenatge a Albert Manent i Segimon amb motiu dels 70 anys*, 38–46. Barcelona: Publicacions de l'Abadia de Montserrat.

Calders, Pere. 1964a. "La Col·lecció Isard, d'Editorial Vergara." *Serra d'Or*, April 1964, 54–55.

Calders, Pere. 1964b. "Llegir o mirar sants." *Serra d'Or*, May 1964, 50–51.

Calders, Pere. 2019. *Sobre el feixisme, l'exili i la censura: Tria d'articles i contes distòpics*. Edited by Diana Coromines. Barcelona: Rosa dels Vents. Ebook.

Calders, Pere, and Joan Triadú. 2009. *Estimat amic: Cartes, textos*. Edited by Susanna Alvarez i Rodolés and Montserrat Bacardí. Barcelona: Publicacions de l'Abadia de Montserrat.

Camps i Arbós, Josep. 2004. "Les Edicions Proa de Perpinyà (1949–1965)." *Els Marges: Revista de Llengua i Literatura*, no. 72, 45–76.

Camps i Arbós, Josep. 2019. "Semblanza de Josep Queralt Clapés (Badalona, 1896–Perpiñán, 1965)." Biblioteca Virtual Miguel de Cervantes, Portal Editores y Editoriales Iberoamericanos (siglos XIX–XXI) (EDI-RED). http://www.cervantesvirtual.com/obra/josep-queralt-clapes-badalona-1896--perpinan-1965-975107/.

Canal i Artigas, Jordi, and Àlex Martín Escribà. 2011. *La cua de palla: Retrat en groc i negre*. Barcelona: Alrevés.

Cano Bueso, Juan. 1985. *La política judicial del régimen de Franco (1936–1945)*. Madrid: Centro de Publicaciones, Secretaría General Técnica, Ministerio de Justicia.

Canosa, Francesc Ferran. 2013. *Joan Sales, l'home incòmode, la veritat que fa nosa*. Produced by Daltabaix, distributed by Inquiets Media. https://vimeo.com/126174399.

Canyameres, Ferran. 1972. *Diari íntim*. Barcelona: Pòrtic.

Capdevila Candell, Mireia. 2009. "El exilio catalán de 1939. Fuentes historiográficas y documentales para el estudio de un modelo singular." Presented at the XII Jornadas Interescuelas/Departamentos de Historia. Universidad Nacional del Comahue, San Carlos de Bariloche. http://www.aacademica.org/000-008/1120.

Capmany, Maria Aurèlia. 1971. *Salvador Espriu*. Barcelona: Dopesa.

Carbó, Joaquim. 1975. *El teatre de "Cavall Fort."* Barcelona: Edicions 62.

Carbó, Joaquim. 2008. "El meu Esbart Verdaguer." *Assaig de Teatre: Revista de l'Associació d'Investigació i Experimentació Teatral*, nos. 66–67, 62–71.

Carrasco, Sergio. 2020. "Digital Censorship in Spain: Closing Websites by Decree." Liberties (Civil Liberties Union for Europe), February 27, 2020.

https://www.liberties.eu/en/news/digital-censorship-website-closed-spain/18814.
Carrasco-Gallego, José A. 2012. "The Marshall Plan and the Spanish Postwar Economy: A Welfare Loss Analysis." *Economic History Review* 65 (1): 91–119.
Casanellas, Pau. 2019. "'Una orgía de Nihilismo': El Franquismo contra el 68". In *Las convulsiones del 68: España y el Sur de Europa*, edited by Abdón Mateos López and Emanuele Treglia. Madrid: Editorial UNED. Ebook.
Casanova, Agustí. 2011. "Els anys 60 als Estats Units." *Diari de Girona*, November 16, 2011. https://www.diaridegirona.cat/opinio/2011/11/16/anys-60-als-estats-units/529613.html.
Casas Codinach, Sonia. 2012. "Sota sospita, els 462 catalans vigilats pel franquisme. Trobem la llista negra antifranquista més completa." *Sàpiens*, no. 118, July 2012. https://www.sapiens.cat/revista/fitxats-trobem-la-llista-dels-462-catalans-mes-vigilats-pel-franquisme_12101_102.html.
Castellet, José María. 1955. *Notas sobre literatura española contemporánea*. Barcelona: Ed. Laye.
Castellet, Josep Maria, and Joaquim Molas. 1963. *Poesia catalana del segle XX*. Barcelona: Edicions 62.
Cendán Pazos, Fernando. 1960. "En torno a una encuesta sobre el libro español." *El Libro Español: Revista Mensual del Instituto Nacional del Libro Español* 3 (35): 344–51.
Censorship file of *Un amor fora ciutat*. 1970. First edition. File 3960–70. Archivo General de la Administración, Alcalá de Henares.
Censorship file of *Un amor fora ciutat*. 1972. Second edition. File 6106-72. Archivo General de la Administración, Alcalá de Henares.
Censorship file of *Un amor fora ciutat*. 1974. Third edition. File 1561-74. Archivo General de la Administración, Alcalá de Henares.
Censorship file of *Barrabàs*. 1958. File 3483–58. Archivo General de la Administración, Alcalá de Henares.
Censorship file of *Barrabàs*. 1963. File 3309–63. Archivo General de la Administración, Alcalá de Henares.
Censorship file of *Déu ha nascut a l'exili*. 1961. File 3250-61. Archivo General de la Administración, Alcalá de Henares.
Censorship file of *La història de San Michele*. 1964. File 7682–64. Archivo General de la Administración, Alcalá de Henares.
Censorship file of *Incerta glòria*. 1956. File 1059-56. Archivo General de la Administración, Alcalá de Henares.
Censorship file of *Un món per a tothom*. 1956. File 3080-56. Archivo General de la Administración, Alcalá de Henares.

Chislett, William. 2013. *Spain: What Everyone Needs to Know*. New York: Oxford University Press.
Chuliá, Elisa. 1999. "La Ley de Prensa de 1966: La explicación de un cambio institucional arriesgado y de sus efectos virtuosos." *Historia y Política: Ideas, Procesos y Movimientos Sociales*, no. 2, 197–220.
Cifra. 1966. "Concesión de los Premios Nacionales de Literatura." *La Vanguardia Española*, December 21, 1966.
Cisquella, Georgina, José Luis Erviti, and José A. Sorolla. 2002. *La represión cultural en el franquismo: Diez años de censura de libros durante la Ley de Prensa, 1966–1976*. Barcelona: Anagrama.
Citton, Yves. 2017. *The Ecology of Attention*. Cambridge: Polity.
Civtat. 2017. "Camil Geis i Parragueras (1902-1986)." http://www.civtat.cat/geis_camil.html.
Clotet, Jaume, and Quim Torra. 2010. *Les millors obres de la literatura catalana (comentades pel censor)*. Barcelona: Acontravent.
Coca, Jordi. 1978. *L'agrupació dramàtica de Barcelona. Intent de teatre nacional català (1955–1963)*. Barcelona: Institut del Teatre / Edicions 62.
Coll i Alentorn, Miquel. 1992. *Història 2: Textos i estudis de literatura catalana*. Barcelona: Publicacions de l'Abadia de Montserrat.
"Conmemoración del 80 Aniversario del Exilio Republicano Español en México." Posted on YouTube by Ministerio de Justicia, December 5, 2019. https://www.youtube.com/watch?v=dziYErRXM0E.
Coll i Pigem, Maria. 2017. *Al paranimf!* Barcelona: Editorial Base.
Corderot, Didier. 2004. "La revista 'Destino' (1937–1939) y la cuestión de la catalanidad." In *Centros y periferias: Prensa, impresos y territorios en el mundo hispánico contemporáneo: Homenaje a Jacqueline Covo-Maurice*, edited by Nathalie Ludec and Françoise Dubosquet Lairys, 207–18. Pessac: PILAR (Presse, Imprimés, Lecture dans l'Aire Romane).
Cormand, Genís. 1999. "Entrevista a Josep Palau i Fabre." *Informatius*, TV3, posted on May 23, 2019. https://www.ccma.cat/tv3/alacarta/inedits/inedits-josep-palau-i-fabre-/video/5855909.
Cornellà-Detrell, Jordi. 2010. "Traducció i censura en la represa cultural dels anys 1960." *L'Avenç*, no. 359, 44–51.
Cornellà-Detrell, Jordi. 2011. *Literature as a Response to Cultural and Political Repression in Franco's Catalonia*. Cambridge: Cambridge University Press.
Cornellà-Detrell, Jordi. 2013. "L'auge de la traducció en llengua catalana als anys 60: El desglaç de la censura, el XVI Congreso Internacional de Editores i el problema dels drets d'autor." *Quaderns: Revista de Traducció*, no. 20, 47–67. https://www.raco.cat/index.php/QuadernsTraduccio/article/view/265452.

Coromines, Diana. 2019. "Pròleg". In Calders, Pere. *Sobre el feixisme, l'exili i la censura: Tria d'articles i contes distòpics*. Edited by Diana Coromines. Barcelona: Rosa dels Vents. Ebook.

Coromina, Eusebi, and Laura Vilardell. 2019. "L'americà pacífic, de la col·lecció 'Isard': Entre la censura i la recerca d'un nou llenguatge literari." *Catalan Review* 33 (1): 135–56. https://doi.org/10.3828/CATR.33.8.

Cort, Rosa Maria. 1987. "Entrevista a J. V. Foix." *30 Minuts*, TV3, posted on June 27, 2019. https://www.ccma.cat/tv3/alacarta/inedits/inedits-j-v-foix/video/5874089.

CRAI (Centre de Recursos per a l'Aprententatge i la Investigació). 2009. "Els Jocs Florals de La Llengua Catalana a l'exili (1941–1977)." Universitat de Barcelona, March 2009. https://crai.ub.edu/ca/coneix-el-crai/biblioteques/biblioteca-pavello-republica/jocs-florals.

Cronin, Michael. 2017. *Eco-Translation: Translation and Ecology in the Age of the Anthropocene*. Abingdon: Routledge.

Das, Nandita, writer and director. 2018. *Manto* (film). Mumbai: Viacom18 Motion Pictures.

Delgado, Lorenzo. 2003. "¿El amigo americano? España y Estados Unidos durante el Franquismo." *Estudios de Historia Contemporánea*, no. 21, 231–76.

Díaz-Plaja, Aurora. 1966. "El 'Jacinto Verdaguer' educa poéticamente a los niños." *La Vanguardia Española*, December 24, 1966.

Díaz-Plaja, Guillermo. 1967. "Presentación." In *Llibres en Català*, by INLE, edited by Maria Ballester. Barcelona: INLE.

Díez, Emeterio. 2008. "La censura teatral bajo el franquismo: La vicesecretaría de educación popular (1941–1945)." *Teatro: Revista de estudios culturales / A Journal of Cultural Studies*, no. 22, 263–276.

Duch Plana, Montserrat. 2017. "Historia, memoria y política en torno de la transición democrática en España". In *Polítiques memorials, fronteres i turisme de memòria*, edited by Ramon Arnabat Mata, and Montserrat Duch Plana. Tarragona: Publicacions Universitat Rovira i Virgili, p. 47-60.

Eaude, Michael. 2008. *Catalonia: A Cultural History*. Oxford: Oxford University Press.

Edicions 62. 1979. *Edicions 62: Mil llibres en català: (1962–1979)*. Barcelona: Edicions 62.

Edicions Proa Collection. Special Collection. Universitat de Vic – Universitat Central de Catalunya. https://www.uvic.cat/biblioteca/colleccions/fons-especials/edicions-proa.

Editorial. 1970. "Crisis en la Industria Editorial." *El Libro Español: Revista Mensual del Instituto Nacional del Libro Español* 13 (156): 653–59.

Edwards, Kate. 2015. "Culture and Censorship." *Multilingual*, April/May 2015, 22–23.

Estapé, Fabián. 2000. *Sin acuse de recibo: [Las extraordinarias memorias de un gran economista]*, edited by Mònica Terribas Sala. Barcelona: Plaza & Janés.

Estefanía, Joaquín. 2014. *La larga marcha: Medio siglo de política (económica) entre la historia y la memoria*. Barcelona: Península.

Estivill, Assumpció. 2013. "Las bibliotecas populares de Barcelona como espacios de socialización durante el segundo franquismo, 1957–1975." *BiD: Textos universitaris de biblioteconomia i documentació*, no. 30. http://bid.ub.edu/es/30/estivill.htm.

Europa Press. 1968. "Secuestro de la obra *La iglesia en España ayer y mañana*." *La Vanguardia Española*, September 14, 1968.

Europa Press. 1976. "Los editores piden una mayor libertad para sus publicaciones." *La Vanguardia Española*, March 31, 1976.

Evans, David. 2018. "Autarky." In *The New Palgrave Dictionary of Economics*, edited by John Eatwell, Murray Milgate, and Peter Newman. London: Palgrave Macmillan.

Fabre, Giorgio. 2018. *Il censore e l'editore: Mussolini, i libri, Mondadori*. Milano: Fondazione Arnoldo e Alberto Mondadori.

Fagen, Patricia W. 1973. *Exiles and Citizens: Spanish Republicans in Mexico*. Austin: University of Texas Press.

Fernández Moya, María. 2017. "La Formación de Una Industria Competitiva a Nivel Internacional: El Sector Editorial Español 1950–2015." Presented at the XII Congreso de la Asociación Española de Historia Económica, Salamanca, September 6. https://www.aehe.es/wp-content/uploads/2016/01/FERNANDEZ-MOYA.pdf.

Ferrer i Roca, Josep M. 2009. "Escriure i Publicar a Barcelona en els darrers cinquanta anys." In *Llegint pedres, escrivint ciutats: Unes visions literàries de la ciutat*, edited by Carles Carreras, and Sergi Moreno, 295–315. Lleida: Pagès Editors.

Ferriz Roure, Teresa. 2001. *La edición catalana en México*. Alicante: Biblioteca Virtual Miguel de Cervantes. http://www.cervantesvirtual.com/obra-visor/la-edicion-catalana-en-mexico--o/html.

Flotats i Crispi, Rosa. 1997. "John Milton i Josep M. Boix i Selva estudi comparatiu de la traducció d'un clàssic al català: Paradise Lost = El Paradís perdut." PhD diss., Universitat Autònoma de Barcelona.

Flotats i Crispi, Rosa, and Josep M. Boix i Selva. 1994. *Entrevista amb Josep M. Boix i Selva*. Tape.

Fraga Iribarne, Manuel, and Guillermo Díaz-Plaja. 1966. "El INLE da muestras de una vitalidad clara y progresiva." *El Libro Español: Revista Mensual del Instituto Nacional del Libro Español* 9 (102): 385–94.

"Franco's Concordat (1953): Text." Concordat Watch, n.d. http://www.concordat watch.eu/topic-34561.843.

Fuster, Joan. 1962. "Nota del Traductor." In *La pesta*, by Albert Camus. Barcelona: Vergara, 255–6.

Gabancho, Patrícia. 2005. *La postguerra cultural a Barcelona (1939–1959): Converses.* Barcelona: Meteora.

La Gaceta Papelera. 1970. "La Industria Editorial Española ante el Mercado Común Europeo." September 1970. Reprinted in *El Libro Español: Revista Mensual del Instituto Nacional del Libro Español* 14, no. 159 (1971): 141–44.

Galderich. 2015. "El primer llibre català del franquisme: *Mes de Maria Eucarístic* (1939), de Mn. Lluís G. Otzet." *Piscolabis & Librorum* (blog), June 11, 2015. http://librorum.piscolabis.cat/2015/06/el-primer-llibre-en-catala-del_11.html.

Galderich. 2009. "Sonata en tres tiempos (1939) de Miquel i Planas, la primera obra en català des del franquisme clandestí." *Piscolabis & Librorum* (blog), March 2, 2009. http://librorum.piscolabis.cat/2009/03/sonata-en-tres-tiempos-de-miquel-i.html.

Galiana, Pedro Miguel. 2017. "El plan nacional de estabilización económica y el modelo de desarrollo español." PhD diss., Universitat Internacional de Catalunya. http://www.tdx.cat/handle/10803/403408.

Gallén, Enric. 1985. *El teatre a la ciutat de Barcelona durant el règim franquista (1939–1954).* Barcelona: Institut del Teatre.

Gallén, Enric. 2016. "Traducció i difusió de textos dramàtics en temps de censura i moral de postguerra." In *Traducció i censura en el franquisme*, edited by Laura Vilardell, 51–75. Barcelona: Publicacions de l'Abadia de Montserrat.

Gallofré, Maria Josepa. 1991. *L'edició catalana i la censura franquista: 1939–1951.* Barcelona: Publicacions de l'Abadia de Montserrat.

García Berlanga, Luis, director. 1953. *Bienvenido Mr. Marshall* (film). Madrid: Uninci.

Gargatagli, Ana. 2016. "Borges traducido a leyes inhumanas. La censura franquista en América." *1611, revista de historia de la traducción*, no. 10. http://www.traduccionliteraria.org/1611/art/gargatagli4.htm.

Gayà, Miquel. 1986. *Històries i memòries.* Ciutat de Mallorca: Ed. Moll.

Geis, Camil. 1981. *Pas i repàs.* Sabadell: Biblioteca Quadern.

Gili, Gustau. 1944. *Bosquejo de una política del libro.* Barcelona: Gustavo Gili.

Giró, Jordi. 2004. *Els homes són i les coses passen*. Barcelona: Publicacions de l'Abadia de Montserrat.

Girons, Alba. 2011. "Cavall Fort, porta d'entrada del còmic infantil europeu." In *La traducció i el món editorial de postguerra: III Simposi sobre Traducció i Recepció en la Literatura Catalana Contemporània*, edited by Sílvia Coll-Vinent, Cornèlia Eisner, and Enric Gallén, 135–40. Lleida: Punctum and Trilcat.

Godayol, Pilar. 2016. "Josep Maria Castellet, editor de autoras feministas traducidas." *TRANS: Revista de traductología*, no. 20 (October): 87–100. https://doi.org/10.24310/TRANS.2016.v0i20.2066.

Godayol, Pilar, and Annarita Taronna. 2018. *Foreign Women Authors under Fascism and Francoism: Gender, Translation and Censorship*. Newcastle upon Tyne: Cambridge Scholars.

Gómez Pin, Víctor. 1981. *El reino de las leyes: Orden freudiano*. Madrid: Siglo XXI.

González, Pedro. 2009. "La depresión de la autarquía." *Diario Público*, April 3. https://www.publico.es/actualidad/depresion-autarquia-1.html.

Gracia, Jordi, and Domingo Ródenas de Moya. 2011. *Derrota y restitución de la modernidad: 1939–2010*. Barcelona: Crítica.

Gremi d'Editors de Catalunya. 2019. "El Gremi de Llibreters de Catalunya confirma les sensacions positives del Dia del Llibre i calcula en 22 ME la facturació de la jornada." May 6, 2019. https://www.gremieditors.cat/gremi-llibreters-catalunya-confirma-sensacions-positives-dia-llibre-calcula-22-me-facturacio-jornada.

Griffin, Roger. 1993. *The Nature of Fascism*. London: Routledge.

Gubern, Romà, and Kathleen M. Vernon. 2016. "Soundtrack." In *A Companion to Spanish Cinema*, edited by Jo Labanyi and Tatjana Pavlović, 370–89. Malden, MA: Wiley Blackwell.

Güell Ampuero, Casilda. 2006. *The Failure of Catalanist Opposition to Franco (1939–1950)*. Madrid: Consejo Superior de Investigaciones Científicas.

Guzmán, M. de. 1954. "Don Agustín de Semir y la Asociación de Cultura Occidental." *Espíritu* 3: 42–45.

Hargrave, Marshall. 2019. "Boom." Investopedia, July 6, 2019. https://www.investopedia.com/terms/b/boom.asp.

Hart, Patricia. 1987. *The Spanish Sleuth: The Detective in Spanish Fiction*. London: Associated University Presses.

Hendricks, Vincent F., and Mads Vestergaard. 2019. *Reality Lost: Markets of Attention, Misinformation and Manipulation*. Cham: Springer Open.

Herrero-Olaizola, Alejandro. 2007. *The Censorship Files: Latin American Writers and Franco's Spain*. Albany: State University of New York Press.

Hout-Huijben, Lidwina Maria van den. 2015. "El rojo crítico: expansión de la literatura Catalana bajo censura (1962–1977)." PhD diss., University of Groningen.

Hout-Huijben, Lidwina Maria van den. 2007. "La censura y el caso de Manuel de Pedrolo. Las novelas perdidas." *Represura*, no. 4 (October). http://www.represura.es/represura_4_octubre_2007_articulo1.html.

Iglésias, Narcís. 2019. "Language Policies in Contemporary Catalonia: A History of Linguistic and Political Ideas." In *The Rise of Catalan Identity: Social Commitment and Political Engagement in the Twentieth Century*, edited by Pompeu Casanovas, Montserrat Corretger, and Vicent Salvador, 79–106. Cham: Springer International.

INLE [Instituto Nacional del Libro Español]. 1963. "Información del extranjero." *El Libro Español: Revista Mensual del Instituto Nacional del Libro Español* 6 (72): 329–32.

INLE. 1966. "Información nacional. Madrid. Círculo de Lectores." *El Libro Español: Revista Mensual del Instituto Nacional del Libro Español* 9 (98): 145–51.

INLE. 1967–1970. *Catàleg de llibres en català*, edited by Maria Ballester. Barcelona: INLE.

IPA [International Publishers Association]. 1962. *Union Internationale des Editeurs seizième congrès Barcelone 6–12 Mai 1962: Rapports*. Barcelona: Instituto Nacional del Libro Español.

Joan Fuster Collection. Biblioteca de Catalunya, Barcelona. http://www.bnc.cat/cat/Fons-i-col-leccions/Cerca-Fons-i-col-leccions/Fuster-Joan.

Joan Gili / Dolphin Book Company collection, MS1197. Gili Catalan Collection. Senate House Library, University of London. https://london.ac.uk/senate-house-library/our-collections/special-collections/printed-special-collections/gili-catalan-collection.

Jimeno Revilla, Raquel. 2016. "Círculo de Lectores (1962–)." Alicante: Biblioteca Virtual Miguel de Cervantes. http://www.cervantesvirtual.com/nd/ark:/59851/bmczw3d6.

John XXIII (pope). 1959. "Allocuzione Con La Quale Il Sommo Pontefice Annuncia Il Sinodo Romano, Il Concilio Ecumenico e l'aggiornamento Del Codice Di Diritto Canonico." Vatican, January 25, 1959. http://w2.vatican.va/content/john-xxiii/it/speeches/1959/documents/hf_j-xxiii_spe_19590125_annuncio.html.

Joric, Carlos. 2015. "Las tijeras de Franco." *Historia y vida*, no. 564: 62–70.

Josep M. Boix i Selva Collection. Biblioteca de Catalunya, Barcelona. http://www.bnc.cat/cat/Fons-i-col-leccions/Cerca-Fons-i-col-leccions/Boix-i-Selva-Josep-Maria.

Junta Electoral Central. 2014. "Administración Electoral." http://www.junta electoralcentral.es/cs/jec/admelectoral.
King, Martin Luther, Jr. 1968. "Paraules de Martin Luther King." Translated by Francesc Vallverdú. *Serra d'Or*, May 1968, 15–16.
Küng, Hans. 2002. *La Iglesia Católica*. Barcelona: Mondadori.
Larios, Jordi, ed. 2013. *La cara fosca de la cultura catalana: La col·laboració amb el feixisme i la dictadura franquista*. Palma: Lleonard Muntaner Editor.
Larraz, Fernando. 2014. *Letricidio español*. Madrid: Ediciones Trea.
Larruela, Enric. 1985. *Les revistes infantils catalanes de 1939 ençà*. Barcelona: Edicions 62.
LaSexta.com. 2017. "Cronología de cómo un chiste sobre el Valle de los Caídos te puede llevar a juicio." May 24, 2017. https://www.lasexta.com/programas/el-intermedio/noticias/siete-videos-que-cuentan-como-chiste-valle-caidos-llevado-dani-mateo-gran-wyoming-frente-juez-juicio-humor_20170524592565 900cf205e8f6fc3006.html.
Lázaro, Luis Alberto. 2004. *H. G. Wells en España: Estudio de los expedientes de censura (1939–1978)*. Madrid: Editorial Verbum.
Lera, Ángel M. de 1971. "Una Ojeada a Nuestra Actividad Editorial." *El Libro Español: Revista Mensual del Instituto Nacional del Libro Español* 14 (157): 7–9.
Lewis, Paul H. 2002. *Latin Fascist Elites: The Mussolini, Franco, and Salazar Regimes*. Westport, CT: ABC-CLIO.
Lima Grecco, Gabriela de. 2014. "El control del libro durante el Primer Franquismo." *Diálogos: Revista do Departamento de História e do Programa de Pós-Graduação em História* 18 (1): 361–80.
Lladó, Ramon. 2004. "Sobre literatura i sobre traduccions. Entrevista amb Ramon Folch i Camarasa." *Quaderns: Revista de Traducció*, no. 11, 215–22. https://www.raco.cat/index.php/QuadernsTraduccio/article/view/25405/25240.
Llanas, Manuel. 2001–2007. *L'edició a Catalunya*. Barcelona: Gremi d'editors de Catalunya.
Llanas, Manuel. 2006. *L'edició a Catalunya: El segle XX (1939–1975)*. Barcelona: Gremi d'editors de Catalunya.
Llanas, Manuel. 2007. *Six Centuries of Publishing in Catalonia: A Historical Synthesis*. Lleida: Pagès; Vic: Eumo.
Llanas, Manuel. 2011. "Traduir al castellà en un compàs d'espera. Les editorials Aymà i M. Arimany en els anys 40 i 50." In *La traducció i el món editorial de postguerra: III Simposi sobre Traducció i Recepció en la Literatura Catalana Contemporània*, edited by Sílvia Coll-Vincent, Cornèlia Eisner, and Enric Gallén, 177–214. Lleida: Punctum & Trilcat.

Llobet, Alexis. 2012. "Entrevista a Francesc Vallverdú." *Quaderns: Revista de Traducció*, no. 19, 397–410. https://www.raco.cat/index.php/Quaderns Traduccio/article/view/257061.

Ll.S.B. 1966. "Panorama de Actividades Literarias, Editoriales y Libreras." *La Vanguardia Española*, March 3, 1966.

Ll.S.B. 1967. "Panorama de Actividades Literarias, Editoriales y Libreras." *La Vanguardia Española*, April 27, 1967.

López, Carlos. 2016. "Franco's Spain and the Council of Europe." *CVCE*, 4. http://www.cvce.eu/obj/franco_s_spain_and_the_council_of_europe-en-67511746-0b1f-47e6-8762-03a336d23bd0.html.

López Burniol, Juan-José. 2010. "Un economista decisivo." *La Vanguardia*, April 24, 2010.

Lorente Fuentes, María. 2006. "Bajo el estado de excepción: cuatro días después de la muerte de Enrique Ruano, el gobierno toma medidas extremas para restaurar el orden público." In *España, en estado de excepción: 1969*, edited by Juan Carlos Laviana, Daniel Arjona, and Silvia Fernández, 20–33. Madrid: Unidad Editorial.

Luelmo, Francisco José Rodrigo. 2010. "The Accession of Franco's Spain to the OEEC." *CVCE*, 3. http://www.cvce.eu/obj/the_accession_of_franco_s_spain_to_the_oeec-en-d811252e-2b8c-4824-b2de-d8038e1cfadc.html.

M.M. i B. 1963. "Bibliografia Catalana Recent." *Serra d'Or*, April 1963, 45.

Majzoub, Mona K., and Christopher J. Doyle. 2020. "To Inflame the Censors: Hemingway's Use of Obscenity in *To Have and Have Not*". *Detroit Lawyer* (January–February 2020), 14–9.

Manent, Albert. 1984. "Resistència i recuperació catalana durant el franquisme." In *Escriptors i editors del Nou-Cents*, 215–38. Barcelona: Curial Ed.

Manent, Albert. 1986. *El Molí de l'ombra: Dietari polític i retrats, 1946–1975*. Barcelona: Edicions 62.

Manent, Albert. 1993. *Solc de Les Hores: Retrats d'escriptors i de polítics*. Barcelona: Destino.

Manent, Albert. 1999. *En un replà del meu temps: Retrats d'escriptors i de polítics*. Barcelona: Proa.

Manent, Albert. 2010. *La Represa: Memòria personal, crònica d'una generació (1946–1956)*. Barcelona: Edicions 62. Ebook.

Manent, Albert. 2011. "Durant un quart de segle les traduccions al català foren oficialment prohibides." In *La traducció i el món editorial de postguerra: III Simposi Sobre Traducció i Recepció en la Literatura Catalana Contemporània*, edited by Sílvia Coll-Vinent, Cornèlia Eisner, and Enric Gallén, 287–96. Lleida: Punctum & Trilcat.

Manonelles, Manuel. 2005. *A quaranta anys del Concili: Reflexions sobre l'església catalana i universal, quaranta anys després de l'obertura del Concili Vaticà II*. Barcelona: Publicacions de l'Abadia de Montserrat.

Marfull, Miguel Ángel. 2009. "La Muerte Que Levantó a Los Estudiantes Contra La Dictadura." *Público*, January 10, 2009, sec. España. https://www.publico.es/espana/muerte-levanto-estudiantes-dictadura.html.

Marín Silvestre, Dolors, and Agnès Ramírez. 2004. *Editorial Nova Terra 1958–1978: Un referent*. Barcelona: Editorial Mediterrània.

Martí, Montserrat. 1962. "Moviment editorial." In *Llibre de l'any 1962*. Barcelona: Alcides, 1962.

Martí, Montserrat. 1963. "Moviment editorial." In *Llibre de l'any 1963*. Barcelona: Alcides, 1963.

Martín de Pozuelo, Eduardo, and Iñaki Ellakuría. 2008. *La guerra ignorada: Los espías españoles que combatieron a los nazis*. Barcelona: Debate.

Martín Escribà, Àlex. 2020. *Escrits policíacs: De la Cua de palla a Crims.cat*. Barcelona: Alrevés.

Martínez Rus, Ana. 2012. "La represión cultural: libros destruidos, bibliotecas depuradas y lectura." In *Franco: La represión como sistema*, edited by Julio Aróstegui and Manuel Álvaro Dueñas, 365–415. Barcelona: Flor del Viento Ediciones.

Martínez Rus, Ana. 2014. *La persecución del libro: Hogueras, infierno y buenas lecturas (1936–1951)*. Madrid: Trea.

Martínez, Jesús A. 2011. "Editoriales Conflictivas y Disidentes en Tiempos de Dictadura (1966–1975)." *Arbor: Ciencia, Pensamiento y Cultura* 187 (747): 127–41.

Mas Esteve, Antonio. 1971. "El Cobro, Cuestión Difícil de Las Ventas a Plazos." *El Libro Español: Revista Mensual del Instituto Nacional del Libro Español* 14 (159): 138–41.

Mas, Antoni, and Mercedes Gordon. 1966. "El Libro Necesita Agresividad Comercial." *El Libro Español: Revista Mensual del Instituto Nacional del Libro Español* 9 (100): 273–79.

Massot i Muntaner, Josep. 1973. *Aproximació a la història religiosa de la Catalunya contemporània*.

Massot i Muntaner, Josep. 1978. *Cultura i vida a Mallorca entre la guerra i la postguerra: 1930–1950*. Montserrat: Publicacions de l'Abadia de Montserrat.

Massot i Muntaner, Josep. 2016. "Les publicacions de l'Abadia de Montserrat i la Censura." In *Traducció i censura en el franquisme*, edited by Laura Vilardell, 9–33. Barcelona: Publicacions de l'Abadia de Montserrat.

Massot, Josep. 2012. "Joan Sales, la mirada libre de un escritor." *La Vanguardia*, November 19, 2012.

Massot, Josep. 2017. "Club Editor Rescata de Los Archivos de La Censura El Making of de 'El Mar.'" *La Vanguardia*, November 13, 2017, sec. Cultura.

Mayol, Carme. 2005. "La Xarxa de Biblioteques 1915–2004: Una història que mira al futur." *Textos universitaris de biblioteconomia i documentació*, no. 14 (June). http://bid.ub.edu/14mayol.htm.

Mengual Català, Josep. 2013. *A dos tintas: Josep Janés, poeta y editor*. Barcelona: Debate. Ebook.

Mengual Català, Josep. 2017. "La primera editorial que le tomó el pelo a la censura franquista." *Negritasycursivas* (blog), May 12, 2017. https://negritasycursivas.wordpress.com/2017/05/12/la-primera-editorial-que-le-tomo-el-pelo-a-la-censura-franquista.

Mengual Català, Josep. 2019. "Exilio republicano español e industria editorial." *Negritasycursivas* (blog), September 6, 2019. https://negritasycursivas.wordpress.com/2019/09/06/exilio-republicano-espanol-e-industria-editorial/.

Michael, Ian. 1998. "J. L. Gili." *Independent*, May 8, 18–19.

Miguel Fernández, Enrique de, and Vicente Sanz Rozalén. 2009. "US Investments in Spain (1989–2005)." In *American Firms in Europe: Strategy, Identity, Perception and Performance (1880–1980)*, edited by Hubert Bonin and Ferry de Goey, 185–208. Geneva: Librairie Droz.

Minobis, Gregori M. 1963. "Una Encíclica Memorable." *Serra d'Or*, June 1963, 8–9.

Miralles, Carles. 1967. "Elegia per a La Nostra Biblioteca de Clàssics Moderns." *Serra d'Or*, October 1967, 52–54.

Molas, Joaquim. 1966. "Algunes Característiques de La Novel·la Catalana Contemporània." *Serra d'Or*, March 1966, 55–57.

Molas, Joaquim. 1978. "Panorama de La Literatura Catalana de Postguerra." *El País*, February 5, 1978. Available at LiTeCa (Universitat Pompeu Fabra). https://parles.upf.edu/llocs/liteca/biblioteca-panorama-de-la-literatura-catalana-de-postguerra.

Molas, Joaquim. 1991. "Pròleg". In *L'edició catalana i la censura franquista: 1939–1951*, by Maria Josepa Gallofré, V–IX. Barcelona: Publicacions de l'Abadia de Montserrat.

Molas, Joaquim. 2010. "1939: any límit de la literatura catalana." In *Aproximació a la literatura catalana del segle XX*. Barcelona: Base.

Moll, Francesc de B. 1975. *Els altres quaranta anys (1935–1974)*. Mallorca: Moll.

Montejo Gurruchaga, Lucía. 2013. *Discurso de autora: Género y censura en la narrativa española de posguerra*. Madrid: UNED Arte y Humanidades. Ebook.

Morales Pérez, Sonia. 2018. "27 octubre 1964: Primera emisión de un programa en catalán." *RTVE.es*, July 30, 2018. https://www.rtve.es/rtve/20180730/historia-tve-primera-emissio-dun-programa-catala/1772240.shtml.

Morcillo, Aurora G. 2010. *The Seduction of Modern Spain: The Female Body and the Francoist Body Politic*. Lewisburg, PA: Bucknell University Press.

Moreno Cantano, Antonio César. 2016. *Tiempo de mentiras: El control de la prensa extranjera en España durante el primer franquismo (1936–1945)*. Sarrión: Muñoz Moya Editores.

Moret, Xavier. 2002. *Tiempo de editores: Historia de la edición en España, 1939–1975*. Barcelona: Destino.

Muñoz, Vicent Melchor, and Albert Branchadell. 2002. *El Catalán: Una lengua de Europa para compartir*. Bellaterra: Universitat autònoma de Barcelona.

Muñoz i Lloret, Teresa. 2006. *Josep M. Castellet: Retrat de personatge en grup*. Barcelona: Edicions 62. Ebook.

Navarro Rubio, Mariano. 1989. "El fin de la autarquía." *La Vanguardia*, April 23, 1989.

Nortes, Silvia. 2017. "No Laughing Matter: Making Jokes about Franco and ETA Is Off the Table in Spain if You Want to Avoid Trouble with the Law." *Index on Censorship* 46 (2): 85–86.

Nortes, Silvia. 2020. "Silencing the Spanish Media." *Index on Censorship* (blog), March 24, 2020. https://www.indexoncensorship.org/2020/03/silencing-the-spanish-media.

O'Connor, Thomas. 2001. "Imprimatur and Nihil Obstat." In *Censorship: A World Encyclopedia*, edited by Derek Jones, 1147. London: Routledge.

Oliver, Joan. 1964. "Tros de Paper." *Serra d'Or*, November 1964, 82.

El País. 1984a. "Jaime Castell Lastortras, empresario." *El País*, July 6, 1984. https://elpais.com/diario/1984/07/07/agenda/457999201_850215.html.

El País. 1984b. "El Instituto Nacional del Libro Español deja de ser autónomo." October 25, 1984. https://elpais.com/diario/1984/10/26/cultura/467593204_850215.html.

Payne, Stanley G. 2011. *The Franco Regime, 1936–1975*. Madison: University of Wisconsin Press.

Pericay, Xavier, and Ferran Toutain. 1986. *Verinosa llengua*. Barcelona: Empúries.

Piñol, Rosa María. 1996. "Planeta controlará a partir de enero la mayoría de las acciones de Destino." *La Vanguardia*, December 25, 1996.

Pinyol i Torrents, Ramon, and Laura Vilardell. 2018. "La censura franquista contra un intel·lectual addicte al règim. el cas del romanès Vintila Horia i La Traducció al Català de *Déu ha nascut a l'exili*." In *Traduccions i diàlegs culturals amb el Català*, edited by Joan Llinàs Suau, and Miorar Adelina Anghelutӑ, 163–79. Bucharest: Bucharest University Press.

Pla, Xavier. 2007. "Traduccions de la literatura catalana—Joan Sales." *Visat*, April 2007. http://www.visat.cat/traduccions-literatura-catalana/cat/ressenyes/66/115//2/prosa/joan-sales.html.

Pla, Xavier. 2011. "Joan Sales, una traducció i una novel·la sense punt final." *Quaderns: Revista de Traducció*, no. 18: 9–19. https://www.raco.cat/index.php/QuadernsTraduccio/article/view/245267.

Planellas i Barnosell, Joan. 2016. "una església pobra i per als pobres. Del Concili Vaticà II al Papa Francesc." *Revista Catalana de Teologia* 41 (2): 349–74.

Pol, Ferran de. 1960. "La nostra novel·la actual." *Serra d'Or*, April 1960, 18–19.

Pol, Ferran de. 1987. "Vuitantè Aniversari de Joan Gili." *Diario de Barcelona*, June 7, 1987.

Portillo, Luis. 1941. "Unamuno's Last Lecture." *Horizon*, December 1941.

Portolés, José. 2016. *La censura de la palabra: Estudio de pragmática y análisis del discurso*. Valencia: Publicacions de la Universitat de València, Departament de Filologia Espanyola.

Preston, Paul. 1971. *The Spanish Right under the Second Republic: An Analysis*. Reading: University of Reading, Graduate School of Contemporary European Studies.

Preston, Paul. 1994. *Franco: A Biography*. New York: Basic Books. Ebook.

Preston, Paul. 2006. *The Spanish Civil War: Reaction, Revolution and Revenge*. London: HarperCollins. Ebook.

Preston, Paul, and Ann L. Mackenzie, eds. 1996. *The Republic Besieged: Civil War in Spain 1936–1939*. Edinburgh: Edinburgh University Press.

Preston, Paul, and Rob Attar. 2020. "Francisco Franco: Is It Accurate to Call the Spanish Dictator a Fascist?" *History Extra Podcast*, August 16. https://www.historyextra.com/period/20th-century/was-spanish-dictator-francisco-franco-fascist/.

Puelles Benítez, Manuel de. 1998. "La política del libro escolar en España. Del franquismo a la restauración democrática." In *Historia ilustrada del libro escolar en España: De la posguerra a la reforma educativa*, edited by Agustín Escolano Benito, 49–71. Madrid: Fundación Germán Sánchez Ruipérez.

Puigtobella, Bernat. 2020. "Albert Jané i la fosforescència del pensament." *Núvol*, May 7, 2020. https://www.nuvol.com/llibres/assaig/albert-jane-i-la-fosforescencia-del-pensament-99723.

Recasens, María. 1966a. "Novedades del mes de enero." *La Vanguardia Española*, February 10, 1966, sec. Bibliografia Catalana Mensual.

Recasens, María. 1966b. "Novedades del mes de abril." *La Vanguardia Española*, May 5, 1966, sec. Bibliografia Catalana Mensual.

Redacción, and Agencias. 2019. "Los consejos profesionales de TV3 y Catalunya Ràdio acusan de 'censura' a la Junta Electoral." *La Vanguardia*, March 29, 2019.

Redacción. 2019. "La Junta Electoral prohíbe que TV3 y Catalunya Ràdio digan 'presos políticos' y 'exilio.'" *La Vanguardia*, October 8, 2019.

Registre Mercantil de Barcelona. "Register of Companies of Vergara S.A." Sheet no. 2005, order 45. Barcelona: Registre Mercantil.

Reseña, Equipo, and Norberto Alcover. 1977. *La cultura española durante el franquismo*. Bilbao: Mensajero.

Revista de Girona. 2000. "Els secrets del primer llibre en català." No. 199, 6.

Ribes de Dios, Àngels. 2003. "La recepció d'Alphonse Daudet en llengua catalana. Traduccions en volum." PhD, diss., Universitat de Lleida.

Ridruejo, Dionisio. 2007. *Casi unas memorias*, edited by Jordi Amat. Barcelona: Península.

Ripoll Sintes, Blanca. 2015. "La revista Destino (1939–1980) y la reconstrucción de la cultura burguesa en la España de Franco." *Amnis*, no. 14. https://doi.org/10.4000/amnis.2558.

Riquer, Borja de. 2019. "El creixement econòmic legitima el franquisme?" In Domènech, Xavier. "20 preguntes clau sobre Franco." *Sàpiens*, July 16, 2019. https://www.sapiens.cat/epoca-historica/historia-contemporania/guerra-civil-i-franquisme/20-preguntes-clau-sobre-franco_202418_102.html.

Robles Piquer, Carlos. 2011. *Memoria de cuatro Españas: República, guerra, franquismo y democracia*. Barcelona: Planeta.

Rodoreda, Mercè, and Joan Sales. 2008. *Cartes completes (1960–1983)*. Edited by Montserrat Casals. Barcelona: Club Editor.

Rojas Claros, Francisco. 2013. *Dirigismo cultural y disidencia editorial en España (1962–1973)*. Alicante: Publicacions Universitat Alacant.

Rojas Claros, Francisco. 2017a. "La Represión de la disidencia editorial. Denuncias y secuestros de libros en España durante la 'Era Fraga' (1966–1969)." *Represura*, no. 2: 7–40.

Rojas Claros, Francisco. 2017b. "Edición y censura de libros de Marx y Engels durante el franquismo (1966–1976)." *Nuestra Historia*, no. 3, 103–26.

Ruiz Bautista, Eduardo. 2005. *Los señores del libro: Propagandistas, censores y bibliotecarios en el primer franquismo*. Gijón: Trea.

Ruiz Bautista, Eduardo. 2015. "La censura editorial. Depuraciones de libros y bibliotecas." In *Historia de la Edición en España (1939–1975)*, edited by Jesús A. Martínez Martín, 43–66. Madrid: Marcial Pons Historia.

Ruiz Soriano, Francisco. 1998. *La poesía de postguerra: (Vertientes poéticas de la primera promoción)*. Barcelona: Montesinos.
Ruiz, Julius. 2005. *Franco's Justice: Repression in Madrid after the Spanish Civil War*. Oxford: Clarendon.
Rundle, Christopher. 2018. "Translation and Fascism." In *The Routledge Handbook of Translation and Politics*, edited by Fruela Fernández, and Jonathan Evans, 29–47. Abingdon: Routledge.
Sabín, José Manuel, and Elena Hernández Sandoica. 1997. *La dictadura franquista (1936–1975)*. Madrid: Ediciones AKAL.
Sales-Balmes, Lluís. 1966. "La Paraula als editors." *Serra d'Or*, April 1966, 61–69.
Salvador, Tomás. 1960. "Barcelona, capital literaria de España." *La Vanguardia Española*, January 6, 1960.
Samsó, Joan. 1994. *La cultura catalana: Entre la clandestinitat i la represa pública*, vol. 1. Barcelona: Publicacions de l'Abadia de Montserrat.
Samsó, Joan. 1995. *La cultura catalana: Entre la clandestinitat i la represa pública*, vol. 2. Barcelona: Publicacions de l'Abadia de Montserrat.
Sánchez Agustí, Ferran. 2009. *Maquis y Pirineos: La Gran Invasión (1944–1945)*. Lleida: Editorial Milenio. Ebook.
Sánchez Gordaliza, Judith. 2012. "La traducción de 'La plaça del Diamant' de Mercè Rodoreda: formulación y aplicación de un modelo dinámico de análisis traductológico y retraducción al español." 2 volumes. PhD diss., Universitat de Vic. http://www.tdx.cat/handle/10803/119542.
Sánchez Sánchez, Esther M. 2001. "El auge del turismo europeo en la España de los años sesenta." *Arbor: Ciencia, Pensamiento y Cultura* 170 (669): 201–24.
Sánchez Sánchez, Esther M. 2004. "La España de la estabilización y el desarrollo en perspectiva francesa (1958–1969)." *Mélanges de la Casa de Velázquez* 34 (2): 251–69. https://doi.org/10.4000/mcv.1357.
Sánchez, Rafael. 1963. "Editorial Ramon Sopena, un nombre que ha originado cinco empresas dedicadas a los libros." *El Libro Español: Revista Mensual del Instituto Nacional del Libro Español* 6 (62): 43–46.
Sánchez, Rafael. 1966. "Ediciones Fax: Libros para la formación de los que van a formar." *El Libro Español: Revista Mensual del Instituto Nacional del Libro Español* 7 (81): 451–56.
Santonja, Gonzalo. 2003. *Los signos de la noche: De la guerra al exilio: Historia peregrina del libro republicano entre España y México*. Madrid: Castalia.
Santos Recuenco, Eloísa. 2016. "Legislación y documentación." In *Censuras y literatura infantil y juvenil en el siglo XX (en España y 7 países latinoamericanos)*, edited by Pedro C. Cerrillo, and María Victoria Sotomayor Sáez. Cuenca: Ediciones de la Universidad de Castilla-La Mancha.

Sàpiens. 2017. "La llista dels 718 expedientats el 1957 per la tancada a la UB." https://www.sapiens.cat/epoca-historica/historia-contemporania/guerra-civil-i-franquisme/document-la-llista-dels-718-expedientats-el-1957-per-la-tancada-a-la-ub_17029_102.html.

Sayrach, Manuel, and Miquel Àngel Sayrach. 2007. *Pas a pas, camí de l'alba: "Memòria" de l'Acadèmia de Llengua Catalana.* Barcelona: Publicacions de l'Abadia de Montserrat.

Schweid, Richard. 2011. "Spain's Not-So-Free Press." *Columbia Journalism Review*, January/February 2011. https://www.cjr.org/reports/spains_not-so-free_press.php.

Serra, Montse. 1999. "Entrevista a Anna Murià." *Avisan's quan arribi el 2000*, TV3, posted on July 14, 2019. https://www.ccma.cat/tv3/alacarta/inedits/inedits-anna-muria/video/5882833.

Serra d'Or. 1961a. "Enquesta als escriptors catalans: Narradors." June 1961, 15–18.

Serra d'Or. 1961b. "Enquesta als escriptors catalans: Narradors II." August 1961, 12–14.

Serra d'Or. 1963. "Notícies." April 1963, 44.

Serra d'Or. 1966. "El nostre llibre." April 1966, 19.

Serra Ramoneda, Antoni. 2001. *Joan Sardà i Dexeus, semblança biogràfica.* Barcelona: Institut d'Estudis Catalans.

Serrano Suñer, Ramón. 1978. *Entre el silencio y la propaganda la historia como fue: Memorias.* Barcelona: Planeta.

Servicio Informativo Español. 1967. *The Spanish Constitution: Fundamental Laws of the State.* Madrid: Ministerio de Informacion y Turismo.

Servicio Nacional de Propaganda. 1939. "Nota de la censura de libros." *La Vanguardia Española*, March 5, 1939.

Shepherd, John, Peter Wicke, and Paul Wicke. 2003. *Continuum Encyclopedia of Popular Music of the World: Vol. 1, Pt. 1: Media, Industry and Society.* London: Continuum.

Slaven, James. 2018. "The Falange Española: A Spanish Paradox." *Advances in Social Science, Education and Humanities Research* 211 (Proceedings of the 10th International RAIS Conference on Social Sciences and Humanities). https://dx.doi.org/10.2139/ssrn.3266916.

Solé-Tura, Jordi. 1999. *Una Història optimista: Memòries.* Barcelona: Edicions 62.

Solé i Sabaté, Josep Maria. 1985. *La repressió franquista a Catalunya: 1938–1953.* Barcelona: Edicions 62.

Soler Serrano, Joaquín. 1980. "A Fondo con Mercè Rodoreda." *A Fondo*, Televisión Española. Posted on YouTube by EDITRAMA, July 5, 2020. https://youtu.be/GQeqlnFvXzg.

Solsten, Eric, and Sandra W. Meditz, eds. 1988. *Spain: A Country-Study*. Washington, DC: GPO for the Library of Congress. http://countrystudies.us/spain.

Sopena, Mireia. 2006. *Editar la memòria: L'etapa resistent de Pòrtic: 1963–1976*. Barcelona: Publicacions de l'Abadia de Montserrat.

Sopena, Mireia. 2011. *Josep Pedreira, un editor en terra de naufragis: Els llibres de l'Óssa Menor (1949–1963)*. Barcelona: Proa.

Sopena, Mireia. 2013. "'Con vigilante espíritu crítico'. Els censors en les traduccions assagístiques d'Edicions 62." *Quaderns: Revista de Traducció*, no. 20, 147–161. https://www.raco.cat/index.php/QuadernsTraduccio/article/view/265458.

Sopena, Mireia. 2016. "Diligent i irreductible. La censura eclesiàstica als anys 60." In *Traducció i censura en el franquisme*, edited by Laura Vilardell, 35–51. Barcelona: Publicacions de l'Abadia de Montserrat.

Sopena, Mireia, and Olívia Gassol Bellet. 2017. "La cultura catalana, asediada. Un balance crítico de los estudios sobre la censura franquista." *Represura*, no. 2, 95–139.

Spaar, Lisa Russ. 2018. "A Trove of Continental Fiction Explores Loss." *New York Times*, January 5, 2018, sec. Books. https://www.nytimes.com/2018/01/05/books/review/european-fiction-grief.html.

Subirana, Jaume. 1995. "Editorial Selecta." LletrA: La literatura catalana a internet, Universitat Oberta de Catalunya. https://lletra.uoc.edu/ca/edicio/editorial-selecta/detall.

T. A., Mercedes. 1966. "La Ley de Prensa e Imprenta." *El Libro Español: Revista Mensual del Instituto Nacional del Libro Español* 9 (100): 283–91.

Tarde, Gabriel. 1902. *Psychologie économique*. Vol. 1. Paris: Félix Alcan, Éditeur.

Terrades, Toni, and Gustau Erill i Pinyot. 1999. Ferran Canyameres: entre la memòria i l'oblit. Barcelona: Baula. https://www.escriptors.cat/autors/canyameresf.

Tiphaigne de La Roche, Charles-François. 1760. *Giphantie*. Paris: A. Babylone.

Tobarra, Sebastián. 1989. "El grupo Planeta compra el 50% de Ediciones que poseía el empresario Julián Viñuales." *La Vanguardia*, September 8, 1989.

Torres, Estanislau. 1995. *Les tisores de la censura*. Lleida: Pagès.

Triadú, Joan. 1964. "La nova etapa del nostre llibre." *Serra d'Or*, June 1964, 37–39.

Triadú, Joan. 1965. "Aspectes de l'aggioramento del llibre català." *Serra d'Or*, May 1965, 63–64.

Triadú, Joan. 1970a. "Panorama de novel·la traduïda. Una qualitat sempre revulsiva." *Serra d'Or*, October 1970, 61–66.

Triadú, Joan. 1970b. "Punt i seguit: crisi, on és la teva victòria?" *Serra d'Or*, November 1970, 47.

Triadú, Joan. 2008. *Memòries d'un segle d'or*. Barcelona: Proa. Ebook.

Tusquets, Esther. 2020. *Confesiones de una editora poco mentirosa*. Barcelona: Lumen. Ebook.

TV3. 1991. "Entrevista a Pere Calders." *Versió Directa*, TV3, posted on July 21, 2019. https://www.ccma.cat/tv3/alacarta/inedits/inedits-pere-calders/video/5886149.

US Department of State. 1953. "Military Facilities in Spain: Agreement between the United States and Spain, September 26, 1953." Originally published in *American Foreign Policy 1950–1955* (Department of State Publication 6446, 1957). Available online through the Avalon Project, Lillian Goldman Law Library, Yale Law School. https://avalon.law.yale.edu/20th_century/sp1953.asp.

Valencia-García, Louie. 2018. *Antiauthoritarian Youth Culture in Francoist Spain Clashing with Fascism*. London: Bloomsbury.

Vall, Xavier. 1994. "Aproximació a la influència de l'existencialisme en la literatura catalana de postguerra." In *Els anys de postguerra a Catalunya (1939–1959)*, by Institució Cultural del CIC de Terrassa, 59–73. Barcelona: Publicacions de l'Abadia de Montserrat.

Vallverdú, Francesc. 1975. *L'escriptor català i el problema de la llengua*. 2nd ed. Barcelona: Edicions 62.

Vallverdú, Francesc. 1987. "L'edició en català i l'experiència d'Edicions 62." In *Edicions 62: Vint-i-cinc anys: 1962–1987*, by Edicions 62, 109–118. Barcelona: Edicions 62.

Vallverdú, Francesc. 2002. "L'activitat Editorial En Xifres. Taules i Gràfics." In *40 anys de llibres en Català*, by Edicions 62. Barcelona: Edicions 62.

Vallverdú, Francesc. 2004. "Testimonis de Repressió i Censura." In *La repressió franquista als països catalans (1939–1975)*, edited by Pelai Pagès, 181–188. València: Publicacions de la Universitat de València.

Vallverdú, Francesc. 2013. "La traducció i la censura franquista la meva experiència a Edicions 62." *Quaderns: Revista de Traducció*, no. 20, 9–16. https://www.raco.cat/index.php/QuadernsTraduccio/article/view/265449.

Valverde Ogallar, Pedro. 2015. "Leer En Madrid: 100 años de bibliotecas públicas de la Comunidad de Madrid." *Mi Biblioteca* 11 (42): 74–81.

La Vanguardia. 1938. "La fiesta del libro." June 17, 1938.

La Vanguardia Española. 1977. "Hoy se completará la formación del Consejo Rector de RTVE." December 1, 1977.

La Vanguardia Española. 1939. "Orden Público. Manifestaciones del Jefe superior de Policía." June 27, 1939.

La Vanguardia Española. 1953. "Anuncios económicos." November 18, 1953.
La Vanguardia Española. 1968. "Secuestro de la obra *Los escritos del Che*." March 3, 1968.
La Vanguardia Española. 1969. "Texto del Decreto Ley por el que se declara el estado de excepción en todo el territorio nacional." January 25, 1969.
La Vanguardia Española. 1970. "Auto de procesamiento contra Manuel de Pedrolo." June 20, 1970.
La Vanguardia Española. 1972. "Manuel de Pedrolo absuelto de la acusación de escándalo público." April 6, 1972.
Vega, José Antonio. 2019. "Con el Plan de Estabilización empezó todo . . . hace 60 años." *Cinco Días*, July 8, 2019. https://cincodias.elpais.com/cincodias/2019/07/05/economia/1562341276_095104.html.
Vergés, Josep C. 2017. *La censura invisible de Josep Pla*. Barcelona: Sd edicions.
Viladomat, Ramon. 2020. "Entrevista: Jordi Canal." *L'Erol*, no. 143, March 2020, 56–63. https://www.raco.cat/index.php/Erol/article/view/366385.
Vilardell, Laura. 2011. "Una aproximació a la col·lecció Isard." In *La traducció i el món editorial de postguerra: III Simposi Sobre Traducció i Recepció en la Literatura Catalana Contemporània*, edited by Sílvia Coll-Vinent, Cornèlia Eisner, and Enric Gallén, 253–72. Lleida: Punctum & Trilcat.
Vilardell, Laura. 2015. "Albert Camus y la censura franquista en la colección 'Isard,' de la Editorial Vergara." *Represura* 1 (1): 93–108.
Vilardell, Laura. 2016. "La col·lecció Isard, d'Editorial Vergara i la censura: el cas d'*After Many a Summer*." In *Traducció i censura en el franquisme*, edited by Laura Vilardell, 171–80. Barcelona: Publicacions de l'Abadia de Montserrat.
Vogel, Adrián. 2017. *Bikinis, fútbol y rock & roll: Crónica pop bajo el franquismo sociológico (1950–1977)*. Madrid: Ediciones AKAL. Ebook.
Wu, Tim. 2017. *The Attention Merchants: The Epic Scramble to Get inside Our Heads*. London: Atlantic Books. Ebook.

INDEX

Page numbers in *italics* refer to figures; page numbers in **bold** refer to tables.

A tot vent (series), 43, 72, 103
Abedul (series), 89
Abellán, Manuel
  on censors, 17, 18, 25
  on criteria for censorship, 19, 21, 22, 25, 34
  on incidence of censorship, **79**, *80*
  on publishers, 53
  on publishing delays, 80–81, *80*
  on self-censorship, 117–19
acquired censorship, 118
advertising, 70, 71–73, 75, 76
advertising industry, 62
Advisory Board of the Children's Press, 154n35
After Many a Summer (Huxley), 158n64
Agency for Management of University and Research Grants (AGAUR), 3–4
Agrupació Benèfica Minerva, 48, 145n61
Agrupació Dramàtica de Barcelona, 57
Aguilar, Manuel, 70–71
Aguirre, Francisco, 158n67
Agustí, Ignasi, 38, 39, 102
Agustí, Lluís, 39
Ainaud, Josep M., 33, 36, 40
Albertí, Santiago, 7, 53, 121–22
Albor (publishing house), 42, 149n92
Alcides (publishing house), 85
Alcover, Norberto, 22
Aleixandre, Vicente, 148n82

Alfaguara (publishing house), 63–64, 74, 112–13
Allò que tal vegada s'esdevingué (Oliver), 95
Almapres, S.A., 89
Alonso, Miguel, 10
Alpha (publishing house), 34, 52, 85
Altés (printing house), 147n74
Álvarez Arenas, Eliseo, 13
Álvarez Turienzo, Saturnino, 17, 19, 154n30
alzamiento (military uprising in Melilla, 1936), 10–11
Amades, Joan, 53
American culture, 7–8, 62–63, 64. *See also* United States
American Liberty, 89
Amics de la Poesia, 45–46
Amics de Rosselló-Pòrcel, 45, 46
amor fora ciutat, Un (Pedrolo), 5, 130–31, 132
Anagrama (publishing house), 63–64, 156–57n51
Analecta Montserratensia (journal), 146n71
Àncora, L' (series), 57
Andorranes (publishing house), 86
Anglo-Catalan Society, 42
Antich, Marcel·lí, 42–43
anticommunism, 7, 14, 59, 111
Antologia (journal), 47
Antón, Ernesto, 75, 152n11

Antònia i Montserrat Raventós (publishing house), 86
Anuaris de l'Institut (periodical), 47
apertura (openness), 7–8, 15, 61, 65–66
Aplec de cançonetes de Nadal (collection of children's songs), 33
Aproximació a la història religiosa de la Catalunya contemporània (Massot i Muntaner), 132
Ara i Ací (series), 74
Aramon, Ramon, 45–46, 47
Arbeloa, Victor Manuel, 158n69
Arbonès, Jordi, 77, 116, 119, 126, 139n3, 158n67
Archivo General de la Administración (AGA), 4, 103–6, 113
Argentina, 39, 40, 41, 63
Argos-Vergara, 102–3
Arias-Salgado, Gabriel, 5, 23, 55–56, 65, 120, 123
Arias-Salgado Law (Order of April 29, 1938), 16, 19, 26–28, 56, 113–14, 120–26
Ariel (magazine), 47, 49
Ariel (publishing house), 107
Arimany, Miquel
  on associations, 49
  on Catalan publishing, 44, 148n80
  on censorship services in Barcelona, 53
  on clandestine activities, 144n56, 145n61, 145n64, 147n76
  Diccionari català general and, 84
  on distribution, 86
  Fuster and, 154n29
  on Gilian Law, 31
  IPA conference (Barcelona, 1962) and, 66
  on literary awards, 48
  on paper scarcity, 141n26
  as publisher, 47, 52–53, 59, 146n68
  royalties and, 36
Ariola, 89
Ariola-Eurodisc, 89
Arión (publishing house), 78
Arraiza, Lorente, 78
Artís-Gener, Avel·lí (Tísner), 43
Asociación de Cultura Occidental (Association of Western Culture), 56
Associació per la Cultura de Mallorca, 86
Associació Protectora de l'Ensenyança Catalana, 147n77
attention economy, 6, 8, 70–73, 74–77, 88, 90–92, 108
Attention Merchants, The (Wu), 70, 71–73
Austral (collection), 75
autarky, 14
Ayén, Xavier, 106–7
Aymà i Ayala, Jaume, 33, 48, 125. *See also* Editorial Aymà (publishing house)
Azagra Ros, Joaquín, 36

B. Costa-Amic (publishing house), 149n92
Bacardí, Montserrat
  on Catalan language, 39
  on criteria and stages of censorship, 22, 34
  on religious books, 65, 150n104
  on theater, 56–57
  on translations into Catalan, 67, 73–74
Baez, Joan, 81
Baeza, Fernando, 78
Baeza Alegría, Eduardo, 55
Balancí, El (series), 103
Ballester, Maria, 85–86, 96
Balmes (publishing house), 86
Banco Catalán de Desarrollo (Catalan Development Bank), 102
Banco de Madrid, 102
Baratech, Feliciano, 101
Barba, Bartolomé, 55
Barcelona
  book purge (1939) and, 28–30
  censorship services in, 53
  IPA conference (1962) in, 66
  libraries in, 88
  publishers in, 28–30, 50, 97
  Sánchez Bella and, 95

Spanish Civil War and, 28
student protests (1969) in, 95
Barcelona Book Chamber, 29–30, 66
Barcelona City Council, 82
Barciela López, Carlos, 62, 151n4, 151n6
Barcino (publishing house), 52, 140n15
Baró Llambias, Mònica, 27–28, 29
Barrabàs (1961 film), 90, 154n30
Barrabàs (Lagerkvist), 90, 154n30, 156n44
Barral, Carlos, 139n4
Bartra, Agustí, 41, 43
Basque Country, 11
Bastardes, Ramon, 71, 75, 85
Baum, Vicky, 156n44
Bauzá (publishing house), 32
Beauvoir, Simone de, 153n22
Beevor, Antony, 138n25
Benet, Josep, 71, 138n27
Benet i Jornet, Josep M., 69
Beneyto, Antonio, 112, 121
Beneyto, Juan, 12, 19, 20, 22, 30, 32, 55
Benguerel, Xavier, 43
Benoît, Pierre, 153n22
Berenguer, Luis, 17–18
Berenguer Amenós, Jaume, 91
Bernáldez, José María, 100
Bertelsmann (publisher), 84–85
Bhabha, Homi, 37
Bibliodisc, S.A., 89
Biblioteca de Autores Cristianos (series), 65
Bienvenido Mr. Marshall (1953 film), 151n5
bills of exchange, 84
Black Spring (Miller), 139n3
Blair, Ann, 74
Blas, José Andrés de, 118–19, 139n1
BMG Entertainment, 89
Boix, Maur M., 125, 146n72, 149n95
Boix i Selva, Josep M.
  on Catalan language, 82, 142n38
  censorship and, 53, 104–6, 107
  Editorial Vergara and, 88, 100–103

Isard (series) and, 4, 71, 89–92, 153–54n28
  religion and, 65
Bonet, Blai, 113
Bonet Garí, Lluís, 48
book censorship in Francoist Spain
  book purge (1939) and, 28–30
  Catalan language and, 12–13, 21–23, 36–37. *See also* Catalan publishers; writers
  criteria of, 19–20
  incidence of, 79–80, 79
  laws and, 5, 16–17, 32, 80, 92–95, 100. *See also* Order of April 29, 1938 (Arias-Salgado Law); Press and Printing Law (1966)
  procedures of, 20–21
  readers and, 24–25
  stages of, 21–23
  types and levels of censors in, 4–5, 17–19. *See also* civil censors; military censors; religious censors
book sequestrations, 95, 96, 108
bookstores and booksellers, 28–30, 70–71, 83, 86–87, 102
Borrat, Maria Montserrat, 53
Bosquejo de una política del libro (Gili), 31
Branchadell, Albert, 71, 81, 154n34
branding, 71–72
Brod, Max, 153n22
Brossa, Joan, 111–12, 114, 159n1
Bruguera (publishing house), 63–64
Buero Vallejo, Antonio, 118
Burma, 3
Bush, Peter, 159n9

Cabanillas, Pío, 92, 95–96, 158n70
Cahner, Max, 71, 85
Calçada i Olivella, Miquel, 1–2
Calders, Pere
  on Catalan journalism, 115–16
  exile and, 39–40, 113
  on Isard (series), 90

Calders, Pere *(continued)*
  on publishing in Mexico, 43–44
  on readers, 74
  on self-censorship, 112
  on translations into Catalan, 75–76
  on writers, 69
Camañes, Jordi, 131
Camus, Albert, 87, 117, 156n44, 158n68
Candel, Francisco (Paco), 107, 115, 116, 120–21, 126, 157n58, 160n12
Cano Bueso, Juan, 137n11
Cantano, Moreno, 56
Canyameres, Ferran, 42, 121
Capdevila Candell, Mireia, 145n65
Capmany, M. Aurèlia, 56
Capsa Theatre (Barcelona), 95
Carbó, Joaquim, 49
Cárdenas, Lázaro, 43
Carner, Josep, 43, 145n61
Carrasco-Gallego, José A., 14
Carrero Blanco, Luis, 16
Carta abierta a un empresario (Candel), 157n58
Casacuberta, Josep M. de, 140n15
Casals, Montserrat, 85
Casanellas, Pau, 95, 157n55
Casanova, Agustí, 62
Casanovas, Domingo, 125
Castell, Jaume, 102
Castellet, Josep Maria, 44–45, 115, 150n100, 153n21, 159n8
Castiella, Fernando María, 65
Castilla (publishing house), 78
Catalan Independence Referendum (2017), 1–2
Catalan language and culture
  clandestine activities and, 7, 45–50
  collaborationism and, 37–39
  education and, 81–82, 115
  exile and, 7, 37, 39–45, 113
  folklore and, 49, 53–55
  journalism and, 116
  music and, 81
  poetry and, 83, 111
  promotion of, 82–83
  rebirth (1946–1959) of, 5–6, 50–60, *52*, **54**, **58**, 107–8, 114
  repression of, 12–13, 21–23, 36–37
  standardization of, 116–17
  television and, 81
  theater and, 52, 56–57, 81, 82, 95
  See also translations into Catalan; writers
Catalan publishers
  censorship and, 107–9, 132–34, **133**
  challenges and strategies (1939–1959) of, 31–36, **35**
  challenges and strategies (1959–1975) of, 78–88, *79–80*, 103–7
  crisis of, 100–103, **101**
  desarrollismo and, 63–64
  in exile, 41, 42–44
  INLE and, 96, **100**
  IPA conference (Barcelona, 1962) and, 66
  location of, 97–100
  official registration numbers and, 93–94, 100
  rebirth of Catalan letters (1946–1959) and, 51–54, *52*, **54**, **58**, 107–8
  Second Vatican Council and, 64–65
  self-censorship and, 104, 117
Catàleg de llibres en català (INLE), 96
Catalonia
  book purge (1939) and, 28–30
  military occupation of, 12–13
  Spanish Civil War and, 11
  See also Catalan language and culture; Catalan publishers
Catalònia (publishing house), 86
Catalunya Ràdio (radio station), 2
Catalunya Teatral (series), 52
categories, 90, 91–92
Catholic Church
  censorship and, 19
  Francoism and, 7, 13–14, 22–23, 59, 64–65

Index [189]

Second Vatican Council and, 60, 62–63, 64–65, 107
Spanish Civil War and, 10
See also Opus Dei
Cavall Fort (magazine), 81–82
Cela, Camilo José, 112–13, 138n20
Cendán Pazos, Fernando, 72, 75
Cendrós, Joan Baptista, 43, 77
censorship
　concept of, 2–3, 24, 110–11
　in Fascist Italy, 16–17
　in Nazi Germany, 16
　in post-Francoist Spain, 1–2
　See also book censorship in Francoist Spain
censura oficiosa (semi-official censorship), 96
Central de Literatura Catalana, 84
Chandler, Raymond, 64
children's magazines, 154n35
Chile, 39, 40, 41
Chorén Rodriguez, Pilar, 36
Cid (publishing house), 78
Cierva, Ricardo de la, 96, 107, 108, 117
Cinco horas con Mario (Delibes), 118
cinema, 15, 90–91, 154n30
Círculo de Lectores, 71, 78, 84–85, 89
Cisquella, Georgina
　on apertura (openness), 150n103
　on Francoism, 11
　on gifts, 106
　on Press and Printing Law (1966), 92, 93, 94
　on regional languages, 56
　on voluntary consultation, 156–57n51
Citton, Yves, 8, 75, 76
civil censors, 4–5, 17, 18, 21, 124–26
civil rights movement, 62–63
clandestine activities, 7, 45–50
Clásicos Vergara (series), 89
Clotet, Jaume, 140n15&16
Club dels Novel·listes, El (series), 59, 74
Club Editor, 126

Coca, Jordi, 56
Col·lecció el Dofí (series), 52, 57
Col·lecció Juvenil Sant Jordi (series), 52–53, 59
Col·lecció Popular Barcino (series), 52
Col·lecció Tròpics (series), 103, 131
Colección de obras de gran formato (series), 89
Colección nuevos horizontes (series), 89
Colección verdad y vida (series), 89
Colgate, 62
Coll i Alentorn, Miquel, 48, 147n74, 147n76
collaborationism, 37–39
Colomer, Víctor, 140n18
colonial studies, 37
commercial margins, 86–87
Committee on Non-represented Nations, 65–66
Concordat (1953), 14, 23
conscious self-censorship, 118–19
Cops d'ull al retrovisor (Boix), 149n95
copyright agreements, 67
Cornellà-Detrell, Jordi, 59, 67, 69–70, 73, 113
Cortázar, Julio, 153n19
Council of Europe, 65–66
Crespo, Ángel, 19
Crespo, Bernardo, 53, 106
Crexell, Joan, 39
crime fiction, 64
Cruzet, Josep M., 7, 33–34, 48
Cua de Palla, La (series), 64
Cuerpo de Inspectores de Traducción (Translation Inspectorate), 34
currency exchange, 67

Dalí, Salvador, 38
Dante, 147n77
Das, Nandita, 3
Dau al Set, 59
Deffontaines, Pierre, 49
Delgado, Lorenzo, 62, 137n13, 150–51n3

Delibes, Miguel, 118
Denmark, 67
desarrollismo (developmentalism), 15, 61–64
desire, 71–72, 76
Destino (magazine), 38–39, 57, 72–73, 102
Destino (publishing house), 52, 57, 63–64, 83
Déu ha nascut a l'exili (Horia), 104
Diario de Barcelona (magazine), 72–73
Díaz-Plaja, Guillermo, 31, 83, 85–86, 96, 100
Diccionari català general (Arimany), 84
Diccionari general de la llengua catalana (Fabra), 84, 103
Discos Vergara, 89
dissemination, 2–3. *See also* Catalan publishers
Distribuïdora Ifac, 85, 86, 87
distribution companies, 85–88
Divina Comèdia, La (Dante), 147n77
Doctor Givago, El (1965 film), 90
Doctor Givago, El (Pasternak), 90
Documents del Concili Vaticà II (series), 65
Dolç, Miquel, 45–46
Dolphin Book (publishing house), 42, 144n52
Domènech, Ignasi, 51
Doyle, Christopher J., 159n6
Duch Plana, Montserrat, 136n10
Dylan, Bob, 15, 81

Eaude, Michael, 81, 138n18
ecology of attention, 6
eco-translation, 6
Edhasa (publising house), 86
Ediciones Arión (publishing house), 78
Ediciones Castilla (publishing house), 78
Ediciones Cid (publishing house), 78
Ediciones Destino (publishing house), 52, 57, 63–64, 83
Ediciones Fax (publishing house), 100

Ediciones Península (publishing house), 75
Edicions 62 (publishing house), 71, 75, 83, 85, 93, 103
Edicions Destino (publishing house), 52, 57, 63–64, 83
Edicions Nova Terra (publishing house), 60, 64–65, 82
Editorial Albor (publishing house), 42, 149n92
Editorial Alfaguara (publishing house), 63–64, 74, 112–13
Editorial Aymà (publishing house)
  Catalan language and, 52–53, 55
  censorship and, 77, 124–25, 130–31, 139n3
  distribution and, 85
  history and catalog of, 103, 148–49n88
  Oliver and, 83
  Proa and, 43
  Strength to Love (King) and, 152n10
Editorial Barcino (publishing house), 140n15
Editorial Estela (publishing house), 60, 64–65, 69, 82
Editorial Joventut (Juventud) (publishing house), 29, 55, 86
Editorial Labor (publishing house), 70, 84
Editorial Moll (publishing house), 33–34, 52, 86
Editorial Pòrtic (publishing house), 107, 116
Editorial Proa (publishing house), 42–43, 72, 83, 85
Editorial Salvat (publishing house), 87
Editorial Selecta (publishing house), 7, 33–34, 52, 53–55, 84
Editorial Vergara (publishing house)
  censorship and, 106–7
  Círculo de Lectores and, 84–85
  crisis of, 100–103
  history and catalog of, 83, 88–89, 109
  paper scarcity and, 63–64

records and, 88, 89
survey on reading habits by, 72
See also Isard (series)
education, 81–82, 115
Edwards, Kate, 120
Enciclopedia Vergara, 89
Enciclopedias y diccionarios (series), 89
England, 40
Erill i Pinyot, Gustau, 42
Erviti, José Luis
  on *apertura* (openness), 150n103
  on Francoism, 11
  on gifts, 106
  on Press and Printing Law (1966), 92, 93, 94
  on regional languages, 56
  on voluntary consultation, 156–57n51
Esbart Verdaguer, 49
Escarré, Aureli M., 146n72
escritos del Che, Los (Guevara), 95
Espasa-Calpe (publishing house), 75
Espinàs, Josep Maria, 114–15, 117
Espriu, Salvador, 42, 111
Ésser en el món (Pedrolo), 138n22
Estapé, Fabián, 138n16
Estatut de Núria (1932), 11, 12
Estela (publishing house), 60, 64–65, 69, 82
Esteve, Josep M., 88
Estimats Amics (magazine), 47
Estrada, Lluís Vicenç, 100–101, 102
Estudis Romànics (journal), 47
Estudis Universitaris Catalans, 48
ETA (Euskadi Ta Askatasuna), 16, 152n17
Europa Press, 96
European Economic Community (EEC), 65–66
European International Movement, 65
European Recovery Plan (ERP), 14
exhaustion of attention, 74–75
exile, 7, 37, 39–45, 113
existentialism, 123

explicit self-censorship, 118–19
exploiters of politics, 11
Eyeless in Gaza (Huxley), 158n64

Fabra, Pompeu, 48, 84, 103
Fagen, Patricia Weiss, 43
Falangism, 11, 13, 15, 17, 38–39, 50, 57
fame, 75–76, 90, 91
Fascicles Literaris (journal), 113
fascism, 11–12, 111
Faulí, Josep, 41
Fax (publishing house), 100
ferida lluminosa, La (television play), 81
Fernández de Bobadilla, Vicente, 72
Fernández Miranda, Torcuato, 59
Fernández Moya, María, 63, 152n13
Ferras, Gabriel, 150n1
Ferriz Roure, Teresa, 37, 43, 143n45
FET y de las JONS (Falange Española Tradicionalista y de las Juntas de Ofensiva Nacional Sindicalista), 11, 13, 15, 17, 38–39, 50, 57
Figaro, Le (newspaper), 158n68
"Fills de Buda" (song), 132
First Development Plan (1964–1967/9), 63
Fiscalía (Public Prosecutor), 94
Foix, J. V., 45, 83, 114
Folch i Camarasa, Ramon, 44, 91, 153n22
folklore, 49, 53–55
Foment de Pietat (publishing house), 86
Fontanella (publishing house), 63–64
footnotes, 132
For Whom the Bell Tolls (Hemingway), 119
foreign books, 26–27
Fornàs, Josep, 106, 107
Fraga Iribarne, Manuel
  Cela and, 112–13
  literary awards and, 155n38
  as minister of information and tourism, 5, 66, 73–74, 83, 92, 94, 104–5, 107, 112–13, 150n103
  on "Spanish problem," 65
  See also Press and Printing Law (1966)

France, 40, 41, 42–43, 95. *See also* Galimard (publishing house)
Franco, Francisco
  mortal remains of, 135n2
  Spanish Civil War and, 10–11
  See also Francoism
Francoism
  Catholic Church and, 7, 13–14, 22–23, 59, 64–65
  history and ideology of, 11–16, 22–23, 50, 111
  See also book censorship in Francoist Spain
Frankfurt Book Fair (1961), 71
freedom of expression, 92
Frente Popular (Popular Front), 10
Fuentes Quintana, Enrique, 150n1
Fuero de los Españoles (1945), 13–14, 45
Fundació Benèfica Minerva, 148n82
Fundació Bernat Metge (series), 34, 52
Fundació Bíblica Catalana, 52
Fuster, Joan, 111–12, 116, 117, 153–54n28&29, 153n21

Gabancho, Patrícia, 49
Gaceta Papelera, La (newspaper), 86–87, 101
Galí, Francesc, 79
Galiana, Pedro Miguel, 61
Galicia, 11
Galimard (publishing house), 123–24, 125, 126
Gallén, Enric, 81
Gallofré, Maria Josepa
  on book purge (1939), 29–30
  on Catalan language, 55
  on Catalan publishing, 149n96
  on criteria for censorship, 23, 27, 32, 33, 34
  on translations into Catalan, 51
García Berlanga, Luis, 151n5
García Lorca, Federico, 42
García Márquez, Gabriel, 152n17, 153n19

García Venero, Maximiano, 139n10
Gargatagli, Ana, 139n8
Gayà, Miquel, 46
Gaziel (Agustí Calvet), 12–13
Geis, Camil, 33
Geografia de Catalunya (Solé Sabaris), 87
German language, 27
Germanor (magazine), 41
gifts, 106
Gili, Gustau, 31, 140n17, 142n28, 144n52
Gili i Serra, Joan, 42, 147–48n79
Gilian Law (Spanish Book Protection Law, 1946), 31, 34–36, 63–64
Giravolt (television program), 81
Gironella, José María, 38, 142n38
Gómez Pin, Víctor, 117
Gómez Torrano, J., 106
González, Pedro, 36
González Oliveros, Wenceslao, 13
Goytisolo, Juan, 126
Gracia, Jordi, 28
Gran Wyoming, El (José Miguel Monzón Navarro), 2
Grand Hotel (Baum), 156n44
Griffin, Roger, 7, 12, 111
Grijalbo (publishing house), 63–64
Grup Estudi, 47
Gubern, Romà, 140n13
Güell Ampuero, Casilda, 144n53

Hammett, Dashiell, 64
Hargrave, Marshall, 67
Harris, Wilson, 37
Hart, Patricia, 64
Hemingway, Ernest, 119
Herrera, León, 95–96
Herrero-Olaizola, Alejandro, 31, 66, 71, 142n35
història de San Michele, La (Munthe), 158n67
Historia general de las literaturas hispánicas (Díaz-Plaja), 89
historic realism, 150n100

Històries (series), 63–64
Hitler, Adolf, 13, 111
hoja del lunes, La (periodical), 101
Hollywood movies, 15
Homer, 51, 147n77
homosexuality, 130–31
Hout-Huijben, Lidwina Maria van den, 79–80
Huxley, Aldous, 120, 158n64

Ibáñez, C. R., 153n23
Ifac (distribution company), 85, 86, 87
iglesia en España, La (Arbeloa), 158n69
Iglésias, Narcís, 67
illes d'or, Les (series), 33–34
implicit self-censorship, 118–19
importers, 26–27
Incerta glòria (2017 film), 159n9
Incerta glòria (Sales), 123–26, **127–29**, 132
Index Librorum Prohibitorum (Index of forbidden books), 19
Información Comercial Española (magazine), 77–78
information theology, 23
INLE (Instituto Nacional del Libro Español)
  Catalan books and, 77, 96, **100**
  de la Cierva and, 96
  on Círculo de Lectores, 84–85
  creation and role of, 30–31
  on pocket books, 71
  on promotion, 72, 75
  on publishers, 117
  on publishing crisis, 101
  survey on publishers by, 77–78
inner exile, 37, 44–45
installments, 83–84, 88–89
Institut d'Estudis Catalans (IEC; Institute of Catalan Studies), 47, 48, 85, 147n77
Institut Français, 47, 49
Instituto Nacional del Libro Español (INLE). *See* INLE (Instituto Nacional del Libro Español)

Intermedio, El (television show), 2
International Monetary Fund (IMF), 14, 15, 59, 150n1
International Publishers Association (IPA), 66
Introducció a l'estudi de la llengua catalana (Roca Pons), 91–92
Isard (series)
  Boix i Selva and, 4, 153–54n28
  branding and, 72
  censorship and, 104, 107
  distribution and, 87
  history and catalog of, 71, 74, 89–92, 90, 103
  La Pesta (Camus) and, 158n65
  translations into Catalan and, 70, 75–76
Italian language, 27
Italy
  Fascism in, 12, 13, 16–17
  Pla in, 112
  translations in, 67

Jacinto Verdaguer National Literature Prize, 83
Jané, Albert, 81–82, 159n6
Janés, Josep, 32, 36, 86, 148n83
Jimeno Revilla, Raquel, 84
Joanot Martorell Prize, 48, 58–59, 91, 123, 125
Jocs Florals, 12–13, 40–41, 43, 144–45n57
John XXIII, Pope, 62–63, 64–65. *See also* Second Vatican Council (1962–1965)
Joric, Carlos, 28
Josep M. de Sagarra Prize, 83
Josep M. Folch i Torres Prize, 83
Josep Pla Prize, 57, 83
journalism, 116

Kennedy, John F., 62
King, Martin Luther, Jr., 62–63
Küng, Hans, 64

Lacruz, Mario, 102
Lagervist, Pär, 156n44. See also *Barrabàs* (Lagerkvist)
Larraz, Fernando, 18, 19, 39, 143n47, 159n2
Latin American literary boom, 153n19
Law for the Repression of Freemasonry and Communism (1940), 140n14
Law of Political Responsibilities (1939), 27, 31–32
Law on the Principles of the National Movement (1958), 57
Leña verde (Berenguer), 17–18
Lera, Ángel M. de, 153n26
Lesfargues, Bernard, 85, 126, 159n11
Lewis, Paul H., 137n12
ley giliana (Spanish Book Protection Law, 1946), 31, 34–36, 63–64
libraries, 88
Librería Editorial Argos, 102
Libro Español, El (magazine), 31
Liñán, Fernando de, 95–96
Literary Circle, 49
literary prizes and awards, 48, 58–59, 83, 91. See also Premi Joanot Martorell
Llanas, Manuel
  on Barcelona Book Chamber, 141n23
  on book purge (1939), 29
  on cinema, 156n44
  on criteria for censorship, 34, 51
  on distribution, 85
  on National Catholicism, 64
  scholarship on Catalan publishing and, 4
  on translations into Catalan, 56, 67, 69–70
Lletres (magazine), 41
Llibres a la mà (series), 57
Llibres de l'Óssa Menor, Els (series), 36, 84
Llibres en català (catalog), 85–86
Lliga Espiritual de la Mare de Déu de Montserrat, 152n16

London Club, 49
López, Carlos, 65
López-Llausàs, Antoni, 86
Luján, Néstor, 39
Lumen (publishing house), 63–64, 156–57n51

Madrid
  censorship services in, 53, 55, 106, 122
  publishers in, 100, **100**
Madrid Treaty (1953), 14
magazines and journals, 41–42, 46–47, 72–73, 81–82, 102. See also specific publications
Majzoub, Mona K., 159n6
Maluquer, Jordi, 116
Manent, Albert
  on associations, 48
  on Catalan publishing, 39
  on clandestine activities, 46, 47, 145–46n67
  Edicions 62 and, 71
  on Editorial Aymà, 148–49n88
  on Fraga Iribarne, 73
  on inner exile, 44
  Jocs Florals and, 41
  on payments, 116
  on repression of Catalan language, 36–37, 142n32
  on Sagarra, 148n83
Manent, Marià, 42, 55
Manonelles, Manuel, 64
Manto (Das, 2018), 3
Manto, Saadat Hasan, 3
Manuales Vergara (series), 89
Mapamundi (series), 89
mar, El (Bonet), 113
Mare nostrum (television program), 81
Marías, Julián, 118
Marín Silvestre, Dolors, 151n8
Marshall Plan, 14, 62
Martinell, Maria, 69
Martínez, Federico, 125

Martínez, Jesús A., 93, 153n21
Martínez Pavía (publishing house), 86
Martínez Rus, Ana, 31–32
Martín-Gamero, Adolfo, 96
Martorell, Oriol, 89
Martos, Luis, 17–18
Mas, Antoni, 70
Mas Esteve, Antonio, 84
Mas i Perera, Pere, 40–41
Masoliver, Juan Ramón, 38
Massot, Josep, 85, 113
Massot i Muntaner, Josep, 55, 104, 132, 146n71
Mateo, Dani, 2
matrimonio y sus alternativas, El (Rogers), 126, 129
Maucci (publishing house), 32
Mauriac, François, 156n44
Mayol, Jaume Aymà, 88
Meditz, Sandra W., 62
Mengual Català, Josep, 28, 30, 33, 41, 120
Mentora (publishing house), 86
Mes de Maria Eucarístic (Otzet), 32–33
Mexico, 39–40, 41, 43–44, 63, 100, 113
Miguel Fernández, Enrique de, 61, 151n7
military censors, 4–5, 17–18
Millà (publishing house), 52
Millán, Manuel Sancho, 124
Millán Astray, José, 11, 22
Miller, Henry, 139n2
Millet i Maristany, Fèlix, 48, 145n61, 147n74, 148n82
Ministry of Commerce, 77–78
Ministry of Information and Tourism (MIT)
  Arias-Salgado and, 5, 55–56
  Catalan journalism and, 116
  creation and role of, 18
  Fraga Iribarne and, 5, 65, 73–74, 83, 92, 94, 104–5, 107, 112–13, 150n103
  Incerta glòria (Sales) and, 123–26, 127–29
  INLE and, 31
  ministers (1974–1977) of, 95–96
  Robles Piquer and, 107
  Sánchez Bella and, 76, 80, 95–96, 108
  See also Press and Printing Law (1966)
Minobis, Gregori M., 64
Mirador (magazine), 38–39
Miramar, 47–48
Mitologías ilustradas (series), 89
Mola, Emilio, 10
Molas, Joaquim
  on Catalan culture, 37
  on Catalan publishing, 50, 56, 138n28
  on clandestine activities, 145n65
  on "historic realism," 150n100
  on literary awards, 59
  on writers, 69
món per a tothom, Un (Pedrolo), 121–22
Monde, Le (newspaper), 152n17
Mora, Víctor, 112
Morales Pérez, Sonia, 81
Moreno Sánchez, Fernando, 130
Muñoz, Vicent Melchor, 71, 81, 154n34
Muntanyola, Ramon, 47
Murià, Anna, 40
music, 81
Mussolini, Benito, 12, 13, 16–17, 111

Nadal Prize, 39, 57
National Book Fair, 31
National Book Institute (INLE). *See* INLE (Instituto Nacional del Libro Español)
National Catholicism, 13–14, 22–23, 64–65
Nature of Fascism, The (Griffin), 12
Nauta (publishing house), 83
Navarro Rubio, Mariano, 15, 152n12
Nazi Germany, 12, 13, 16
new book service (*servicio de novedades*), 86
newspapers, 72–73
Nieto, Ramon, 119
nihil obstat ("nothing hinders"), 21, 32–33, 39, 60, 125–26

1984 (Orwell), 106–7
Nit de Santa Llúcia (literary award), 48, 58–59, 83
Nortes, Silvia, 2
Nosaltres els valencians (Fuster), 153n21
Nostra Revista, La (magazine), 41
Nostres Clàssics, Els (series), 52
Nou testament de Montserrat (1961), 60
Noucentisme, 59
Nova Cançó (movement), 15–16

Obra Cultural Balear, 86, 154n34
Obra del Diccionari, 86
Obres poètiques (Foix), 83
Odyssey (Homer), 51, 147n77
official registration numbers, 92, 93–94, 100
official silence (*silencio administrativo*), 92, 93, 94
Oficina Romànica, 86
Oliver, Joan
  on censorship, 111, 113
  Editorial Aymà and, 43, 130
  on literary awards, 83
  as playwright, 95
  on self-censorship, 119
  as translator, 153n22
Òmnium Cultural, 154n34
Opus Dei, 15, 23, 59
oral agreements, 103–4
Order of April 29, 1938 (Arias-Salgado Law), 5, 16, 19, 26–28, 56, 113–14, 120–26
Order of December 23, 1936, 26
Order of July 14, 1966, 155n38
Order of July 15, 1939, 30
Order of March 15, 1941, 32
Order of May 23, 1939, 30–31
Order of November 24, 1962, 63
Orfeó Català, 52
Organisation for Economic Co-operation and Development (OECD), 15, 111, 150n1

Organisation for European Economic Co-operation (OEEC), 14
Oromí Inglés, Miguel, 124
Orwell, George, 106–7
Otzet, Lluís G., 32–33

Pablo Muñoz, José de, 122, 124, 125–26
Pacem in Terris (John XXIII), 64
Pact of Forgetting (1977), 8, 16, 23, 113–14
Palau i Fabre, Josep, 45–47, 143n46, 146n69, 147–48n79
Palmolive, 62
Pàniker, Salvador, 113–14, 118, 119, 126, 129–30, 160n12
paper scarcity, 27–28, 34, 46, 63–64, 78, 88
para-fascist regimes, 7, 12, 111
Parcerisas, Francesc, 69
Pas i repàs (Geis), 33
Payne, Stanley G., 95
Pedreira, Josep, 36, 84, 85
Pedrolo, Manuel de
  censorship and, 4, 5, 110, 121–22, 126, 130–31, 132, 138n22
  on role of writers, 115
  on *San Camilo, 1936* (Cela), 112–13
Pemartín, Julián, 31
Península (publishing house), 75
Pérez Embid, Florentino, 124–25
Pericay, Xavier, 59
Pesta, La (Camus), 87, 117, 158n65
Pi de la Serra, Quico, 132
Pi i Sunyer, Carles, 143n43
Piernavieja, Miguel, 125
Piñol, Rosa María, 57
Pinyol i Torrents, Ramon, 4
Pire, Dominique, 156n44
Pla, Josep, 32, 111, 112
Pla, Xavier, 113
plaça del diamant, La (Rodoreda), 121
Plana, Adelina, 102–3, 106, 157n60, 158n66
Planas, Ramon, 114
Planeta (publishing house), 57, 63–64
Plaza y Janés (publishing house), 63–64

pocket books, 64, 71, 88–89
Poesia (magazine), 46–47
poetry, 83, 111
Point Counterpoint (Huxley), 158n64
Pol, Ferran de, 69, 82, 153n22
Pol, Varela, 78
Polígrafa (publishing house), 63–64
Polo, Pedro, 147–48n79
Polos de Desarrollo (Development Poles), 15
Pons, Ventura, 95
Pont, El (magazine), 146n68, 146n71
Pont Blau (magazine), 41
Porcel, Baltasar, 4–5, 113, 114, 115, 119, 120
Porter Moix, Miquel, 28–29
Porter Rovira, Josep, 28–29
Portolés, José, 25
Portuguese language, 27
Premi Ciutat de Barcelona, 91
Premi Ignasi Iglésies, 91
Premi Joanot Martorell, 48, 58–59, 91, 123, 125
Premi Josep M. de Sagarra, 83
Premi Josep M. Folch i Torres, 83
Premi Josep Pla, 57, 83
Premi Nadal, 39, 57
Premi Prudenci Bertrana, 83
Premi Sant Jordi, 83
Premi Víctor Català, 91
Premio Nacional de Literatura Jacinto Verdaguer, 83
Press and Printing Law (1966)
  articles and key concepts of, 5, 17, 23, 66, 80, 92–95, 100, 108, 150n103
  Pàniker on, 113–14
  strategies to overcome censorship and, 103–7
  translations and, 104
  writers and, 122, 126, 129–31
Press Law of April 22, 1938, 16, 26. See also Order of April 29, 1938 (Arias-Salgado Law)
Preston, Paul, 10, 12, 16

Primer Plan de Desarrollo (1964–1967/9), 15
Primo de Rivera, Miguel, 135n2
prior censorship, 16–17, 20–21, 93
prior deposit, 92, 94
Procel, Lluís, 85
promotion, 90–91
propaganda, 24
Prudenci Bertrana Prize, 83
pseudonyms, 44, 47
Publicacions de l'Abadia de Montserrat, 64–65, 93–94
publishers
  desarrollismo and, 63–64
  as readers, 25
  self-censorship and, 104
  See also Catalan publishers; Spanish-language publishers
Puig Antich, Salvador, 16
Puig i Cadafalch, Josep, 48
Puig i Ferrater, Joan, 42–43
Puig Quintana, Pere, 147n77
Puigtobella, Bernat, 81–82
Purina, 62

Quaderns (clandestine booklets), 46
Quaderns de l'Exili (magazine), 41
Quaderns d'estudis polítics, econòmics i socials (magazine), 41
Queralt i Clapés, Josep, 42–43
Qüestions de vida cristiana (magazine), 64–65

Rafael Dalmau (publishing house), 52
Raguer, Hilari, 150n101
Rajoy, Mariano, 135n1
Ramírez, Agnès, 151n8
Rat Penat, Lo, 154n34
readers, 24–25. See also attention economy
reading habits, 72–73
real estate, 62
records, 89

Redreçament (magazine), 51
regionalisms, 11, 22
Reguera, Andrés, 96
religious books, 21, 60, 64–65, 108
religious censors
    Catalan books and, 39
    Incerta glòria (Sales) and, 124–26
    Mes de Maria Eucarístic (Otzet) and, 32–33
    profile and role of, 4–5, 17, 21, 60
represa, La (Manent), 146n70
repression, concept of, 24
Reseña, Equipo, 22
resistance, 2–3
Ressò (magazine), 47
Ressorgiment (magazine), 41
returns, 86
Revista de Catalunya (magazine), 41
Revista Europa (magazine), 72–73
Riba, Carles
    Catalan culture and, 7, 114
    censorship and, 51
    clandestine activities and, 7, 45
    death of, 60
    inner exile and, 44
    self-publishing and, 53
    as translator, 51, 147n77
Ribes de Dios, Àngels, 91
Ridruejo, Dionisio, 21
Ripoll Sintes, Blanca, 57
Roberts, Cecil, 153n22
Robles Piquer, Carlos
    on Catalan publishing, 73
    on censorship, 157n57
    censura oficiosa and, 96
    Fraga Iribarne and, 66
    INLE and, 31
    on Marshall Plan, 151n5
    MIT and, 107
Roca Pons, Josep, 91–92
Ródenas de Moya, Domingo, 28
Rodoreda, Mercè, 117, 121, 122, 143n46
Rodríguez Casado, Vicente, 66

Roig Gironella, Juan, 125
Rojas Claros, Francisco, 65, 93, 150n103
Romea Theatre (Barcelona), 82, 95
Romero, Emilio, 141n25
Romeu, Josep, 147–48n79
Rosa Mística (Geis), 33
royalties, 36, 66
Ruano, Enrique, 94
Rubió i Balaguer, Jordi, 48, 147n76
Ruiz, Julius, 14, 137n11
Ruiz Bautista, Eduardo, 141n24
Ruiz Soriano, Francisco, 34
Rundle, Christopher, 12, 16

Sagarra, Josep M. de, 147n77, 148n83
Sales, Joan
    on Catalan language, 82, 117
    on Catalan publishing, 87, 149n89
    on censorship, 122
    on distribution, 85
    exile and, 41
    as publisher, 74
    See also *Incerta glòria* (Sales)
Sallent (printing house), 146n69
Salvador (printing house), 49
Salvador, Tomás, 83, 155n37
Salvat Ediciones (publishing house), 87
Samsó, Joan
    on associations, 49
    on Catalan culture, 39, 56, 136n7
    on clandestine activities, 45, 46, 47–48, 145n63
    on collaborationism, 38
    on *Destino* (magazine), 57
    on Esbart Verdaguer, 147n78
San Camilo, 1936 (Cela), 112–13, 138n20
Sánchez, Pedro, 135n2
Sánchez Agustí, Ferran, 152n17
Sánchez Bella, Alfredo, 76, 80, 95–96, 108, 141n25
Sánchez-Juan, Sebastià, 30, 49
Sant Jordi Prize, 146–47n73
Sant Jordi's Day (April 23), 75, 82–83, 130

Sanz Rozalén, Vicente, 61, 151n7
Sardà, Joan, 150n1
Sardà i Dexeus, Joan, 15
Sarsanedas, Jordi, 49
Sartre, Jean-Paul, 158n68
Sbert, Antoni M., 143n43
Second Francoism, 59, 114
Second Republic (1931–1936), 10–11
Second Vatican Council (1962–1965), 60, 62–63, 64–65, 107
secondhand bookstores, 29–30
Seeger, Pete, 15, 81
Segundo Plan de Desarrollo (1969–1971), 15
self-censorship
  definition of, 117
  publishers and, 104, 117
  Setze Jutges and, 16
  writers and, 25, 112–13, 117–20, 132
self-censorship and, 117
self-publishing, 53
Semir, Agustín de, 56
Sercali (publishing house), 86
Serra d'Or (magazine)
  advertisements and, 72–73
  on Catalan culture, 154n30
  as first authorized journal, 47
  literary prizes and, 83
  official registration numbers and, 94
  on *La Pesta* (Camus), 153n25
  self-censorship and, 104
  Strength to Love (King) and, 152n10
  on translations into Catalan, 69
Serra Pujol, Lluís, 102
Serrahima, Maurici, 47–48, 131
Serrano Suñer, Ramon, 11, 26, 30, 34, 136n4
servicio de novedades (new book service), 86
Servicio de Ordenación Editorial (Editorial Management Service), 94
Setze Jutges (Sixteen Judges), 15–16, 81
Shepherd, John, 89

silencio administrativo (official silence), 92, 93, 94
Siles, Rafael Giménez, 32
Simenon, Georges, 42, 74
Sindicato Español Universitario (Spanish University Union), 140n15
social movements, 62–63
Soldevila, Carles, 91
Soldevila, Ferran, 147n76
Solé i Sabaté, Josep Maria, 27
Solé Sabaris, L., 87
Solé-Tura, Jordi, 38
Solsten, Eric, 62
Sopena, Mireia, 19, 95, 106, 149n90, 150n104
Sopena, Ramon, 88
Sorolla, José A.
  on *apertura* (openness), 150n103
  on Francoism, 11
  on gifts, 106
  on Press and Printing Law (1966), 92, 93, 94
  on regional languages, 56
  on voluntary consultation, 156–57n51
Spaar, Lisa Russ, 123
Spanish Book Protection Law (Gilian Law, 1946), 31, 34–36, 63–64
Spanish Civil War (1936–1939), 5, 10–11, 16, 28. See also Order of April 29, 1938 (Arias-Salgado Law)
Spanish-language publishers, 63, 71, 75, 77–78
Stabilization Plan (1959)
  Catalan publishers and, 23, 107
  currency exchange and, 67
  development and, 61
  Opus Dei and, 15, 59
  Second Francoism and, 150n103
  See also *desarrollismo* (developmentalism)
Starr, Ringo, 154n33
Strength to Love (King), 152n10
subscriptions, 84, 87

Sunyer, Ramon, 46
supra-text, 37
Surís, Nicolau, 88, 100–101, 102

Tàpies, Antoni, 59
Tarde, Gabriel, 74
targeted advertising, 75, 76
Tarradell, Miquel, 47
teatre per a nois i noise, El (Theater for boys and girls), 82
Tebé, Tomàs, 146–47n73
teca, La (Domènech), 51
Teixidor, Joan, 38
Tele/Estel (weekly publication), 102, 116
Tele/eXpres (newspaper), 102
television, 81
Televisión Española, 81
Temps (journal), 47
Tercer Plan de Desarrollo (1972–1975), 15, 16
Terrades, Toni, 42
theater, 52, 56–57, 81, 82, 95
tierra y sus límites, La (Editorial Salvat), 87
Tiphaigne de la Roche, Charles-François, 74
Tísner (Avel·lí Artís-Gener), 43
Torra, Quim, 140n15&16, 151–52n9
Torres, Estanislau, 25, 110, 121, 132, 159n8, 160n12
tourism, 8, 15, 23, 62
Toutain, Ferran, 59
translations into Catalan
  boom (1969–1975) of, 5–6, 8, 67–77, *68*, *73*, 97, *97*–99, 103, 107
  censorship of, 34, 51, 56–57, 59
  exile and, 42–43
  Isard (series) and, 89–92, *90*
  religious books and, 60
  royalties and, 36
  self-censorship and, 119
translations into Spanish, 59, 60, 67

Trevor-Roper, Hugh, 137n12
Triadú, Joan
  on advertisements, 72
  Ariel (magazine) and, 47, 147–48n79
  Calders and, 43–44
  on Catalan publishing, 103
  on clandestine activities, 145n66
  on readers, 74
Tribunal de Orden Público (Public Order Court), 94
Tribunal de Responsabilidades Políticas (Tribunal of Political Responsibilities), 13, 22
Trident, El (series), 57
Tusquets, Esther, 117

ulls i la cendra, Els (Torres), 159n8
Umbral, Francisco, 119
unconscious self-censorship, 118–19
UNESCO (United Nations Educational, Scientific and Cultural Organization), 48
Unió Excursionista de Catalunya (Catalan Hiking Union), 49
Union Académique Internationale (International Academic Union), 147n74
Unión Musical Española, 86
United Artists, 89
United Nations (UN), 14, 59, 111
United States, 7, 14, 59, 61–63
Uruguay, 40

Valencia-García, Louie, 150n103
Vall, Xavier, 123
Vallespinosa, Bonaventura, 56–57
Vallverdú, Francesc
  on *apertura* (openness), 150n103
  on Catalan publishing, 50
  on censorship, 22, 158n68
  on publishers, 25
  on translation boom, 67

on translations into Catalan, 68, 69–70, 73, 76, 77
as translator, 152n10
Vanguardia Española, La (newspaper)
  advertisements and, 72–73
  "book censorship note" in, 28
  on book purge (1939), 29–30
  on book sequestrations, 95
  on censorship representatives, 53
  on new releases, 83, 84
  Pàniker and, 129–30
  on Pedrolo, 160n15
  on *La Pesta* (Camus), 153n25
  repression of Catalan language and, 13
Vargas Llosa, Mario, 152n17, 153n19
Vázquez Montalbán, Manuel, 126
Velero (series), 89
Verdaguer, Jacint, 7, 33, 53–55
Verdura, Josep, 77, 82
Vergara. *See* Editorial Vergara (publishing house)
Vergés, Josep, 38
Vernet, M. Teresa, 91
Vernon, Kathleen M., 140n13
Verrié, Frederic-Pau, 47, 66, 145n58
Versions de poesia catalana (Verrié), 66
Vidal, August, 91
Villaronga, Agustí, 159n9
visibility, 91
Vogel, Adrián, 150n2
voluntary consultation, 17, 92–93, 94, 107, 130

Wallace, William, 2
Wicke, Paul, 89
Wicke, Peter, 89
World Bank, 14
World War II, 7, 13, 22–23, 40, 50
writers
  on Arias-Salgado Law (Order of April 29, 1938), 120–26
  clandestine activities and, 45–46
  collaborationism and, 37–39
  concept of censorship and, 110–11
  economic situation of, 116
  exile and, 39–40, 44–45, 113
  Press and Printing Law (1966) and, 122, 126, 129–31
  as readers, 25
  role of, 114–16
  self-censorship and, 25, 112–13, 117–20, 132
  standardization of Catalan language and, 116–17
  strategies to overcome censorship and, 132–34, **133**
  translation boom and, 68–69, 91
writers' gatherings, 45–46
Wu, Tim, 8, 70, 71–73, 76

Xammar, Eugeni, 143n41
Xirau, Ramon, 43
Xuriguera, Ramon, 42–43

Zendrera, Josep, 29, 34

www.ingramcontent.com/pod-product-compliance
Lightning Source LLC
Chambersburg PA
CBHW030653230426
43665CB00011B/1070